An Azorean in Canada

An Azorean in Canada

A Memoir

Roberto Machado

Roberto Machado

Copyright © 2023 by Roberto Machado

All rights reserved. No part of this book may be reproduced in any manner whatsoever without written permission except in the case of brief quotations embodied in critical articles and reviews.

ISBN 978-1-7390220-0-6
Ebook ISBN 978-1-7390220-2-0

Printed in the United States of America

Published in Canada by Roberto Machado Presents

Cover design by Daniel Swanson
Photograph Insert design by Daniel Swanson

First Edition

For my wife and daughter, with all my love.

EPIGRAPH

Il y a un temps pour vivre et un temps pour témoigner de vivre. Il y a aussi un temps pour créer, ce qui est moins naturel. Il me suffit de vivre de tout mon corps et de témoigner de tout mon cœur.
Camus,
Noces à Tipasa

Ce qui m'effraie, ce n'est point tant le choix des mots ou des tournures, ni les subtilités grammaticales – qui sont, finalement, à la portée de tout le monde : mais c'est la position du romancier, et celle, plus dangereuse encore, du mémorialiste.
Marcel Pagnol,
La Gloire de mon père

CONTENTS

DEDICATION v
EPIGRAPH vii
PREFACE xiii

ONE

The Early Years

1 | Life in São Miguel, Açores, 1952-1969 — 2

2 | The Arrival in Toronto — 22

3 | Bloor Collegiate Institute, 1970-1973 — 26

4 | The Summer Language Bursary Program, Summer of 1972 — 31

5 | A Farewell to Bloor Collegiate Institute, June of 1973 — 37

6 | University of Toronto, Saint Michael's College, 1973-1977 — 42

7 | Ontario-Québec Permanent Commission, Summer of 1975 — 59

8 | The West End YMCA, 1976-1978 — 68

CONTENTS

9 | A Long-Distance Relationship, 1976-1978 75

10 | Faculty of Education at the University of Toronto, 1977-1978 80

photo insert 85

photo insert 86

photo insert 87

photo insert 88

photo insert 89

photo insert 90

photo insert 91

photo insert 92

photo insert 93

photo insert 94

photo insert 95

photo insert 96

photo insert 97

photo insert 98

CONTENTS

photo insert 99

photo insert 100

photo insert 101

photo insert 102

photo insert 103

TWO

The Middle Years

11 | The Wedding, July 29th, 1978 106

12 | A Honeymoon in Portugal, August of 1978 110

13 | Grand River Collegiate Institute, 1978-1979 122

14 | Harbord Collegiate Institute, A Dream of a School, 1980-1997 135

15 | School of Graduate Studies at the University of Toronto, 1985-1989 155

16 | Harbord Collegiate Institute, 1980-1997 (continued) 161

17 | Malvern Collegiate Institute, 1997-2000 189

CONTENTS

18 | Back at Harbord Collegiate Institute, 2000-2010 196

19 | A Ph.D. in Québec Literature, 2010-2017 224

THREE

The Late Years

20 | Retirement Living, 2018- 276

EPILOGUE 315
ACKNOWLEDGMENTS 323
PHOTOGRAPH CREDITS 329
ABOUT THE AUTHOR 331

PREFACE

An Azorean in Canada: A Memoir traces my adventures and misadventures from the moment I was born in 1952, in Ponta Delgada, São Miguel, Azores, to the moment that I emigrate, in December of 1969, and set foot in Toronto, to the present day. It deals with a variety of universal themes such as infancy, adolescence, adulthood, immigration, discrimination, resilience, adaptation and survival in a new country. The tome is divided into three parts which are subdivided into chapters each one with its own title. The third part is followed by an Epilogue summarizing the highlights of my life and times and an Acknowledgments section. It also includes an insert containing authentic photographs with their respective captions.

An Azorean in Canada: A Memoir includes factual socio-economic and cultural information about life in the Azores in the 1950s and '60s and the general conditions that led to widespread emigration to America, Canada, France and elsewhere, in the XX century. However, the bulk of the story pertains to life in Canada where I have lived, studied, worked and raised a family for the last fifty-three years. From specific references to common individuals, to important political personalities and to historical and cultural events stretching from the early 1970s to the present, I allude to and comment on many of them. So, in this regard, *An Azorean in Canada: A Memoir* is also about the work in progress that Canada remains to this day.

Professionally speaking, I was a high school teacher and department head of French and Modern Languages and, in that capacity, I have much to say about pedagogy and public education. Also, being a firm believer in life-long learning, after retiring from teaching in 2010, I went back to the University of Toronto to do a Ph.D. in Québec literature which I completed in 2017.

In addition, throughout the book I reminisce with fondness about my involvement with an amateur theatre group at the University of Toronto, La Troupe des Anciens, since 1975, and my association, since 2010, with a not-for-profit, the Canadian Education Exchange Foundation (CEEF), specializing in international student exchanges for adolescents. These two organizations brought me much personal satisfaction and pleasure during my leisure time.

An Azorean in Canada: A Memoir will be of utmost interest to members of the Portuguese community, especially those with an Azorean background, who emigrated to Canada, USA, France, Brazil and elsewhere since I am one of their own. Furthermore, past, present and future teachers will find the book educational, informative and entertaining. Finally, anybody out there contemplating doing graduate work, joining an amateur troupe or a not-for-profit, will find in my book all the encouragement needed to actually do it. The rewards will be countless.

ONE

The Early Years

1

Life in São Miguel, Açores, 1952-1969

I was once a very cute and curious little boy. Now, at the age of seventy, although I have remained curious, the cuteness has long since vanished. This is the story of my life journey on Earth, a miniscule planet belonging to the Milky Way, one of the many galaxies that make up the Universe. My name is Roberto Augusto Machado. My life adventure started on August 13th, 1952, the day I was born in a small city by the name of Ponta Delgada, in the island of São Miguel, in the Azores (Açores), an autonomous region belonging to Portugal situated in mid-Atlantic between Europe and North America. At around 9:15 p.m. I came into this world weighing 3,500 Kg and, like most babies, the first thing that occurred to me upon opening my eyes and looking at my surroundings in my parents' bedroom, was to cry because, I am sure, I felt lost in a strange new environment.

Elzira, my mother, who was 28 years old at the time, was not only re-lived to find out that I looked normal but also delighted to welcome me into her life; she had already been married for five years when I decided to show up and join her and my father, António, who was already 35. They had gotten married on December 21st of 1947 and, as the years had passed, she had become more and more anxious about motherhood so that by 1952 she clearly thought that it was never going to happen to her. Well, it did.

In those days, fathers did not attend the birth of their children in order to be part of such a unique experience. It was not the manly thing to do. Luckily for Elzira, when the much-anticipated moment arrived, she was left in the capable hands of an experienced midwife who, needless to say, knew exactly what to expect and do in such circumstances and, therefore, took complete charge of the situation at hand, especially when she realized that my mother was clueless about the entire affair. After many hours of pain and suffering, accompanied by much encouragement from the midwife, Elzira finally gave birth. Once the mess was cleaned up, my father came into the bedroom to comfort his wife and to inspect me. He was most pleased with what he saw. I was a beautiful boy. As the next few years came and went, I remained an only child. There would be no opportunity for sibling rivalries in my life.

My earliest memories are rather pleasant. I was fortunate enough to have grown up in a comfortable two-story home that belonged to my paternal grandmother who happened to be a widow. It was a four-bedroom house. It was occupied by herself and three out of four of her adult children who, after they had gotten married, just stayed on where now they were raising their own children. It was not an unusual family arrangement by local customs and standards by any stretch of the imagination. Each couple had a separate bedroom and, as kids arrived on the scene, they shared it with their parents when they were toddlers. Being an only child, the obvious advantage for me was that there was no shortage of cousins of my own age with whom to play and socialize daily. So, I never felt alone; there was always a cousin, girl or boy, willing to play with me. Between 1952 and 1955 alone no less than five of my cousins were born: Fátima, Graça, Eduarda, Carlos and Henrique. The late comer was Cecília, who arrived in 1958.

This closeness, for the adults living in the family home: my grandmother, my uncles and my aunts, however, was a different story as anyone who has lived in a crowded and multi-generational household can attest to; the most common one was the total lack of privacy which sometimes can lead to jealousies, conflicts and even animosity between family members. The good news is that young children are seldom aware of the rifts between adults going on in the background and, from time to time, in the foreground, too. For the vast majority of them the pleasure of having another child to play with whenever they feel like it overrides all the negatives associated with the inconvenience of putting up with the adults who had begotten them.

Most Azorean women of my mother's generation, she was born on April 13th, 1924, were expected once they got married, especially if their husbands had the financial means that permitted it, to become housewives and, eventually mothers. Elzira was not an exception to this rule. Throughout my entire childhood and adolescence, I was privileged to have at all times her full attention, protection, support and unquestionable love. Consequently, I grew up to be a self-assured and outgoing young boy, one that made friends easily and who possessed a sense of adventure. I don't remember ever being afraid of anything until much later in life.

These personality traits of mine were further developed thanks to my father's influence. Professionally, he was a competent public servant; he worked for the Governo Civil, the main department of the local regional government, and was well-liked and respected by his colleagues. Socially, he enjoyed the company of many friends because of his friendliness and easy-going manner. He was a born leader and was fun to be with. Come to think of it, he possessed what the French refer to as *joie de vivre* which was communicative. So, as a result of his many personal and professional attributes, and the fact that he had some financial means at his disposal, I was directly exposed to many social and cultural events that stimulated my body and mind. One might say that he spoiled me with his unconditional love and by showering me with all sorts of gifts that most children of my own age did not have: a tricycle, a bicycle, roller skates and hockey sticks, balls of all sizes, a train set, toy cars and boats of all shapes and sizes, puzzles of all kinds, comic books, and the list just goes on. Needless to say, my immediate cousins who had siblings did not consider themselves as lucky as I was. They had to share among themselves whatever they had. However, by playing with me they, automatically, were playing with everything that was mine. I was not a selfish child. I did not mind sharing because I enjoyed the company of other children. They were fun to be with.

Aside from the many toys at my disposal, there were also nice clothes that my parents, this was strictly my mother's domain, used to buy for me not only for my birthdays but also for special occasions such as Christmas, Carnival, Easter, the famous Festas do Senhor Santo Cristo dos Milagres, a major religious event in São Miguel, first communion, family weddings, etc.

In the Ponta Delgada of my childhood, for any boy or girl under the age of 10, there were essentially only three public celebrations noteworthy during the whole year: the first one was Christmas, *Natal*, the second one was the cult of the Senhor Santo Cristo dos Milagres, Lord Holly Christ of Miracles, a bust of Ecce Homo believed to have been a gift from Pope Paul III, in the XVI century, to a few nuns in São Miguel who went to Rome because they wanted to establish a new convent in the island. The last one was Carnival which enabled the young to put on costumes and attend a few neighborhood parties where goodies were made for the occasion, such as *malassadas*, a type of doughnut, music was played, confetti thrown about, and where some dancing for the teenagers occurred. These three festivities were totally different from one another but all demanded a lot of effort and enthusiasm from the local adult population in order to stage them.

In short, until the age of 9, I lacked absolutely nothing. To use a cliché, life was good. And then catastrophe struck.

On August 22nd, 1961, nine days after my 9th birthday, my father died unexpectedly in New York City where he had gone on a personal business trip. For my mother and myself, this was a tragedy of major proportions. Overnight, it changed dramatically our lifestyle. From living a carefree life, a life of abundance, all of a sudden Elzira, who was just a simple housewife and mother, a woman with limited education, was left a widow at the age of 37. She did not have a trade and much less a profession. She felt utterly vulnerable. Going forward, she would have to watch every single penny in order for the two of us to survive on whatever my father had been able to put aside during their last fourteen years of married life.

One of the first consequences that resulted from my father's sudden passing was that Elzira was kicked out of the old matron's house by one of my mother's brothers-in-law. Instead of coming to the emotional support of the widow and her son in distress when they most needed it, and out of all sorts of preexisting rivalries and jealousies that existed between all four siblings, and with the complicity of my paternal grandmother, this troubled man came to the conclusion that this was the opportune moment to get rid of the two of us. Fortunately, my maternal grandfather unexpectedly came to our rescue by allowing his oldest daughter, my mother, to return home and share his house without having to pay rent.

It goes without saying that returning to her parents' home was not an easy decision on Elzira's part. Fourteen years had passed since she had lived with them. Furthermore, she had enjoyed, thanks to her husband, an easy life without financial worries of any kind. Now she was returning to their house with a young son. She would have to share daily life once again with someone who was a bully. Her father had married my maternal grandmother when she was 17 years old and, by the time she had turned 18, she had already given birth to Elzira. As the years passed, she would give birth to another three children, two boys and another girl. The fact remains that my grandfather had ruled over them all with an iron fist. I don't think that he ever displayed any affection and much less love for any member of his immediate family. Consequently, daily life for his wife and four children had been mostly unpleasant. They lived in fear of this man. He was both abusive and nasty. In short, he was a tyrant at home. So, Elzira knew fully well what to expect by returning to her parents' home. Life was not going to be rosy going forward for old habits seldom change as time marches on. But she felt that she had no choice. She needed help and some support, badly.

It did not take long for her father to start showing his true colors once again. To further complicate matters, Elzira was counting on him to help her finalize António's unfinished business dealings with the American companies at the time of his death, a situation rendered more difficult because neither of them spoke English and had to rely on third parties for additional help.

Women in São Miguel in the early 1960s were not expected to know anything about business. Elzira only had superficial knowledge of her husband's business affairs. Therefore, she needed the presence of a man in order to be taken seriously and to command respect in a world totally dominated by men, and the only one available was her father in spite of all his personality flaws. The least that can be said about this period in her life is that it was most stressful and, indeed, painful. It took the rest of 1961 and all of 1962 to bring António's business dealings in America to a somewhat successful conclusion. I say a somewhat successful conclusion because the American companies took advantage of the fact that the little businessman from Ponta Delgada, António, had died to delay paying the balance of the money that they owed his widow for as long as they possibly could.

In the end, Elzira was left with just enough money to live from day to day if there were not any unexpected and unnecessary expenses. She made enormous sacrifices herself so that I lacked nothing. Her immediate goals were to make sure that I would finish elementary school, go on to high school and, ultimately, to university, something that António had always wished for me, something that he even had left written in a note before his ill-fated trip to America.

António himself had become an orphan at the age of 13 when his father, Manuel Augusto Machado, passed away mysteriously in Lobito, Angola, one of the former Portuguese colonies in Africa, where he was setting up an electric power station and, because of the financial hardship caused by his premature death, he had never completed his high school education which prevented him from advancing in his chosen career within the regional government of the Azores. He had come to see higher education as the means by which one could succeed in any chosen professional field, as an invaluable tool that opened all sorts of doors that otherwise might remain closed. In other words, he equated higher education with a certain degree of personal and professional satisfaction, fulfillment and happiness.

In the Azorean diaspora, one hears frequently that once an Azorean, always an Azorean. As someone who spent my formative years in that miniscule part of the world, I can vouch for it. Azoreans are sentimentalists at heart and, even though they have emigrated to all four corners of the world, they never forget their roots. So, before I continue my life trajectory, this is the opportune moment to say a few words about this unique archipelago named Azores.

The Azores, located in mid-Atlantic, was discovered by a Portuguese navigator, Diogo de Silves, in 1427. Its coordinates are: 30° 30' and 40° N and 25° and 31° 30' W. It is 1,500km from Europe and 4,000km from America. The archipelago consists of nine volcanic islands divided into three groups. The Eastern Group is composed of São Miguel and Santa Maria, the Central one is made up of Terceira, Graciosa, Faial, São Jorge and Pico and, finally, the Western Group has two islands, Flores and Corvo. The closest island to Europe is Santa Maria and the furthest is Flores. Between Santa Maria and Corvo there is a distance of approximately 600km or 336 nautical miles. Given its strategic location, the Americans saw fit to build two air bases in the archipelago, one in Lajes, Terceira, in 1943, and the other one in Santa Maria, in 1944. It goes without saying that the US paid good money to the central Portuguese government in Lisbon for the use of the two airports for many years. Unfortunately, the Azores itself never saw much of that money being reinvested in its own economic development which explains, at least partly, the continued emigration of its population throughout the 1900s and, especially, in the 1940s, 1950s and 1960s. The language spoken in the Azores is, of course, Portuguese.

São Miguel, the largest island in the archipelago, is 65km in length by 14km in width. Its total land mass is 759,41km². It's also the most populated with about 140,000 people as of 2020. Its capital city, Ponta Delgada, was established in 1518. It had a population of approximately 69,000 inhabitants in 2011. Today, it's by far the most important city of the Azores and its capital. The main campus of the Universidade dos Açores was founded there in 1976.

When I was growing up in the 1950s in Ponta Delgada, children started school at the age of 7. Until that age they were under the supervision of their mother. Elementary school itself consisted of four grades. At 10, pupils faced a choice: they could enroll in either an academic high school called *liceu* or in a trade school called *escola industrial*. I enrolled in the Liceu Nacional de Ponta Delgada, named today Liceu Antero de Quental after the most important Azorean poet who was born in São Miguel. The secondary program consisted of seven grades, with formal exams at the end of the second, fifth, and seventh. If successful, afterwards, students could proceed to higher education, the so-called privileged and happy few, which obliged them to travel to continental Portugal since there was no university in the Azores, or they could directly join the workforce.

In December of 1969, when I emigrated to Canada, I was enrolled in grade 6 of high school. I should have been already in grade 7 but, lamentably, I had failed grade 3 because of low marks in a few subjects. In those days, if a student failed a couple of subjects, automatically he had to repeat the whole program of studies the following school year. There was no remedial summer school to upgrade one's marks. I was part and parcel of a backward education system that penalized students needlessly, students who were ready to be promoted to the following grade in some subjects but could not do so because of the built-in unfairness inherent in a system that separated students from their peer group, other students with whom they had been ever since grade 1 in some cases, just because they had failed a couple of subjects.

The immediate impact of policies such as the one I just described is that it destroys an adolescent's sense of worth and self-esteem going forward at a critical point in his or her life. This ill-conceived policy in the field of education is typical of countries, usually poor ones, that make it as difficult as possible for the vast majority of its students to acquire a reasonable degree of literacy and numeracy and this explains the vast numbers of illiterate people in some areas of Portugal, especially in the Azores. Ironically, in the long run, this reality prevents the country itself from attaining its full potential globally relegating it to the tier of the so-called underdeveloped countries. When will politicians finally realize that a country's most important resource is its people?

As an aside, by contrast, when I arrived in Toronto in 1969 and enrolled in my neighborhood high school, Bloor Collegiate Institute, I noticed right away that much was done differently when it came to the field of education starting, of course, with the promotion of students from one grade to the next. Students who failed specific subjects were asked to attend summer school to upgrade their mark or, if for whatever reason that was not possible, they would have to repeat the failed subjects the following school year without having to repeat all the other subjects in which they had done well. Another difference that I found remarkable was the fact that students did not have tutors after school. Throughout most of my student life in Ponta Delgada, I had attended *explicações*, private tutoring at the students' expense, paid by their parents, of course, because my own teachers were not available for extra help. In Toronto, teachers were not only available and willing to help before or after school but they were also friendly and very approachable. They enjoyed teaching their subjects and expected all students to do as well as they possibly could.

Looking back, although some of my high school teachers in Ponta Delgada must have been competent in their field of expertise, I don't remember a single one who was approachable and friendly. They created an invisible barrier between themselves and the student body, the pompous idiots. The difference between them and their Canadian counterparts was like night and day. The result: in spite of a mediocre command of English upon arrival in Toronto, I quickly thrived in all subjects at Bloor Collegiate. So much so that one of my weakest school subjects, French, in Ponta Delgada, became within a couple of years of my arrival, my best subject. In fact, thanks to my Canadian teachers' level of expertise of their subject matter, coupled with huge doses of energy and enthusiasm on their part, the methodology that they employed, and the constant encouragement provided to all students, after finishing my high school studies I enrolled at the University of Toronto as an undergraduate student in French and Spanish and, afterwards, at the Faculty of Education of the same university in order to obtain the necessary certification to become a high school teacher of those two languages. Who could have predicted that from failing French in Ponta Delgada I would one day be teaching it at the high school level in my adoptive country? And when one considers that later I went on to complete two graduate degrees: an M.A. in French literature and a Ph.D. in Québec literature, it cannot be considered nothing short of a miraculous turn of events by any standard.

But returning briefly to my infancy, I must say that I remember with fond memories my elementary school teacher, Dona Mariana Carreiro, the word *dona* in Portuguese denotes respect for a woman. Indeed, she was already an older woman, perhaps in her late fifties, when I showed up in her grade one class. Among the local parents, she had developed the reputation over the years as a competent, no-nonsense type of teacher whose children had been her charges. Consequently, when my father found out that she was going to be the teacher to take pupils from grades one to four in September of 1959, he did not hesitate for a second to enroll me in her class. I quickly found out that she was strict but fair.

It's not so much the day-to-day running of a classroom that a young child remembers most but rather the special events that happened from time to time. In grades one and two, she picked me and three other boys, the most confident ones in her class, I suppose, to recite a poem at

Christmas time in front of all the parents who gathered for the happening in the Ginásio do Liceu, the local high school gym. That experience became a highlight in my young academic life. It was the first time that I found myself on stage in front of so many curious faces looking directly at me. The occasion terrified and elated me at the same time. These two ever so brief moments on the spotlight went well for me: they brought about the usual applause at the end of the poems. It was an experience that I never forgot. And, as it turned out, it would not be the last time that I would be on stage in my long life. More about this subject later.

Aside from these happy memories, what I remember most about Dona Mariana is that she would not hesitate to give a misbehaving student the strap. She would ask the poor fellow to come to the front of the class and extend his right hand with the palm facing up and promptly apply a certain number of thrashes, depending on the gravity of the "crime" committed by the victim who would end up invariably crying in pain. The reason why this punishment was always done in front of the entire class was obvious to the rest of us: it was a direct reminder as to what would happen if one of us dared to misbehave. Nowadays, it would have been perceived as child abuse and the teacher would be fired on the spot for such atrocious actions. In my days, however, parents always sided with the teachers and viewed them as second parents who could not do any wrong. If you were given the strap, it was because you had deserved it. No point complaining about it at home because they would never side with you, anyways.

By contrast, my memories from high school tend to be much more vivid than the ones from my elementary school days, especially those connected with my teenage years, a time when I started paying more attention to girls even though they were very much absent from all my classes. In fact, boys and girls were separated by sex not only in elementary school but also in high school. Consequently, we, boys, only saw them before school, at lunch time, when most of us walked home for the long break before afternoon classes resumed, or after school. During classes they were nowhere to be seen as they attended theirs in a different section of the *liceu*. Despite these needless social restrictions, groups of two or three boys, all friends, of course, would stand in strategic street corners to see groups of girls, all friends, too, go by at key times during the day. If a couple of boys were particularly interested in a couple of girls, they would follow them at a certain distance until they disappeared into their respective abodes. With the passage of time this distance got shorter and shorter and, if a girl showed any sign of some mutual interest, the more courageous boys would engage in some small talk with her and their relationship eventually would move on to exclusive dating without any parents knowing anything about it, it goes without saying. This type of premature courtship required a lot of time and patience to produce positive outcomes for all concerned. That said, it was fun to engage in it.

In my case, most of the time, I stuck together with my male friends. We had known one another for ages, so it seemed, by the time we were in high school. Before my teenage years, when I was 11 and 12, what brought us closer as friends was that some of us also played sports together. Soccer was our favorite, a typical choice for any boy born anywhere in the Portuguese-speaking world.

From the age of 13 onwards, the gang would get together at a favorite café, such as O Gil, Gil being the owner's given name, after school for conversations that would last until supper time. Everything under the sun was discussed at length. The topics ranged from politics, to music, to sports, to girls, to plans for the weekends, etc. None of us was ever in a hurry to return home. On weekends, especially on Saturday afternoons or evenings, there were classes on Saturday mornings, it was not unusual to go to the movies at the Teatro Micaelense. Aside from providing an escape from daily life by travelling the world virtually, this particular outing gave the boys the opportunity to see girls at intermission time. In those days it was customary to stop the movie halfway through so that the audience would go to the bar and order a drink or a snack. But because the girls were usually in the company of their parents or older siblings, there was seldom an opportunity to chat with them at intermission. But you could observe them from a distance and that was more than enough to satisfy most of us. Deep down, most of us were rather shy and, consequently, lacked the confidence to approach girls in the first place. Every now and then, especially at Carnival time, there were dances and these were very popular with all of us boys and girls because they were so infrequent.

Daily life in the summer time was drastically different from our winter routine because there was no school and we, high school students, did not work. As a matter of fact, I do not recall ever hearing about one of my friends working during the summer vacation. In a society that hardly had enough jobs to employ its adult population, there would not be any part time work for its adolescents anyways. Creativity was the key word in order to remain active and enjoy the freedom during the hot summer days. It was a time to relax and enjoy going in the morning to a beach called Praia do Pópulo, in São Roque, a small town to the east of Ponta Delgada, or to the local municipal swimming pool, located on the east end of Avenida Marginal, also referred to as Avenida Infante Dom Henrique, followed by lunch at home and, afterwards, at some point in the afternoon, a trip to a favorite café until dinner which was in turn followed by an outing to the Marginal in the evenings. Aside from going to the beach or to the swimming pool, going to the Marginal was the most fun because that's when boys and girls got together away from their parents' constant watch in order to chat and get to know one another. All these activities were group activities. Everything was prearranged ahead of time. I do not remember ever being alone at the beach, at the café or at the Marginal. Life was never boring. There was always something to do outside of the home. None of us missed watching TV in the comfort of our homes for the simple reason that it was not available in the 1960s in the Azores and, finally, when it became available in the next decade, it changed dramatically people's habits, as it did everywhere else in the world. Instead of looking for opportunities to mingle and socialize in the evenings, people started to stay home to watch TV programs, especially soap operas from Brazil.

The long summer vacation also gave me the opportunity in at least a couple of occasions to visit other islands in the archipelago. In 1967, I had the chance to travel by ship to the island of São Jorge with a friend of mine whose aunt and her husband lived there. They had a beautiful country home located on the south side of the island with a gorgeous view of the island of Pico, only 18km away, which derives its name from its most spectacular physical feature, that is to say, its mountain. At 2351m, it's Portugal's highest mountain. Tourists nowadays visit the island purposely to climb it in order to enjoy, from its top, on a clear day, the view of the surrounding islands: Faial, São Jorge, Graciosa and Terceira. It's a stunning sight to behold. In any case, my friend's relatives were an older childless couple who were delighted to have the two teenagers stay with them for a month or so. They did everything to keep us entertained in an island where there wasn't much to do, especially for people of our age. They made it a point of honor to take us to all corners of their beautiful island, an island that has recently become also a tourist attraction for all sorts of folks interested in hiking in a setting that is most idyllic. Besides its natural, unspoiled beauty, São Jorge is, as everyone knows, especially for cheese aficionados, world famous for the Queijo de São Jorge, a delicacy. While on the island my friend and I also met some of the local teenagers who were quite friendly towards us and who kept us involved in local activities such as weekend dances and the odd deep sea fishing expedition, which definitely was a first for both of us. All in all, my stay in São Jorge remains to this day one of my most treasured memories.

A couple of years later, in 1969, the last summer that I would spend in the Azores, a few of us decided to travel to the closest island to São Miguel, an island a mere 85km from Ponta Delgada, Santa Maria, to go camping there for a month in a place called Praia Formosa, fairly close to the biggest town in the island, a place named Vila do Porto. The location of our camp site was directly across from the white sandy beach, so unusual in the Azores as most are dark grey because of the volcanic origin of the islands, and in the immediate vicinity of a small motel. Once again, this trip turned out to be a wonderful experience. At night, four of us shared a small tent and the rest of the day was spent at the beach or in the small dining area of the motel where in the evenings pop music was played on a record player. We listened to the Beatles, the Rolling Stones, Roberto Carlos, etc., and, whenever a slow song was played, there was the possibility of some dancing as well with the local girls. Spending that much time with my friends, was a wonderful way to say goodbye to them because my trip to Canada was already looming large in the horizon. Essentially, it was only four months away.

These trips within the archipelago were not a first for me. When I was 6 years old, in the summer of 1958, my parents had taken me to Santa Maria where at the time the busiest international airport in the Azores was located. As a boy, I was in love with airplanes and in São Miguel, in spite of being the largest of the islands, there was only a miniscule airport located in Santana, close to Rabo de Peixe, on the northern side of the island and, therefore, not easily accessible on a daily basis to the people that lived in Ponta Delgada. Only rarely did our family go there, usually to say goodbye to a family member who was emigrating to America or Canada. So, this particular trip to Santa Maria gave me the opportunity to see firsthand all sorts of large airplanes that were constantly either arriving or departing on the way to North America or Europe. I was in heaven for a day. It was with a lot of convincing and coercing that my parents dislodged me from the terminal area to see the rest of the small island.

Just a few short months later, in October, they took me again on another trip, this time a seven-day cruise of all the islands in the archipelago aboard a ship called Carvalho Araújo. It was such a pleasure to travel from island to island and to visit some local sites. In Terceira, for instance, we had a chance to go to Lajes, a town where the Americans had built an airfield; in Faial, we visited the site of the Vulcão dos Capelinhos, a volcano that had erupted in 1957 just offshore and had destroyed all sorts of houses in the surrounding area prompting a wave of refugees to go to America under the sponsorship of a young senator at the time from Massachusetts by the mane of John F. Kennedy. In Pico, at a place named Lajes do Pico, we actually saw from the upper deck of the ship a whale being cut at a local whale factory. The smell was nauseating. Whaling was still allowed in the Azores at that time and it was a source of much needed revenue for the *picoenses*, as the inhabitants of the island are referred to. But what I remember most about the trip is the times when we had to disembark offshore in rough seas, because the particular island did not have a dock, and board a small motor boat called *lancha* that would take us to the port area. I was terrified. Just the idea of walking down the narrow metal ladder to the waiting motor boat in rough seas, gave me nightmares. But I survived the experience and its memory, although not pleasant, has stayed vivid in my mind.

Friends have always been important to me. Elementary school provided the opportunity to make some new ones who were not from the neighborhood; but it was in high school that I significantly increased my circle of friends. After my father's passing, especially, they played a decisive role in my daily life and I don't know how I would have survived without their friendship and daily presence in my life. So, a word or two about them is in order now.

My favorite partner in elementary school was Marco António. His father, Mr. Moura, worked for Radio Marconi and he liked to speak French with the two of us when we started high school (French was the first foreign language to be introduced in those days as part of the high school curriculum). Going to Marco António's home on Saturday afternoons was fun because, after homework was done, the two of us would go down to the backyard and shoot around a soccer ball to get rid of some excess energy. I remember the Moura family for another reason: Marco António's dad was the proud owner of a brand-new pale green Fiat 500 and, on occasion, he would give his son and friends a ride to school. To this day, I remember the unique smell inside the cabin of that brand-new car. Also, in the winter time, Mr. Moura used to put on driving gloves, a characteristic that always struck me as unusual because he was the only man that I knew who had that rare habit in

Ponta Delgada, a city that never gets really cold in the winter. The man had style.

Next to Marco António, stood Emanuel. The Vasconcelos', his parents, had a summer home, nestled amid several *estufas de ananases*, pineapple greenhouses, in Fajã de Baixo, a town relatively close to Ponta Delgada. Every once in a while, during the long summer vacation, I was invited to spend the day there and that was always a lot of fun because we would build kites from scratch and then try to fly them in a setting where there was almost never any sea breeze, a fact that made kite flying almost an impossibility, but that did not stop us. Emanuel had been a late arrival for the Vasconcelos. He had a much older brother who was a university student in the field of mathematics at the Universidade de Coimbra. As most Azorean university students studying in mainland Portugal in those days (there was no university in the Azores until the mid-seventies), he used to return to São Miguel on vacation in the summer. At the time, he was dating a beautiful young woman who, when I was in grade one, had been a teacher candidate in Dona Mariana Carreiro's class, my elementary school teacher. When she saw me for the first time at the summer house, a couple of years later, she still remembered teaching a young Roberto and asked me if I remembered her. Out of shyness and cowardice, I, blushing, said that I did not, although I did remember her vividly on account of her beauty and kindness towards me in that grade one class. After this blatant, unexpected, and totally unnecessary lie, I felt terrible about it and regretted having been such an idiot by not telling her the truth. She deserved better than that because she was such a caring person. Simply put, I did not have the courage afterwards to confess to her that I had lied, and I have lived for the rest of my life with guilt feelings about that moment of weakness.

Moving on to high school, my best friend was Luís whom I called França, because França was part of his family name, and because it sounded out of the ordinary. Although we were attending different high schools, our friendship flourished because we had girlfriends who were also neighbors and friends; until my departure to Canada the two of us were inseparable. Luís went on to become an important visual artist in Portugal.

Another friend was Zé, a nickname for José, whom I called Cabral, again because that name was part of his family name. He was the son of a medical doctor, and this is the fellow who in the summer of 1967 invited me to accompany him to the island of São Jorge where his father's sister lived with her husband. Cabral, like his dad, went on to become a medical doctor himself.

Still another friend was Necas, the short form for Nectário, the son of an optometrist, and yet another one was Tó, a nickname for António, the son of a pilot working for SATA, the Azorean Airliner, who just happened to be piloting the twin-engine Hawker Siddeley HS 748 manufactured by Avro, a British company, the day that my mother and I left Ponta Delgada to Santa Maria to board there a CP (Canadian Pacific) airplane that would take us to Montréal, Canada. I will never forget the kind gesture displayed by Tó's father as he asked one of the flight attendants to bring me to the cockpit so that I would see the island of Santa Maria emerge from the sea on that beautiful sunny morning of December 22nd, 1969. It was an unforgettable experience. I was saddened to find out a few years later that Tó had perished quite young from a self-inflicted gunshot to the head because his father was having an affair with his girlfriend. And there were other friends, too many to be mentioned here. All of them were excellent company and kept me interested and engaged in all sorts of activities and issues of the day.

In the late 1960s, most of my friends were in one way or another committed to political, social and educational reforms in a Portugal still dominated by a fascist government, that of António Salazar, which forbade and punished severely any political dissention. The Salazar years were certainly a very dark period in Portuguese politics which caused massive emigration from a country where so many of its citizens were illiterate and utterly poor in the mid XX century and saw no future to better themselves if they were to stay put, especially in the Azores, where professional opportunities for so many were non-existent.

It goes without saying that these friendships came to an abrupt end when I emigrated to Canada in December of 1969, shortly after having turned 17, in August of that year. When someone emigrates, it's very much like a premature death of that individual for all those left behind. In the space of just a few seconds one disappears from the daily life of relatives, friends and acquaintances. Time marches on for everyone and eventually and inevitably all concerned get used to the new reality. Most relationships do not survive a sudden physical separation.

For a while there were still a few letters written back and forth but, with time, those slowly became more and more infrequent and, eventually, stopped altogether. I was busy in my new country, which I loved from the very beginning, and so were my friends back home. Eventually, many of them, in turn, left the Azores to pursue higher education in mainland Portugal. *C'est la vie*! Such is life!

Between 1969 and 2018, I had a chance to get together in Ponta Delgada with only two of my former close friends: França, in 1987, and Cabral, in 2018, who happened to be there on vacation at the same time as me. Two chance encounters. Both occasions provided a unique opportunity to touch base after so many years had gone by, and to take stock of what we had done in the intervening time. The former had become an arts instructor and the latter a surgeon. Cabral was divorced. Both lived in continental Portugal and only returned occasionally to São Miguel on vacation. It was during these two brief encounters in São Miguel that I realized how many of my former friends had left the island, for one reason or another, to put down new roots elsewhere. I happened to be just one out of many.

Essentially, the years that I spent in Ponta Delgada can be divided into two very distinct periods: before and after my father's passing. Before his death, my life was carefree, after it, it was full of worries of one kind or another. Sadly, my father was going to be absent from my life at a time when I was going to need him the most for support and guidance, during my adolescence and young adulthood, just like his own father had been absent for him since 1930 when he had died unexpectedly in one of the former Portuguese colonies in Africa. My dad had been only 13. History has a nasty habit of repeating itself. Fortunately for me, the company of my good friends somehow compensated for the irreparable loss of my father.

To sum up, many years have passed since those dark days of the early 1960s when my personal world was turned upside down. Life has certainly taken many twists and turns but let me assure you, dear reader, that Elzira's laser-focused goal of seeing her husband's dream come to fruition, combined with her unwavering support and her capacity for self-sacrifice, eventually paid dividends. Without her protection and support I would not have amounted to much. But more about it in the next chapters.

I said it before, but it's worth repeating, life can change dramatically in the space of just a few seconds. It happened again to me in 1969, just like it had in 1961. In late 1969, I started a new chapter of my life in a beautiful new country in North America, an officially bilingual country full of immigrants from all over the world – Canada. It was the best thing that ever happened to me.

2

The Arrival in Toronto

In the evening of December 22nd, 1969, after having boarded a Canadian Pacific flight in Santa Maria that took the my mother and me first to Montréal followed by an Air Canada connecting flight to Toronto, we finally arrived at our destination. It was snowing and no one from our family was waiting for us at the airport. My uncle, my aunt and my two cousins had already been to the terminal earlier that evening but had returned home because they were not expecting us anymore on account of the bad weather. In fact, there had been a delay in Montréal because of a snowstorm. Canada, land of snow! As I quickly found out in the next few days, one of the most popular topics of conversation in my new country was the weather, especially winter weather.

Given that there wasn't anybody at the airport to welcome us, one of my first duties was to figure out how to use a public telephone with limited English skills. It was a frustrating experience. We did not have any Canadian coins. With my broken English, I finally got some good Samaritan to make the call for me by showing him on a piece of paper the number that needed to be dialed. Luckily, someone answered at the other end and the fellow gave the receiver back to me. My relatives had just arrived home from the airport and promised to pick us up shortly afterwards.

While waiting to be picked up, and since there was nothing else to do, it was time to start looking around more closely at our new surroundings in the terminal building. Everything was in English and French, the two official languages of Canada. I did not understand much of what was being said over the public address system nor, for that matter, what was displayed on the signage everywhere. That's when I realized for the first time the biggest handicap that was facing me – the lack of English or French language skills. It was not going to be easy to adapt to my new life without improving rapidly my command of English. The challenge ahead seemed enormous and it scared me. Would I be able to be up to the task? That said, the terminal itself was a hub of activity; in those days there wasn't much in terms of security and passengers and the public at large walked around freely everywhere. Furthermore, there were airplanes arriving and departing constantly and crew members in lovely uniforms walking about in all directions. It was most entertaining. Also, everything smelled so differently.

Finally, our relatives, my uncle José, my father's youngest brother, my aunt Eduarda, my mother's younger sister, and my cousins Carlos and Paula, showed up and after hugs and kisses they took us to their car, a metallic blue Dodge Coronet, parked at the terminal's parking garage. We placed the luggage in the trunk and off we were on our way to Bartlett Ave., in Toronto, where they lived in a rented house that belonged to a Portuguese friend of theirs. Everywhere we drove the streets were covered with snow. After getting off the car, in front of the house, I noticed the snow neatly piled on the front yard and it was then and there that I touched it with my bare hands for the first time in my life. I had no gloves, anyways. I was 17 years old. The snow's very fine texture and coldness amazed me. It was odorless and looked and felt like something out of this world. I had only seen it from time to time in movies such as *Doctor Zhivago* and *A Man and a Woman*, back in Ponta Delgada.

After showing us the house and where we were going to sleep, I was going to share a bedroom with my cousin in the finished basement whilst my mother was going to share one with her niece on the main floor, we went to bed as both my mother and I were physically and emotionally exhausted. It had been a very long day. The very next day we met the elderly French-Canadian couple, M. and Mme Doucette, who lived in the flat on the second floor. They were extremely friendly and welcoming.

Luckily for all concerned, we were just a few days away from Christmas Day and the New Year's celebrations. School was also on winter break. Consequently, there was lots of free time to get to know my relatives daily Canadian habits among which was the daily consumption of TV programming by the whole family, especially my two cousins. Indeed, a lot of time was spent in front of the little screen. For me, come to think of it now, that habit was not necessarily a waste of time as I learned a lot of English just by watching with my cousin some of his favorite shows such as *Star Trek*, with William Shatner, Rowan and Martin's *Laugh-In* and *The David Frost Show*. It was like taking a crash-course in spoken English, just what I needed before starting school in January of 1970.

Christmas and New Year came and went rather quickly. During the festivities, my mother and I met some of the Portuguese families with whom my uncle and aunt socialized at parties on a regular basis. A few days after the holidays, we finally saw my other uncle João, my mother's youngest brother, and my aunt Vidália, the couple who had sponsored us to come to Canada. They had driven to Fall River to celebrate the holidays with my aunt's side of the family who lived in that corner of Massachusetts. João, when I was growing up, had always been my favorite uncle because he was the youngest of my uncles and because he was a lot of fun to be with. I had been the ring bearer at his wedding, and he had shown me how to ride my bike, something that a young child never forgets.

In early January of 1970 all Ontario students returned to school after the Christmas holidays and my uncle João and a personal friend of his, an engineer of Azorean descent who worked for Ontario Hydro, at the corner of University Ave. and College St., took me to the Toronto Board of Education main office building located almost next door to it, and I submitted an official document from the Liceu Nacional de Ponta Delgada, my high school in São Miguel, certifying that I had completed five years out of the seven required to get a high school diploma. The document was in Portuguese and, consequently, needed to be translated so that someone could assess properly my credentials and give me equivalency in Ontario. On January 13th, 1970, Mrs. Lemieux, a Supervisor at the Evaluation Centre of the Ontario Department of Education, determined that "on the basis of the information in your report from a secondary school in Portugal, you have standing equivalent to the Ontario Grade eleven level." My fate was sealed. I was, however, devastated by the news. In my humble opinion, given that I had completed successfully five years of studies in Ponta Delgada, and on account of my age, I had turned 17 in August of 1969, I should have been placed in grade 12. It was a definite set-back. I was going to be in a class with students who were a couple of years younger than I was, and I was facing the real possibility of not being promoted to the next grade in June on account of my lack of English fluency. My predicament made me apprehensive, and the immediate future did not look promising. Would I be able to succeed? The future would tell.

3

Bloor Collegiate Institute, 1970-1973

I was told to enroll at Bloor Collegiate Institute, my neighborhood high school. When I arrived at the main office to register in the company of my uncle João, we were told to see the school's principal, Mr. Stubbs, an older gentleman who, upon finding out that my family name was Machado, that my country of origin was Portugal, and that I was not fluent in English, suggested that I go next door and enroll in a technical school, a suggestion that if it had been acted upon would have blocked any possibility of me attending university upon graduation. This man was clearly under the impression that anyone arriving from Portugal was uneducated and, therefore, not university material. It was my first contact with blatant discrimination based on country of origin. However, after being told of my aspirations, I intended to attend university, he relented and registered me officially. I became at that moment a Bloorite, as students attending the school are called. Right after completing the paperwork himself, he nevertheless took the trouble of showing me my locker in the basement, gave me a lock and demonstrated a couple of times how to work the number combination to get it to open. I was placed in Miss Huggins's home form class. All students belonged to specific home form classes at the beginning of each school day. She also taught the class English. Because of my lack of fluency in

English, I was also going to be taking a special class of English as Second Language (ESL) for recent immigrants. My other subjects were: French, Mathematics, History, Geography and Physical Education. I specifically remember with fondness my teacher of French, Mme Turcotte, a French Canadian. For me, it was the first time that I had as a teacher of French a native speaker of the language teaching her mother tongue to non-natives, mostly anglophones. Her total command of all aspects of the language made a world of difference in a classroom setting and it was an experience that I did not forget going forward. At the end of the school year, in June, I managed to pass French and Math. ESL did not count as a credit in those days. Miss Huggins wrote in my report card under comments: "Robert is working very hard and I am sure that once he has mastered English he will do very well." She clearly saw potential in me. That summer, the summer of 1970, my first summer in Canada, I had to attend summer school to continue upgrading my English skills, especially my oral ones which were inferior to my written ones.

Also, what is noteworthy is that just before the end of the summer vacation I landed my first Canadian part-time job. I somehow found out that a big new restaurant, The Old Spaghetti Factory, was opening shortly in downtown Toronto and that management was looking for part-time help to put the finishing touches on the premises. They needed students to sweep floors, put the tables and chairs in the right places, hang some pictures up and the like. I went to the address and was hired on the spot. That said, within a few days, once the place was spic and span, management let us go. Luckily, school was about to restart. My cousin Carlos and I celebrated the end of the long summer vacation by going to the National Exhibition grounds, known as the Ex, a huge amusement park by the waterfront where we went on all the rides and ate hots dogs with French fries and drank Coke.

In the meantime, Elzira was taking government sponsored adult English classes for New Canadians to have a minimum working knowledge of the language so that she could survive and "prosper" in Canada. She found her classes challenging to say the least. Once the six months of classes were over, a friend of the family found her a job in a cosmetics factory, Elizabeth Arden, in downtown Toronto. The work was easy to do and, consequently, my mother started to relax a bit, finally.

In September of 1970, I was enrolled again in grade 11, except in French and Mathematics, the two subjects that I had managed to pass the year before. I would be taking those at the grade 12 level. Mentally, I was more than ready this time around to be as successful as possible in all subjects. Mr. Juergen Hoffmann, my history teacher, was also my home form teacher in 1970-71. As the year progressed, he noticed my hard work, determination and excellent marks and provided lots of encouragement. The result? That June I graduated from grade 11 with Honors. Mr. Hoffmann wrote on my report under comments: "I am very pleased with this report Roberto. Well done." He also rewarded my hard work by choosing me to represent the school by participating in a federal government summer student exchange program called the Young Voyageurs Program. It consisted of a 10-day trip by airplane to Ladner, one of Vancouver suburbs, in British Columbia, on the west coast of Canada which included, on the return leg of the trip, a two-day visit to Ottawa, the country's capital followed by a final train ride from Ottawa to Union Station in Toronto. I received a congratulatory letter from the Minister Without Portfolio, the Honorable Robert Stanbury in which he said:

> As Minister responsible for Canadian Citizenship, it gives me great pleasure to congratulate you on the honor of being chosen to participate in the Young Voyageur program which is coordinated and financially supported by the Government of Canada.
>
> I hope you enjoy the exchange and will be most interested in having your impressions arising from it when you have time to write.

Thanks to Mr. Hoffmann, I was well on my way to discover other parts of my vast adopted country.

In the late Spring of 1971, my relatives bought a house in Mississauga, a city to the west of Toronto. My mother and I moved there with them. Their decision to live in the suburbs caused all sorts of problems for myself and my mother. High school students in the 1970s were obliged to register in their district high school. If you moved out of the district, automatically you had to change schools. Consequently, when in June of 1971 Principal Stubbs found out that I had an address in Mississauga, he quickly made the decision to enroll me in a high school in that city. But good old Mr. Hoffmann came to my rescue and pulled some strings at the school's office so that I could stay at Bloor Collegiate, a school that I had become very familiar with and in which I was doing so well.

Consequently, in September of 1971, I was enrolled in grade 12, except in French and Physics – they were at the grade 13 level. Mr. McDonagh was my home form and English teacher. If one of my highest marks in grade 11 had been Physics with Mr. Saylor, it was my lowest mark ever in grade 13 with the same teacher. It was all about mathematics and the fact that I was not taking Math did not help. By contrast, my highest mark ever at the end of grade 12 turned out to be in grade 13 French. Slowly but surely, I was coming to an important conclusion: if I were to be accepted at university, I would be furthering my studies of modern languages, possibly French and Spanish with the objective of teaching them myself at the high school level.

The rest of the school year was uneventful except for the commuting. My mother was still working in Toronto and I was studying there, too, but living too far, in Mississauga. So, in December of 1971, she found a flat in a home owned by an elderly Italo-Canadian couple, Mr. and Mrs. Bellissimo, located at 745 Lansdowne Av., fairly close to the subway line and within walking distance of Bloor Collegiate, for a reasonable rent and the two of us moved out of our relatives' home in Mississauga. It was one of the best decisions that she ever made in her life. The number of hours travelling back and forth was dramatically reduced for both of us and, in my case, I could concentrate on my studies because there were no family distractions of any kind, especially television. For the next four years we would live on the second floor of that house.

Early in 1972, in February, my mother's mother, Margarida, passed away in Ponta Delgada at the age of 65. I still remember Elzira siting on the edge of her bed and crying upon finding out the sad news in a letter. Ever since my father's passing in 1961 and until December of 1969, mother and daughter had been inseparable and had become very close. My mother was also Margarida's first born. As a result of her loss, she started making plans to return that summer to São Miguel in view of accomplishing two objectives: sell my grandfather's house and bring him to Canada.

At about the same time of my grandmother's passing, my teacher of grade 13 French, Mme Carter, made her class aware of an educational opportunity run by the federal government of Canada in conjunction with provincial ones that literally changed the course of my future studies and of my life: she told us about the Summer Language Bursary Program. Bursaries of $600.00 were available for any deserving student who was at least 17 years old and a Canadian citizen or a landed immigrant. I fitted the criteria and, more importantly, Mme Carter was willing to write a reference letter on my behalf. I started looking forward to the summer of 1972 with trepidation.

4

The Summer Language Bursary Program, Summer of 1972

Ah, the Summer Language Bursary Program! It was a federal government sponsored program for senior high school students as well as college and university ones who could get a bursary and attend it literally for free, so to speak. I chose École française d'été, at the Université de Montréal.

On June 9th I received a letter from the Université de Montréal that said the following:

Monsieur,

Nous avons bien reçu votre demande d'admission à l'École française d'été 1972.

Nous constatons que votre dossier est complet et nous avons le plaisir de vous informer que votre demande a été acceptée.

Nous vous rappelons que tous les étudiants doivent se soumettre à un examen de classement. Vous devrez donc vous présenter à la salle Z-110 (entrée U-1 de l'Immeuble principal) le jeudi matin, 29 juin 1972 à 10 heures; à cette fin, le plan ci-joint vous sera très utile.

Aline Dagenais
Directeur
École française d'été

N.B. Vous êtes prié de conserver la carte d'étudiant ci-incluse qui vous sera nécessaire pendant la période de l'École française d'été.

The program itself was six weeks long; it ran from Thursday, June 29th to Friday, August 11th. In its promotional brochure, Université de Montréal claimed that:

L'École française d'été is designed to attract a wide variety of students: Junior College and University students (aged 18 or more as of July 1st) who are anxious to improve their proficiency in French; civil servants, professional people and persons from the business world who wish to become bilingual; teachers of French who wish to improve their knowledge of the language; people interested in French for cultural enrichment. The French summer school is an excellent opportunity for teachers of French who have never lived in a French environment.

I took the train from Toronto's Union Station to Montréal's Central Station, Gare centrale de Montréal, where Mr. Eduardo de Paiva Melo, his wife and two young daughters, were waiting for me. They had settled in that beautiful city after emigrating from São Miguel. He worked for the city in the area of outdoor maintenance. They were very good friends with my uncle José. Furthermore, they were *compadres* which means that my uncle and his wife were godparents to one of their daughters. They quickly took me to the residence at the Université de Montréal that I would call home for the next six weeks. Upon arriving at my destination, I introduced myself to the person on duty and Mr. Melo was impressed with my level of fluency in the French language and told me that he doubted that I would be requiring his help any time soon. He was right about that.

École française d'été remains one of my best summers ever. I found myself in one of the world's greatest francophone cities, living in a university residence with breakfast, lunch and dinner provided daily, except on weekends, and attending grammar and literature classes in the morning and early afternoon followed by all sorts of cultural, sports and social activities in the evening. All this offered in a language that I had come to love, French. It was an unforgettable experience, one that confirmed my choice for a future professional career. It was also an amazing opportunity to meet Canadian students from other provinces and territories.

Particularly, I remember Gerri, the short form for Geraldine, a girl from Winnipeg, Manitoba, who had travelled by train with a girlfriend of hers, Darlene, all the way from her native city to Montréal, a trip that took three days. In fact, Gerri and I became such good friends that in December of that same year I travelled by airplane to Winnipeg just to see her. I figured that a girl who had the sensitivity to quote a few words from Saint-Exupéry's *Le petit prince*, as she did in a drawing that she offered me, was well worth a trip to frigid Winnipeg in the middle of the winter. I stayed at Paul's home who happened to hail from Winnipeg too. In any case, I don't remember the details of the planning anymore but he had agreed to host me for a few days in the basement of his parents' lovely home.

My Winnipeg trip was a memorable one if nothing else because I saw for the last time Gerri and witnessed with my own eyes the flatness of the landscape in and around the city and the huge amounts of snow everywhere.

I particularly recall with fondness Gerri inviting me for dinner at her family's home where I met her parents and sister; they received me warmly. I had brought with me, by way of thanking her for all her troubles, a Gilles Vigneault record. We had seen the *chansonnier* perform live that summer and both of us had been blown away by his songs, his incredible level of energy on stage and his showmanship. On another occasion, Gerri and I went to a restaurant called The Fireplace, on Pembina Highway, for dinner where we enjoyed a meal and where we had a chance to be alone and reacquaint ourselves. During the evening, I became aware that her feelings towards me had changed, that the magical moments that we had shared at Université de Montréal were no longer there. I was disappointed. I decided to return to Toronto as soon as possible. Our long-distance correspondence lasted for a few more weeks with letters going back and forth between the two of us before it stopped altogether. Eventually, like most long-distance relationships, it fizzled out for lack of oxygen. During the last fifty years I have wondered occasionally what became of her and if she had a happy and fulfilling life. She deserved it.

Before leaving Winnipeg, I gave Paul's mother, Mrs. Adams, as a token of my appreciation for hosting me for a few days, a Beethoven album. She was a sophisticated woman who enjoyed listening to classical music. I think she appreciated the gift although she probably already possessed that particular album. Paul was kind enough to drop me off at the airport and I flew back to Toronto. I have never returned to Winnipeg.

I also had the pleasure of meeting Jim, short for James, another fellow from Winnipeg. Come to think of it now, there was a large contingent of Winnipeggers attending École française d'été that particular summer. He had just finished his undergraduate degree at the University of Manitoba that summer which meant that he was older than most of us. He had driven from Winnipeg to Montréal by car. He had just purchased a beautiful 1972 silver Camaro. A dream of a car for any dashing young man such as himself. Needless to say, he became instantly popular among the rest of us because of that car. He used to drive us around Montréal in the evenings before we would end up inevitably at the Café-Campus, a local hang out for university students. A pub that served beer, some fast food and where dancing also happened on weekends. In Jim's case, he was attending the summer program because he wanted to improve his French and because he intended to live and work in Montréal, which he actually ended up doing in the fall of 1972. When I visited him in his tiny apartment in Nun's Island in the summer of 1973, he was already working for a laboratory company as a sales representative.

All of us were so young and foolish back in 1972. In those days, cigarette smoking, beer-drinking and sexual experimentation were common occurrences on campus residences. I remember vividly a group of us:

Jim, myself, Gerri, Darlene and Jo-Anne, a girl from Vancouver, coming back from an outing to the Café-Campus a bit drunk. We decided to continue the conversation in Gerri's room. Single rooms were rather small in the residence and the five of us in a room was just one too many. At one point I stretched out in Gerri's narrow bed and before long I was joined there by Jo-Anne. Before I could count to three, we were necking right in front of everyone. When Jim and Darlene decided that they had had enough and left, Jo-Anne got up as well and at that moment I asked her if she wanted company. She said "yes". We took the elevator up to her room all the while kissing and once in the room proceeded to do some more necking accompanied by heavy petting. It was as far as it went.

When I saw Gerri the next day, at supper time, in the cafeteria, I intended to apologize for what had taken place in her room but before I could do it, she was the one who asked me point blank what had happened in Jo-Anne's room. When I said "not much", she believed me and dropped the subject. From that evening onwards, at the end of the day, we used to get together either in her room or mine for some kissing, necking and petting. That was as far as both of us were willing to go. We never engaged in sexual intercourse itself.

The organizers of École française d'été were truly committed to making sure that all of us enjoyed ourselves. There was no shortage of activities from which to choose. Some of the most memorable ones were a weekend trip to Québec City, a jewel of a city in North America, an outing to Jerry Park to see a game between the Alouettes baseball team and another team, a visit to Terre des Hommes, the follow-up of Expo 69, an evening with French Canadian *chansonniers*, one of whom was no other than the great Gilles Vigneault himself, many frequent visits to Le Vieux Montréal, etc. I was in heaven and I don't think for a moment that I was the only one.

In any case, after the summer course was over, Jim invited me, Paul, and a guy from Newfoundland to drive back with him to Winnipeg, a journey that would take several days. The Camaro could accommodate only four people. I declined the kind offer because I needed a summer job to make some money before classes resumed in September. But the other two accepted and the unfortunate fellow from Newfoundland ended up being operated for appendicitis in northern Ontario, in a small town named Kenora, therefore delaying the return trip to Winnipeg for Jim and the other fellow by a couple of days.

I got my first real Canadian summer job after returning from Montréal. From a heavenly experience at the beginning of the summer I went to a hellish one in the later part of the same summer. I worked from 4 to 12 o'clock at the Rowntree chocolate factory. The work was not hard to do but it was tedious, mindless work. I worked alongside an older woman who had been working at the factory for years. She was a very kind woman and when I left to return to school, she offered me a lovely pen in its case which I still possess to this day. She knew that I loved studying and figured that I would make good use of it. She was right.

As a diversion from the tediousness of the job at the chocolate factory, an Italian friend of mine from high school, Orlando Buonestella, and I used to go to the film showings at the Revue Cinema, an art house and repertory theatre, located at 400 Roncesvalles Avenue, not too far from High Park. The price of admission was more than reasonable and the cinema itself not too far from our neighborhood. Orlando and I considered ourselves film buffs and at the Revue we were exposed to films by Fellini, Bergman, Werner Herzog and others. After each showing we would go for coffee and discuss the pluses and minuses of the production. These were animated conversations that lasted a couple of hours or so before we would go our different ways.

5

A Farewell to Bloor Collegiate Institute, June of 1973

1972-73 marked my last year in high school. It was the easiest of them all. I had already completed two grade 13 credits the previous year. I needed to complete another four to get my High School Honour Graduation Diploma and move on to university. My timetable allowed for a lot of free time between classes which I put to good use by reading all sorts of books. Aside from the odd weekend get together with my relatives in Mississauga or the odd party at my favorite uncle's home in Etobicoke, one of Toronto's boroughs, life just seemed to be unfolding as it should.

A major highlight in the fall of 1972 was the much-anticipated hockey tournament between Canada and the former Soviet Union (USSR) known as the Summit Series; it kept me, and everybody else in Canada, glued to the TV screen for the entire 8-game series. The first four games were played in Canada and the next four in the Soviet Union. Before the Series started, most Canadian hockey fans, especially the pundits, were convinced that the professional athletes from the National Hockey League (NHL) that made up the Canadian team were far superior to the Soviet ones in every aspect of the game. That opinion changed overnight. We were all shocked with the result of game one: USSR 7 – Canada 3. The Canadian team had been clobbered and, as we watched the Soviet team outperform the Canadian one in all aspects of the game, we realized that the Series was not going to be a walk in the park for the Canadian contingent. That said, the outcome of game one was the best way to stimulate interest in everybody as the Series unfolded across Canada and, afterwards, in the Soviet Union. At the end of the Canadian leg of the Series, the Soviets had won two games and tied one. The Canadian roaster had managed to win just one game at home. The outlook did not look promising at all as the Series moved to Moscow. It got even worse after the first game there with the result of USSR 5 – Canada 4. The Soviets had taken three games to one lead in the Series and were playing in their country now. Most Canadian fans did not think that Canada would be able to recover from such a deficit and much less win the Series. Luckily for Canada, its team won the next three games and Paul Henderson made history by scoring the winning goal with just seconds left on the clock in the final game. In doing so, he became instantly a national hero, made all of us proud, and established Canada's reputation as the country to beat in ice hockey. To this day, although many people refer to hockey as the national game of Canada because of its popularity, in fact that distinction is reserved to lacrosse, a game invented in Canada. Regardless, many boys and girls love passionately the game and start playing it when they are quite young. It's a passion that will last their entire lifetime.

The next memorable event that stands out for me took place on Friday, November 3rd, at 2:30 p.m. That's when Bloor Collegiate celebrated the Forty-seventh Annual Commencement during which I was granted the Grade 12 diploma. I had come a long way since arriving in Canada with limited English skills.

Another key event for me that has stood the test of time is the Canada-wide tests for Admission to College and University that took place on December 6th, 1972, at our school. Essentially, there were two types: The Canadian Scholastic Aptitude Test (CSAT) and the Canadian English Language Achievement Test (CELAT). I did well in both and the next step in the early months of 1973 was the choice of a university. Students could choose three different ones in order of preference. After visiting the campuses of York University and of the University of Toronto, I was leaning towards the former because the tour for incoming undergraduate students had been so interesting and informative. There was, however, a major drawback, the distance to the main campus. My third choice was Queen's University located in Kingston, a city to the east of Toronto and Canada's first capital. I had no intentions of attending it because the cost of tuition and accommodation would have been prohibitive, but I had to pick three universities and Queen's had a fine reputation. To make a long story short, I was accepted by all three universities and, luckily, common sense prevailed in my final decision - I chose the University of Toronto and one of its most respected and old colleges, St. Michael's College or St. Mike's, for those of us with fond memories of our undergraduate days spent there. It's a decision that I have never regretted making. It's there that I was fortunate enough to meet people who would become lifelong friends and, in a few cases, colleagues of mine in my chosen profession. Furthermore, the University of Toronto was the closest of the universities to my place of residence; in ten minutes by subway, I could be on campus.

Finally, in 1972, there was my trip to Winnipeg in December to see Gerri. Emotionally, it turned out to be a major flop and, upon returning to Toronto, I tried to put it out of my mind. Our relationship was over.

At the end of June, my high school days were done and it was time to say so long to some of my favorite teachers. It was a bittersweet moment. Bloor Collegiate had been good to me. I had matured and blossomed in its classes. But, as the saying goes, all good things sooner or later come to an end. Fortunately, that summer of 1973, a few of us Bloorites were employed to staff a summer program by the catchy name of Program Ketchup with the purpose of keeping youngsters occupied during the long summer days by teaching them a few arts and crafts, engaging them in reading activities, and by taking them on outings to local parks. A couple of young women from Saskatoon, Saskatchewan, Terri and Grace, who had moved to Toronto, had posted an ad in our school Guidance Department asking students to apply for an interview. I did and was accepted together with a few of my friends such as Mario Amato, Enrico Iafolla, Jenny Fidel, Joe Curatola, Antonietta Difresca, Virgilio Palermo, Paula Spensieri, Maria de Sousa and others. The summer camp was to take place in the basement of St. Anthony's Catholic Church on Bloor St. West, not far from our school. It turned out to be a wonderful experience which, the following year, my best friend Mario Amato and I ran again under the "new" name of Program Ketchup II. Now, it was our turn to hire Bloor students to join us in this worthwhile endeavor. This time around we were fortunate to find a school by the name of St. Joseph's Elementary School that was vacant in the summertime, also close to Bloor Collegiate. Both programs allowed the staff to gain invaluable skills dealing with young children. It also made all of us more responsible, resourceful, and budding entertainers.

The next event that I remember vividly happened in early September of 1973, on Tuesday, September 5th, to be exact; my mother's father, Virgínio, passed away after being sick and hospitalized for a while at the Queensway Hospital, in Etobicoke, resulting from all sorts of complications related to diabetes. The poor fellow only outlasted his wife by a year and a few months; she had passed away on Wednesday, January 12th, 1972. Another factor that contributed to his quick demise was the fact that he was living in a country whose language he did not understand and in a hospital setting where no one spoke Portuguese. He felt totally isolated. He was like a fish out of water. The only regular visitors that he could look forward to seeing were my mother, his son João, and his other daughter Eduarda, who could only drop by briefly to comfort him after their workday was over. He simply gave up and decided to let go. He was going to be seventy years old on November 9th. He is buried at the Holy Cross Cemetery, 8361 Yonge St., Thornhill, Ontario, where one can find a Doric bronze memorial with his name engraved on it. I have kept both fond and nasty memories of him. The fond ones have to do with the month-long that I lived with my grandparents in the spring of 1960 while my own parents were on a trip to continental Portugal, and the nasty ones encompass the period between December of 1961 and December of 1969, the period during which my mother and I had to live in his house after my father's death. The kindness that he had displayed in 1960 and while my father had been alive just about evaporated overnight and, as time went on, especially during my teenage years, although we lived in the same house, I tried to ignore the man. That said, he did not have to welcome the two of us into his house. Yet, he did it, which just shows that most people are made up of a combination of good and bad traits in constant struggle for supremacy.

After my mother and I left for Canada in December of 1969, finally my grandparents were left all alone. Three out of their four children were now living in Canada with their respective families, and the other one, an army career man, was fighting in a war of attrition, a losing cause, in Africa, between Portugal and the natives of its colonies. Both of my grandparents were dead within three years of our departure from Ponta Delgada.

6

University of Toronto, Saint Michael's College, 1973-1977

In September of 1973, I started my undergraduate degree at the University of Toronto, the largest in Canada, a university with a sterling international reputation. I was registered at St. Michael's College, founded in 1852. As it turned out, my choice of college was one of the best decisions that I ever made in my life. The next four years provided a lot of intellectual stimulation as well as numerous opportunities to socialize by participating in social, cultural and sports activities that can only be available to someone who enrolls in a large university with tremendous resources at its disposal. Right from the start I made numerous new friends, people who have accompanied me in my life trajectory ever since, either professionally or personally.

In 1973, President John Evans was in charge of the university and in his welcoming letter to the undergrads that year he stated:

> Academic work, although of primary importance, is only part of university life and the student who wishes to derive maximum benefit from the university experience will certainly want to be involved in the wider life of the university. Participation in university government, in clubs and societies, theatre and music groups, athletics, student newspapers, literary journals, social events and countless other activities are open to all interested students.

I wanted to take full advantage of it all and, therefore, I followed his advice to the letter. To that end, prior to arriving on campus, I had chosen my subjects carefully; they were: Modern French Literature, French Language and Composition, Intermediate Portuguese, Beginning Spanish and an Introduction to Sociology. All students had to carry five full-year courses. Also, I had been told about Orientation Week and its varied activities and the possibility of being part of its planning committee. I dove right in. Right away I met two other guys: Charlie Campisi, who was going to study mostly English and Philosophy, and Sal Minardi, who was going to pursue a degree in French and Italian studies. Sal happened to know some of the incoming first-year students coming to the College: Antoinette, Joyce, Angela, Angelo, and others. And because some of them were going to be studying French, like myself, we became good friends which was facilitated by the fact that we found ourselves together in many of the same classes. Frequently, we would have lunch in Canada Room, the main cafeteria at St. Mike's, and spend time in between classes chatting in Brennan Hall, the most popular lounge at the College. It was a lot of fun to spend time with them all because they were full of energy, enthusiasm and initiative. So much so that when Joyce, whose parents hailed from Croatia, invited the group in early October to attend a fundraiser banquet and dance on Saturday, November 3rd, at 6:00 p.m., in the basement of a Croatian church on Manning Ave., Our Lady Help of Christians Church, a number of us welcomed her enterprise with open arms anticipating a great time. In my case, I purchased my ticket to the event not knowing that Bloor Collegiate was holding its Forty-eighth Annual Commencement at 8:00 p.m. that very same evening. On October 18th the school sent out a formal invitation to all its graduates. For a few days after receiving mine I debated whether to let down my new friends in order to walk across the stage one more time to receive personally my Honour graduation diploma and socialize perhaps for the last time with some of the students and staff who had been part and parcel of my life ever since my arrival in Canada. Finally, I opted for the banquet and dance at the

Croatian church. Emotionally, I had already moved on and felt that the Commencement was going to be for all intents and purposes a repeat of the previous year's one when I had been granted the grade 12 diploma. Besides, I had already said my good-byes to my favorite teachers and friends at the conclusion of the school year that June.

As a direct consequence of having volunteered for Orientation Week, I quickly got familiar with the workings of Student Union and the Senate; the latter was composed of fifteen members elected by the Student Body for a one-year term. The idea of running for Senator and "defend" students' rights appealed to me. I stored the idea in the back of my mind for future reference. In the meantime, I was going to enjoy as much as possible all sorts of planned events such as dances, plays, concerts, sports, etc., all of which were readily available at my fingertips.

And that's how I met Marie while attending a dance, staged in Upper Brennan. She was two years ahead of me. She was specializing in French and Italian and wanted to be a high school teacher. We exchanged phone numbers and for the next while we dated on a weekly basis. She lived in Scarborough and was registered at Scarborough College, one of the two satellite colleges associated with the University of Toronto, the other one being Erindale College, in Mississauga. She also used to work part-time on Saturdays as a bank teller on College St. So, our routine that first winter was something like this: I would meet her by the bank after work and we would go for dinner somewhere. Afterwards, we would take a walk to Toronto City Hall or to Hart House, both places invariably deserted at that time of day, where we would talk and neck for a while. In the summer, on account of the good weather, we used to go to parks and we would engage in similar activities there. Frequently, we would also go to movies and plays. We even went on a special outing to see La Comédie-Française in its *Tournée Canadienne* of 1974, at the O'Keefe Centre. Alas, the venue, too large, was not appropriate for the staging of a play, or any show for that matter and, furthermore, the two plays that the famous troupe chose to perform were not very well known to the public at large: *La Station Chambaudet*, by Eugène Labiche and *Mais n'te promène donc pas toute nue!* by Georges Feydeau.

That spring, Marie graduated from Scarborough College with her BA and she invited me to attend the graduation party staged at the Scarborough campus. I, of course, was delighted to accept it. I borrowed my cousin's blue Ford Mustang and drove to her house to pick her up. I had very little practical driving experience at the time and at a street corner not too far away from her home, I realized that I had driven too far into the intersection and into the lane of incoming traffic. I proceeded to back up a little without noticing that there was a car right behind mine. Bang! I had smashed into the front grill of the other car causing some minor damage. After telling the other driver that I did not have insurance, he was kind enough not to call the cops on me, he just took my phone number and address. It was understood that he would contact me with regards to the costs of repairing his car. It was a terrible start for what otherwise turned out to be a fun evening. She had done it! She had gotten her degree. I hoped to be able to imitate her at some time in the near future. In September, she would be attending the Faculty of Education.

We had many things in common: she was the first one from her family to attend university and me too; she was an excellent student and me too; she wanted to be a high school teacher and me too; she enjoyed the theatre and me too; she was kind and generous and me too; finally, both of us wanted to experiment a bit with sex without going all the way, of course, because, after all, she was not only Italian but also Catholic and going all the way was something reserved for married couples. It was an exciting period in my life. That said, the fact remains that by the time I graduated from St. Michael's College, in 1977, we had already stopped dating altogether. She had found somebody else to love and me too. Life went on.

Relationships that one considers so important at a point in one's life, with the passage of time, and as one meets other people, sometimes just fall apart. Such is human nature. Many years later, at a conference for teachers, we met by chance and I found out from her that she had married an Italian guy who taught French at York University and that she was the proud mother of five daughters. I was very happy for her.

In 1973, my professor of Modern French literature was Jean-Claude Susini and on my very first class, as we were all sitting around a large rectangular table at Teefy Hall, I looked to my right and saw a relatively young man with long hair and I asked him in French, of course, if he was taking the course, like the rest of us. He looked at me with a big smile and said: "No, I am teaching it." I had confused him for one of us undergrads, a gaffe of enormous proportions, so I thought. Apparently, not for him though. As the year progressed and he got to know me better as a serious-minded student, my awkward remark never surfaced in our conversations. He probably had forgotten about it. He was one of the few professors that I came across who would be able to lecture without any notes in front of him. He was a source of inspiration and, therefore, it was a pleasure to be in his classes. Aside from being a scholar, he was also entertaining, approachable and friendly, a terrific combination.

I remember running into Professor Susini in the Quad, in the fall of my second year, after the elections for Senate were over, and him asking me if I had won the race for senator. When I told him that I had not, he said: "Not to worry, Roberto, great men like Victor Hugo also lost when they ran for politics the first time. Try again."

A couple of years later, when I was no longer in his classes, he invited myself and Michel, a fellow undergrad who was involved in the staging of the yearly French Play, to accompany him home and partake in the drinking of a couple of beers. The topics of conversation kept on jumping from subject to subject and before we knew it his wife at the time invited us for supper and made a spaghetti dish that was delicious. And many more years later, when I was already a teacher myself and married, I invited him, divorced at the time, and Jean-Paul Ginestier, a fellow teacher at Harbord Collegiate Institute where both of us taught, and his wife Anne, to come for supper at my own house in Mississauga.

During the evening summer projects came up and when he found out that my wife and I were travelling to his native France that summer, he graciously invited us to drop by his house in Le Vigan where he spent most summers, which we did to our greatest pleasure.

It's funny how some people never forget certain happenings in life, trivial or not. One of the dishes that my wife prepared for that special dinner was *rissóis de bacalhau*, a traditional Portuguese delicacy made with cod. Decades later, after remarrying and retiring and having moved to Windsor where his new wife taught French at the University of Windsor, in our sporadic correspondence my email, he still remembered how delicious that particular dish had been. Incredible!

After I started teaching high school and whenever I happened to visit St. Michael's College, either on account of the French Contest or the staging of the French Play, I always made it a point of dropping by his office for a little chat. And, when my daughter Natasha was born in 1989, he took the trouble of giving me a gift for her, a puzzle that he had picked up at some antique show. A very touching gesture on his part that I have never forgotten.

In between these times, there was still another occasion when he invited myself and my wife and some other friends to his house in the east part of Toronto. He was living alone at the time and worked very hard at preparing a delicious dinner that included as one of the courses a mouth-watering couscous dish.

I was hoping to see him in person again in 2019 when the University of Toronto's Troupe des Anciens celebrated its 50th anniversary. Unfortunately, he could not attend the wonderful celebration.

As an undergrad, I wanted very much to be involved in all sorts of activities on campus. In my second year, I ran unsuccessfully to be a senator and serve on Student Council. It did not work out. Not one to be discouraged easily by defeat, I ran for President of the Cercle Français, this time successfully. It was a position from which I derived a lot of personal gratification and, as a bonus, it opened up all sorts of other doors for me and, more specifically, a chance to participate as an actor in the staging of the French Play whose director was Professor Paulette Collet. The Cercle Français was responsible for coming up with activities where students could practice French outside of a normal classroom setting. So, aside from the usual wine and cheese parties and crêpe lunches, staged on St. Michael's campus, there were also outings to local French restaurants and to Le Théâtre du P'tit Bonheur, the precursor of the Théâtre Français de Toronto, to watch *Les Fourberies de Scapin*. These activities were open to all students of French and the faculty of the Département d'études françaises. It was during one of these occasions, a wine and cheese party, staged at Brennan Hall, that I met the unforgettable Professor Collet, otherwise referred to by all of us who participated in her plays throughout the years as "Madame".

Again, like Professor Susini, she was one of those scholars who would play a huge part in both my student and personal lives. She invited me in 1975 to play the role of Capitaine des Pompiers in *La Cantatrice chauve*, by Ionesco. It was a dream of a role in a play that came to symbolize the theatre of the absurd. The last time that I had been on stage had been in May of 1969 in Ponta Delgada, when *As Professias do Bandarra*, by Almeida Garrett, a Portuguese playwright and poet, was staged at the Teatro Micaelense as part of the festivities associated with the Festas do Senhor Santo Cristo dos Milagres. Then I had played a minor role, a silent one. Now, I was given a wonderful opportunity to shine on stage in a language other than my mother tongue. That's when I truly caught the theatre bug, so to speak, a bug that has stayed with me until now. That year, *La Cantatrice chauve* was going to be played in conjunction with *George Dandin*, one of the many Molière plays.

I was fortunate enough to be coached by a perfectionist, Madame, who demanded and expected only the best from each and every member of an amateur troupe made up of mostly anglophones who were in the process of mastering French. I quickly realized that I did not know much about acting and much less about enunciation. Fortunately, I had fallen into the hands of a Molière expert and a theatre enthusiast who had wanted herself to become an actress at some point in her life before turning to teaching. Rehearsals took countless hours during the week, after classes, and on weekends leading to the show. Madame herself led by example: she was willing to sacrifice a lot of her free time to offer to the public at large an outstanding production in French at a time when the number of plays being staged in the language of Molière was insignificant in Toronto.

The following year, in 1976, she asked me to play the role of Zapo, in Arrabal's *Pique-nique en campagne*, another play typical of the theatre of the absurd, as part of a double bill; the other play being *Les Précieuses ridicules*, by Molière. The shows were going to take place during the Semaine francophone and, as a guest of honour, Fernando Arrabal himself had been invited to attend one of the performances. It was a unique opportunity to shine again on stage. At the end of the show Arrabal stepped on stage to thank the actors for their effort and to answer questions from the public at large. I have kept a photo of myself standing next to the great playwright and my script of the play where he wrote: "*Para Roberto Machado, con todo cariño. F. Arrabal (en recuerdo de tu excelente interpretación de Zapo).*" What else could a simple amateur actor from Toronto ask from a vedette such as himself? Thanks to Madame, I had reached the pinnacle of my theatrical career, so I thought.

But that performance was not going to be the end of my association with Madame. After going on to the Faculty of Education at the University of Toronto in 1977 to obtain my professional certification as a high school teacher of French and Spanish in Ontario and establishing myself professionally at Harbord Collegiate Institute, a high school within a mere 20-minute walk from the St. George campus, I was invited by Madame once again to play the role of Géronte, an old man, in a play by Jean-François Regnard entitled *Le Légataire universel*. It was 1984 and the play was going to mark the official opening of the new theatre at St. Michael's College, a theatre that would provide a steady home, finally, for La Troupe des Anciens. Sadly, the play could only be staged on June 15th, too late in the school year to attract any university students still left on campus. That said, for me, it was another chance to step on stage and to learn a role written in verse, a first for me. Again, in 1987, she asked me to interpret the role of Damis in the staging of *Tartuffe*, another play in verse, and in 1997, the role of M. Loyal, in the same play. The year before, in 1996, Madame had tapped on my shoulder to replay the role of Capitaine des Pompiers. It had been 20 years since I had played that role for the first time. The opportunity brought back lots of good memories and it was fun to reimagine how the role could be played differently.

In the early 1990s, Madame thought of the idea of staging special matinées for high school students of Core French and French Immersion before the evening shows for the public at large. As a high school teacher of French programs in an academic high school, I was invited to bring my senior students to one of the shows and that tradition went on until I retired from teaching.

Starting in 2000, as a member of Troupe des Anciens, I became more and more involved with other aspects of the production, namely stage directions, publicity and, more recently, ticket sales. Informally, I also became the unofficial "archivist" of La Troupe des Anciens. I had collected over the years many programs, posters, photos, videos, etc. associated with each of the productions. In other words, I had accumulated a treasure trove of material that proved to be most valuable when it came time to the publication of the "coffee-table" book marking the 50th Anniversary of the Troupe des Anciens. Even now, in 2019, Madame still counts on me to play minor roles from time to time. In an amateur troupe such as ours everybody must pitch in whenever and wherever there is a hole to be plugged.

All the experienced gained in the world of the theatre prompted me, in 2010, upon retiring from the Toronto District School Board and after two promotions as Head of Modern Languages in two high schools: Malvern Collegiate Institute and Harbord Collegiate Institute, to consider and undertake a Ph.D. in this fascinating domain. I chose a *Québécois* playwright by the name of Marcel Dubé and some of his plays in the 1950s, 1960s and 1970s, to be the focus of my thesis. I analyzed this body of work from a socio-semiotic point of view. Born in 1930, Dubé dominated the emergent typical Québec theatre scene for decades. He deserved that someone take yet another look at his body of work out of gratitude for his enormous contribution to an amazing art form – the theatre world.

Another instructor who played a critical role in my life was Professor Laura Fernanda Bulger. When I met her in 1973, she was a lecturer in the Department of Hispanic Studies. She had met in Lisbon John, a Canadian citizen, who was the Head of the Science Department in a high school in Toronto. They had married and now the couple had settled in Etobicoke. I had chosen Portuguese as one of my subjects because I wanted to perfect my knowledge of the language and become more familiar with the literature of the Portuguese-speaking world. During our first-class usual introductions and after hearing that I had completed my fifth year of high school in Portugal, she said that I was going to be rather bored in her class because none of the other students was as fluent as me. She was right, of course. The reason I mention her is that in the future our paths would cross frequently. I explain. After teaching that course, she got a job at Harbord Collegiate where she taught Portuguese and Spanish in grades 11 through 13. She taught there from 1975-1980. In 1980, she returned to the University of Toronto to teach Portuguese, and I took over as teacher of Portuguese and Spanish at Harbord Collegiate. From that point on, we became very close colleagues and friends. She had started a unique cultural event at Harbord Collegiate called Noite de Teatro, a play in Portuguese. I continued that tradition from 1981-1989, the year that my daughter was born. This extra-curricular activity connected me with the theatre world in very practical terms. I had had numerous opportunities to act in plays but not to direct any of them. Now, it gave me the opportunity to do so, gaining, therefore, invaluable experience in all areas of a stage production, including publicity. No one wants to stage a play without an audience in attendance.

Professor Bulger eventually got her Ph.D. from a Portuguese university while teaching at Glendon and moved back to her native Portugal. In the intervening years, while at Glendon, she worked tirelessly to establish a minor program of studies in Portuguese at the college. Regretfully, we did not succeed in bringing it to fruition in spite of all her efforts which were countless. I say we because I was heavily involved in the process too. It was many years after she had left Canada that such a program would see the light of day at York University's main campus. Our only consolation was that we had prepared the groundwork for the next group of Lusophones who tried to establish such a program at that university. In the meantime, we had fought the good fight!

In 1989, when my daughter was born, Laura and her Canadian husband, John, were about to leave Canada for Portugal. They were going to put roots in Porto. Professor Bulger had found a job in a Portuguese university and her husband, who had just retired as Head of Science in his high school in Toronto, was looking forward to tutoring English to Portuguese students in Portugal. Throughout the 1980s, Laura and I had come to appreciate one another's qualities as hard workers, organizers and fighters in education. Before they left to Portugal, they visited us in Mississauga and brought a gift for Natasha, our daughter. Something that touched my wife and I very much but that was not unexpected given the nature of the woman and of our relationship.

Many years later, when she came to Toronto to participate in a conference, it was around Thanksgiving. My daughter was doing a masters in Forestry Conservation at the University of Toronto and dating already a fellow student who would become eventually her husband, I made it a point of honor to fetch her at the hotel where she was staying so that she would partake in our Thanksgiving dinner. She was very happy to see all of us after so many years had passed. The first time that she had seen my daughter she had been a baby. Woefully, Laura was suffering from Crohn's disease, a disease that had taken her to England in search of a cure forcing her to be separated from John for long periods of time. There, she spent almost two years undergoing various treatments without much success. The fact remains that her disease destroyed her marriage; she and John had decided to divorce amiably. In any case, she appreciated our gesture and we had a chance, in a relaxed environment, to reminisce about many things. The last time my wife and I saw her was in her native Lisbon in 2013. When she found out that we were going to be in Lisbon, she got all excited and immediately invited us for a get together. She met us at our hotel and took us for lunch in downtown Lisbon, by the Tagus River. Afterwards, she showed us her condo and her neighborhood and made plans for another get together after our return from the Algarve. Again, she met us at our hotel and we spent a couple of very happy hours in one of the hotel's restaurants. Regretfully, that was the last time we saw her alive. Afterwards, we still wrote emails back and forth and it was in one of them that she informed me that she was back in a Lisbon hospital suffering from a serious case of leukemia. It was through a friend of hers, Professor Onésimo Teotónio Almeida, from Brown University, that I found out she had died at the hospital. My wife and I were very saddened by the news.

After this long aside, it's time to return to my undergraduate adventures. In 1974, I was chosen to represent the Portuguese students' point of view in the Department of Hispanic Studies Staff-Student Advisory Committee. It was another very valuable opportunity to voice student concerns and aspirations when it came to the delivery of Portuguese courses. Although at the time I did not think that all participatory opportunities in the field of education would bring about noticeable improvements and positive change overnight, especially in education where things happen ever so slowly, inevitably some good comes out of the many hours that one spends in this type of meetings. There were seven students and seven professor representatives in this committee. One representing Portuguese studies, myself, the other six, Spanish studies. As I remember, one point that was made time and again by the student representatives was that all courses leading to specialty should be taught in the target language. Although some of the faculty of the Department of Hispanic Studies were internationally recognized scholars, a few of them were not fluent speakers of Portuguese or Spanish. In fact, some of them taught the material of their literature courses in English. We, the students in the committee, were totally against this practice. On the other hand, the faculty representatives were lukewarm to the idea of change. One thing that we students took away from the meetings was how much professors enjoyed listening to themselves. Like I said, invariably someone always learns something from meetings of this nature, if nothing else how to conduct them in a polite and efficient manner. For me, they also provided a glimpse into the inner workings of a large Department at the University of Toronto.

My third and fourth years at St. Mike's were extremely busy from both intellectual and social points of view. I continued my involvement with the Cercle Français and its activities and, starting on the 6th of November, 1975, the rehearsals for *La Cantatrice chauve* commenced in earnest too. The two shows for the public at large were scheduled for January 30th and 31st of 1976, at the Vic Theatre, right in the middle of the winter. The choice of dates was, as usual, entirely left in the capable hands of our artistic director, Professor Collet. That said, in the middle of a bitterly cold winter, and there were many, you would think that people hesitated a bit before setting out to see a play at the University of Toronto. Not so. Madame's reputation for putting on a good show was already well established by the time that I started acting in them. The two-hour rehearsals were brutal though, as Madame, being the perfectionist that she was and is to this day, demanded the best that we could offer in terms of talent. Besides, as I pointed out before, most of us were not native speakers of French and Madame was forced frequently to stop the rehearsal to correct our pronunciation so that these rehearsals turned frequently into phonetics and diction lectures. Once a teacher, always a teacher; Madame never missed an opportunity to enrich us and all of us were the better for it.

As the date for the shows got closer and closer, so did the frequency of the rehearsals, including some on weekends. It is said that actors, even amateur ones, will do anything in order to shine. We were a dedicated and committed group to the success of the enterprise and none more so than Madame herself. The result was that even in a so-called theatre like the Vic Theatre, which was nothing more than a lecture hall, the shows were always a hit. At intermission, one of the actors passed a hat and people paid what they could to defray the costs associated with the production. Most university students in attendance, being notoriously cheap by nature, contributed next to nothing, of course. Most of the money raised came from the parents and relatives of the cast as well as from the francophone community. As for us, members of the troupe, none of us cared much about the financial aspect of the production. We were in it because we loved the theatre, that's all.

After our second and last show, after returning the costumes and accessories to Madame's office to be cleaned and stored for January of the following year, Madame had made a tradition of hosting a wine and cheese party at St. Mike's where we would reminisce about the high and low points of the present production. Some speeches were made, some gifts were handed out at around midnight and, after all food and drink was gone, and after many kisses and hugs were exchanged, we all went home happy to have been part of such a unique event. To this day, I have very fond memories of that very first show in which I participated. I had learned lots and made some friends for life.

As a byproduct of my heavy involvement in the French Play, my overall average dropped. But what the heck, it had been worth it! After having taken another Portuguese course in my second year, an Introduction to Luso-Brazilian Literature, with Professor Parker, starting in my third year, I was obliged to focus mainly on French and Spanish courses in view of obtaining a double specialization. There was no more room in my timetable to accommodate anything else. My goal was to become a high school teacher of French and Spanish, those were the most popular modern languages, aside from English, of course, being taught in high schools across the province of Ontario and especially in and around Toronto, its most multicultural city. In those days, Portuguese had just been introduced in two high schools run by the Toronto

Board of Education: Harbord Collegiate and Central Commerce High School, two schools with good Portuguese representation in their student body. That fact was something to keep in mind going forward in my chosen profession.

At the beginning of the 1976 summer, the Bellissimos, our landlords, decided to put up their home for sale and kindly asked the two of us to start looking for another flat. As it so happened, one of their sons, who lived at 725 Lansdowne Avenue, just a few houses down the road from theirs, had just sold his house to a Portuguese couple, Mr. and Mrs. Afonso, who wanted to rent the upstairs flat to help pay the mortgage. They had two youngsters, a girl, Sonia, and a boy, David, both of whom were still too young to attend school. So, it was agreed that my mother would babysit them while their parents went to work. Within days, we moved our few belongings from one flat to the next and life just went on to everybody's satisfaction. The two children were a distraction for my mother and kept her from thinking about her own health issues. As for me, now I was living just across from my best friend Mario Amato. It suited me just fine.

In the fall of 1976, I only needed to take two French courses and two Spanish courses to get my double specialist qualification. Regrettably, all the Spanish courses were half courses. Anyone who has taken half courses knows that they are much more intensive than a full course. All the course work is concentrated in a semester. Be that as it may, there was no other alternative but to put up with it. Also, this being my last year of undergraduate studies, I needed to make sure that my overall average did not suffer as a result of my extra-curricular activities. I needed good marks to be accepted at the Faculty of Education.

For the last six years I had been a Landed Immigrant in Canada. In order to become a teacher in Ontario I thought that it would be a good idea if I finally became a Canadian citizen. To that effect, I was given an appointment at the Court of Canadian Citizenship (Storefront) located in those days at 900 Dufferin St., for Wednesday, September 15th, at 6:45 p.m. I was told to bring with me the following original documents:

a) Passport on which you and/or your family originally entered Canada, b) Immigration Identification Card or Record, c) Two pictures approximately 2" x 1 " including signature on the front on the bottom. Finally, I was told that there would be a fee of $12.00 cash, certified cheque, a money order payable to the Receiver General for Canada. At the office, a bureaucrat informed me that Citizenship involved three steps: 1. The Application; 2. The Hearing, and 3. The Court Ceremony. Now that the Application was completed, it would be posted for three months, as required by law, and shortly afterwards, I would receive a letter from the office advising me of the date of my Hearing. So, to prepare for the upcoming Hearing, I was given a sheet containing twelve possible questions that the Judge could consider asking me to assess if I was a deserving candidate. All of them had to do with the geography and the government of Canada. Out of these three steps, by far the most interesting one was, of course, the Court Ceremony. I was told to memorize, if at all possible, the Oath of Allegiance: "I swear that I will be faithful and bear true allegiance to her majesty, Queen Elizabeth the second, her heirs and successors, according to law, and that I will faithfully observe the laws of Canada and fulfill my duties as a Canadian citizen, so help me God."

On January 14th, 1977, at the Court of Canadian Citizenship, located at 55 St. Clair Ave. East, in Toronto, in a very emotional and touching ceremony, under some pomp and circumstance, I proudly became a Canadian Citizen. It was a privilege and honor of the highest order for me.

One of my two French courses that year was Woman in French-Canadian Literature and to my great surprise and jubilation the professor delivering it was no other than Professor Collet herself. Upon seeing me in her class on the very first day, she proceeded to recruit me for the next French Play to be staged in January of 1977. How could I refuse? I could not and, frankly, over the decades have known very few people who have declined the offer. The funny thing is that she still did not know for sure what plays she was going to stage when I asked her about it but she assured me that she had a role for me, anyways. Before long, she revealed it: I was going to play Zapo in *Pique-nique en campagne* by Arrabal who was going to be invited for the première. The University of Toronto had money for such cultural events in those days!

The rehearsals started on November 17th and the shows were scheduled for February 5th, 7th and 8th, 1977. *Pique-nique en camapagne* was going to be played in conjunction with *Les Précieuses ridicules*, by Molière. Just like *La Cantatrice chauve* had been played in conjunction with *George Dandin*. Whenever Madame chose a one-act play by Molière, she would choose another short play as part of a double-bill performance. Usually, Molière was the second play to be performed in honor of the great man; this time, however, Arrabal's play was going to have that honor because the playwright himself was going to be present for the performance.

Having participated the previous year in the French Play was a tremendous advantage. I knew exactly what waited me and prepared accordingly for another "marathon" commitment of my time and energy. In short, all three shows were a tremendous success and, as I said before, I felt very privileged after the final bow to stand next to Arrabal himself who graciously signed my script. After the closing show, the usual wine and cheese party followed it at St. Mike's and, after saying our goodbyes, we all went home tired but extremely happy and satisfied with the success of the shows.

After four years at St. Mike's, I was ready to graduate and move on to the Faculty of Education where I would learn, hopefully, to be an effective teacher of French and Spanish and, perhaps, Portuguese too. That said, as you will see in the next few chapters, I never really have left St. Mike's.

7

Ontario-Québec Permanent Commission, Summer of 1975

Dear Mr. Machado,

I am very pleased to confirm that you have been selected to participate in the Ontario-Quebec Summer Student Job Exchange Program. You will find below information on the job you are being offered with the Quebec Government.

Ministry: Tourisme, Chasse et Pêche
Position : Exploitation des Parcs
Salary : $120.00 par semaine
Location : Parc des Laurentides
Date: 20 mai – 5 septembre

In order to place the maximum number of students in the available jobs, and to inform the selected students as soon as possible, we would ask you to seriously consider the job we are offering you and give us your firm decision. It is unfortunate when positions are left vacant due to later withdrawals and insufficient time to find alternative candidates. Therefore, we would ask you to send us a written reply either accepting or not accepting the offer, and your letter must be postmarked no later than April 18. If you mail your reply after this deadline, or if we do not hear from you, the job will automatically be offered to another candidate.

When we receive confirmation of your acceptance of this offer, we will be forwarding you information regarding accommodation, travel subsidy, name of person to whom you should report in Quebec.

Congratulations, and I look forward to hearing from you.

Maurice Demers,

Executive Secretary/Secrétaire général

Of course, I accepted the position right away. I was eager to return to a province that had welcomed me so warmly in 1972. In addition, I wanted to be totally immersed in the French language again. Therefore, the first thing I did upon receiving the excellent news was to go out and purchase a car to get to Parc des Laurentides, north of Québec City. I bought a second hand 1974 red and white Camaro on April 28th. It reminded me very much of Jim's silver Camaro, a car that had been thoroughly enjoyed in the summer of 1972 during the six weeks of École française d'été. On May 5th I received the rest of the information as promised by M. Demers. My boss was going to be M. Bernard Chartrand, with an office at the Vieux Moulin; a telephone number followed these precious details just in case I would get lost. Also, he was kind enough to provide me not only with the name of another Ontario student, John, who had been placed at Parc des Laurentides, but also his phone number. Upon receiving this information, I contacted John and drove, with Marie by my side, to Streetsville, a neighborhood in Mississauga, where he was living with his parents in order to meet him personally. I quickly found out that, like me, he was in love with everything French. It was agreed that I would be giving him a ride to our common destination at Parc des Laurentides. John turned out to be a hell of a nice guy and we did many things together that wonderful summer of 1975.

So, on Saturday, May 17th, John and I set out on our long drive to Québec City. We shared the driving although the terms of my insurance did not cover for it which meant that, in case of an accident, any claims submitted to the insurance company if the person driving the car was anybody else except myself would be automatically denied. Luckily, the trip was uneventful. For the next couple of days before proceeding to Parc des Laurentides we stayed in one of the student residences belonging to Université Laval, in St. Foy, a suburb of Québec City. The rooms were basic but comfortable and the cafeteria was open for business: breakfast, lunch and supper; in addition, the prices were more than reasonable too. And, best of all, Vieux Québec was only a short drive away. That summer, John and I made it a habit, whenever we drove together to Québec City from Parc des Laurentides, on our couple of days off every week, to stay at that student residence.

On early Tuesday morning, May 20th, we drove to Parc des Laurentides, a large, unspoiled, beautiful provincial park much admired by the *Québécois* and all sorts of tourists looking to spend time in northern Québec, especially Americans, located right in the middle of highway 175 linking Québec City to Chicoutimi. In those days, at the entrance of the park, there was a gate and one had to stop and say to the people manning the little office where one was coming from and where one was going. As we were getting closer and closer to our destination, we were shocked to notice that the ground underneath the trees was still quite white – the snow had not melted yet in this part of our country! Upon arrival at the Vieux Moulin, we were welcomed by M. Chartrand and treated to a wonderful breakfast during which we met the other people who would be working in different areas of the park. John and I were separated. I was going to be working at Camping La Loutre, located in a gorgeous setting next to Lac Jacques-Cartier, the biggest of the many lakes dotting the park. He, on the other hand, was going to be in the Vieux Moulin area. M. Rivard, an older gentleman, would be my immediate boss. My other colleagues were Luc, Denis and a couple more fellows whose names escape me now. Luc was a veteran. He was older than the rest of us and he had already worked at the park for a few years when I met him. He had lost the right eye as a young boy and wore a black patch over it. That handicap did not stop him from driving a car, a Chevrolet Nova, a name that became the butt of many jokes in Latin America because it literally means in Spanish "It does not work", and much less from operating a mountain bike which he brought to the park occasionally. He also had a chalet in Stoneham, a short distance to the south of the park where he used to entertain some of us occasionally. He was heavily into drugs. Except for him, the rest of us were all university students. A few of us, like myself, had never been close to nature. We had much to learn that summer about working in a provincial park.

After breakfast, M. Rivard showed me and the other people assigned to Camping La Loutre the house where we were to live; it was a decrepit old house that offered a minimum of comfort; he would be living in the one next door, a much better one and, afterwards, he took us to our office at the entrance of Camping La Loutre. The campsite itself was almost next to L'Étape, a restaurant and gasoline station halfway between Québec City and Chicoutimi and Lac-Saint-Jean. He explained our duties and, after a short question and answer period, he dismissed us until lunch time. We were given time to settle down in our house. In the meantime, at the office, he was left to work on a rotating timetable for all of us.

Before the campground was to open to the public the following weekend, there was a lot of work to be done on the grounds: the individual campsites had to be cleared, the Men's and Women's washrooms freshly painted and cleaned, the locks in the trailer park primed, and the list went on and on. After the park officially opened, we worked for a certain number of hours at the office, welcoming and registering the campers, assigning campsites, collecting fees and issuing receipts, and the rest of the time we maintained and patrolled the camp grounds. Breakfast, lunch and dinner were in the kitchen of the main restaurant at the Vieux Moulin. The Chef and his helpers took pride in their work and, accordingly, prepared excellent meals for the numerous restaurant guests and, indirectly, for us, the staff. *Vive la gastronomie québécoise!*

Within the next few days, we all adapted to our new work routine. At meal times, I used to see John every once in a while. The rest of the time, I was strictly dealing with my francophone coworkers and mostly

Québécois campers. This was ideal to improve my French. Every once in a blue moon, American campers passed through the park, too. And, because they could not say much in French, they were ecstatic to find out that I was fluent in English. Most of them used to arrive at the office in incredible trailers. They were a home away from home, literally. Many times, after my shift was done, I was invited by them to drop by for a beer and to chat. Life was good.

Whenever John and I were free from our duties for a couple of days, not always on weekends because those were very busy days for camping, we used to drive to Québec City for entertainment. There was never a shortage of things to do in Québec City and we took full advantage of it. At some point that summer, a few of my friends from St. Mike's arrived for École française d'été at Université Laval. They were Antoinette, Joyce, Angela and Sonya. It was fun spending some time with them now and again. And, when my birthday came around on August 13th, we all drove in my Camaro to the Vieux Québec to celebrate the occasion in a local restaurant. How we all fitted in that car is beyond my comprehension.

One afternoon, I got a phone call from John at the office. He had met two American women in their early thirties who were staying at his campsite and he had befriended them. They were teachers vacationing in Québec. He was inviting me to go down to Québec City for an evening of fun with them. Normally, John and I did not drive all the way to Québec City just for an evening. It was not worth it on account of the distance involved. But he promised me that we would have a good time and I accepted the invitation. The four of us hit it off right away. We walked for a bit in the neighborhood of the Château Frontenac, along the boardwalk looking at the sights, and afterwards went to our usual brasserie where we did much talking and drinking. Late at night we returned to the park. I was too drunk to drive. So, John took the wheel and I sat in the back seat with the teacher with whom I had been talking most of the evening. Before long, we were necking. Once at their tent, John and the other woman started making out and shortly afterwards the two of them left to go to John's room. I was left in the tent with my companion who quickly proceeded to undress herself and me. The rest is history. We got together with the two teachers a couple more times at the park, went boating with them in one of the lakes, drank a few more beers at their campsite and, a few days later, they left on their journey across the province of Québec never to be heard from again.

In early July, I returned to Toronto for Marie's sister's wedding. I asked M. Rivard for a few days off which he promptly accorded me. Since there was no way that I would be driving all the way from Parc des Laurentides to Toronto and then back within just a few days, I asked him, whose main residence was in St. Foy, if I could park my car on his driveway while I was gone. He graciously agreed to my request. From Québec, I took a bus to Montréal and from there another one to Toronto arriving at my home very early on Friday morning. Since I needed a car for the wedding, I phoned my favorite uncle and asked him if I could borrow his wife's Camaro for the next day, Saturday, the day of the wedding. It seems that everybody had a Camaro in those days. He agreed to it. So, on Saturday morning I went to his home in Etobicoke, one of Toronto's boroughs, to pick up the car and then drove to Marie's home to meet her. The two of us quickly reconnected and after bringing each other up to date on the latest news, we prepared for the wedding ceremony. Much later, during the reception, I inadvertently found out that during my absence she had been dating occasionally another fellow. I was a bit surprised but not shocked. On Sunday morning I returned the car to my uncle's home, saw Marie briefly one more time, and off I went to the bus terminal to initiate my return trip to Parc des Laurentides. The crazy things that one does in the name of love.

Back at Camping La Loutre, every once in a while, on clear nights, Luc used to invite me for a motorcycle ride where he made it a point of not just riding on highway 175 at top speed but also of taking some dirt road that led, I thought, to nowhere. All of a sudden, he would stop, shut off the engine, and the total silence and the bright sky full of stars would amaze the two of us. We would be wonderstruck, especially after smoking a couple of joints. After a few laughs for no reason at all, we would climb back on the motorcycle and we would be on our way home. At first, these night escapades scared me to death and they made me nervous, especially the very first one; the ride itself at night and the stop in the middle of the forest, where an encounter with a bear or with a moose would not be out of the question, concerned me. Luc, however, experienced none of my apprehensions. He was a cool guy. With time, I came to appreciate the uniqueness of these nighttime rides. The risks that young people take for a thrill are many and I had my share of them that summer.

If one considers that highway 175 was notorious for accidents involving vehicles and moose, the chances that Luc took, and me along with him, were nothing short of absolutely insane. I had seen the total devastation caused when a car hit a moose every now and then. People and animals died on impact periodically on that road because of such unlucky encounters. But we were young and foolish and we did not think that such disasters would happen to us. I consider myself lucky to have survived in one piece these nocturnal adventures and to be able now to tell a story with a happy ending.

On two occasions while driving along highway 175, I had close encounters with disaster. The first time was during one evening of heavy fog. After dinner, I had stayed for a while chatting with John at the Vieux Moulin. When I finally decided to return to Camping La Loutre, I could not see twenty feet ahead of me. It was one of the scariest moments of my life driving in a highway that I was not very familiar with and in such foggy conditions. The fog disoriented me and when I put the high beams on, it would be even worse. At one moment I found myself on the dirt shoulder of the road. I stopped the car to find out where exactly I was. If I had driven just a few more inches, the car would have gone down a ravine. Just then a truck drove by my car at top speed sounding the horn. Frankly, to this day I don't know how I ever got back safe and sound to Camping La Loutre. The second time was even more serious although it was in plain daylight: I was driving to meet John to go to Québec City when a mosquito got into my left eye; I momentarily closed both eyes trying to dislodge it. It's never a good idea to close one's eyes while driving. When I reopened mine, I was driving in the opposite lane and a pick-up truck was approaching fast in my direction. I swerved to my right and the other driver also pulled to his right in just the nick of time avoiding hitting me by an inch or so. He was driving on the shoulder of the road. I felt the rush of air through the open window as he passed me. I don't know how I did not lose control of the car driving along at 60 miles an hour when I swerved to the right. And, looking at the rearview mirror, I could see the other motorist raising an enormous cloud of dust. How he managed to control his truck is a mystery to me. That man saved my life and his that day. I guess it was not our time to die right then and there. Sometimes one needs to be lucky to live to an old age.

Before my stint at Camping La Loutre was officially over, it was supposed to finish on September 5th, I returned to Toronto. My courses at the University of Toronto were about to resume. I said my good-byes to M. Rivard, to Luc, Denis and all the other folks that I had the pleasure of meeting including the talented and friendly Chef who had fed me so well all summer long. John did not return to Toronto with me. He stayed on to complete his stint at Parc des Laurentides making in the process a few much needed dollars. Both of us had had a tremendous summer experience. We had improved significantly our knowledge of French, we had learned lots about the history, culture and the traditions of the proud *Québécois* people. I set out to Montréal and from there to Toronto alone. It was a long drive.

Alas, I knew that what awaited me in Toronto was not too pleasant. My dear mother had been diagnosed in the spring of 1975 with scleroderma, a disease that attacks one by one all the major organs of the body, and during the summer she had spent almost two months undergoing all sorts of probing tests interned at Mount Sinai Hospital. Her prognosis was atrocious, she would never be able to work again.

She was devastated and so was I. It literally meant that she would have to make ends meet with just a small disability pension. Luckily, I had made good money during the summer and did not have to rely on her anymore for financial support. Somehow, we would manage, and we did. In the spring I had been awarded The Spanish Prize by the Council of the Faculty of Arts and Science; in the fall, I qualified for a bursary tenable only at St. Michael's College. Every little penny helped and was much appreciated. Going forward I would have to apply for OSAP, the Ontario Student Assistance Program, a very worthy program that gave out a combination of a Canada Student Loan and a grant. Of course, the loan would have to be repaid in the future but the grant was free money. I would also have to work part-time in order for the two of us to maintain a decent lifestyle.

In late August, out of the blue, I found out that one of my Portuguese cousins, Maria da Conceição, and her mother, Dona Izalda, who lived in Ponta Delgada, were visiting family and acquaintances in Massachusetts and that they wanted to fly to Toronto to visit their side of the family during a weekend. In the meantime, they were staying in the home of a former neighbor of theirs, a family that had emigrated and settled in Somerville in 1967. Since they did not speak English, they would be accompanied on the trip to Toronto by one of the daughters of the couple, someone who spoke the language fluently and would serve as an interpreter at the airport. That's how I met Filomena, my future wife, although at the time I did not know it. During the weekend that my cousins stayed in Toronto, Filomena and I got to know each other a little bit, especially when I offered to give her a ride to her cousin's house where she would be staying for the weekend. I found out that she was dating someone and that her relationship with her current boyfriend was going nowhere. I was practically in the same predicament as she was. My relationship with Marie was on the rocks. That said, none of us was ready to give up just yet on our then partners. Before Filomena returned to Boston, however, we exchanged phone numbers, a gesture that changed the direction of our lives.

8

The West End YMCA, 1976-1978

In the summers, like most Canadian students, I tried to find work in order to save money to pay for university tuition and to satisfy personal needs. No reasonable university student in Canada can expect his or her parents to pay for his or her studies when one is already a young adult. I was no exception to the rule. After programs Ketchup and Ketchup II, and the unique experience at Parc des Laurentides, I was more than ready to start looking for a part-time job throughout the year as quickly as possible to contribute some money at home, supplement my student's lifestyle and, at the same time, hopefully gain some more experience in the field of education. I found it, starting in January of 1976, at the West End YMCA where Mr. Franco Savoia, a true gentleman, was its director.

There, I was also very fortunate to meet a fellow Azorean, Mr. João Medeiros. He was coordinator of Portuguese programs at the West End YMCA. He had earned a degree in Social Work from York University and was very much committed to improving life for all people, especially within the Portuguese community. He had written a paper in July of 1975 entitled "Toronto Portuguese Community Development and Organization: Past and Present." It was a detailed, statistical analysis of the situation. He had also reviewed recently with Sidney Pratt, a friend, a book entitled *Portuguese Immigrants and the Myth of Success* written by Grace M. Anderson, a professor at Wilfrid Laurier University, published in 1974, in which the two of them concluded that "The image she projects of the Portuguese and the explanations for immigration that she provides are superficial, incomplete, and biased." In the mid-1970s very few people understood what was really going on in the Portuguese community established in Toronto. João's commitment to social justice issues led him to come up with the idea, together with Mr. Domingos Marques, a friend from mainland Portugal, of publishing a new newspaper called *Comunidade, O Jornal Comunitário Português*. Domingos was its director and João the editor. The title said it all. It was a monthly, essentially a labor of love, that after running its course ceased to exist, as many newspapers eventually do. However, while it did exist, it raised some very important social justice issues as well as the Portuguese community's profile. Furthermore, it brought together some very fine people who would go on to improve the quality of life for folks who could not do it on their own.

In 1977, *Comunidade* started publishing some articles in English, too. The Honorable William Davis was Premier of Ontario and when this feature was brought to his attention, he wrote a few lines to the editor congratulating him for taking this important initiative. In the newspaper's February issue one can read the following: "It is to *Comunidade*'s credit that it has come such a long way in such a short time. Please be assured that we in the Ontario Government wish you every success in the days ahead." It goes without saying that the newspaper could not have survived if it were not for a generous subsidy from the Ministry of Culture and Recreation (Wintario). Subscriptions and advertisements were not enough to keep it afloat.

The newspaper dealt with a lot of topics that were relevant and, consequently, of the utmost importance within the Portuguese community. In July of 1977, for instance, the newspaper ran an article about the murder of the Portuguese shoeshine boy Emanuel Jaques, only 12 years old, at the Charlie's Angels massage parlor located at 245 Yonge St. Before being murdered Emanuel had been repeatedly sexually assaulted and then strangled and finally drowned. It was a crime that galvanized the Portuguese community and that was directly responsible for its loss of innocence. The rest of that summer many Portuguese kids were kept indoors for fear of another murder. Another article in the same issue dealt with the high number of delinquent children in the Portuguese community and what to do about it. And yet another one tackled an Education system, Ontario's, that left behind many of its students, students who would never graduate. There was also an article entitled "Emigration in the History of Portuguese Society". Finally, something lighter in tone called "A Visita", "The Visit", written by João in which he delves into the pleasures of visiting friends to maintain relationships alive. *Comunidade* was an important means of maintaining the Portuguese community informed about what was going on in Canada and back home in Portugal.

Also, on July 9th, 1977, *Comunidade* celebrated its second anniversary with a terrific party at the Ukrainian Hall, located close to the corner of College and Spadina, with more than 200 guests in attendance. Myself, Margarida, São (Conceição), and a few more of us who worked at the West End YMCA were recruited for the occasion to serve the food. Like I said, *Comunidade* was a labor of love.

Aside from being involved in the publication of the newspaper, Domingos and João had another very worthwhile project underway; it was a book celebrating the first twenty-five years of the establishment of Portuguese immigrants in Canada. The first ones had arrived in 1953 and 1978 marked the 25th year of their arrival. Its title was *Portuguese Immigrants, 25 Years in Canada*. Their book, like the newspaper, had received a grant from the Ministry of Culture and Recreation in order to see the light of day.

For the next few years, I would be involved in the teaching of ESL classes to Portuguese adults who wanted to gain a basic working knowledge of English in order to be able to function more independently and effectively in the community at large and be in a position to defend their interests and rights. Two of my colleagues, Maria Margarida Aguiar and Maria da Conceição Pereira, wrote an article for the February issue of

1977 of *Comunidade* that explained the approach that all of us took in the teaching of the ESL program to adult students. It said:

Our methodology is based on Paulo Freire's theories on adult education, which stress the analysis of the community one works in which leads to a curriculum guideline. This guideline includes a set of themes relevant to the participant's needs. The actual classes involve an initial dialogue on the theme, followed by the language they need to use in their everyday lives.

Most of our students speak Portuguese as their first language and their educational background varies but is generally limited to elementary or less. As well, they are mostly unskilled workers.

The teachers in the program, are university students of Portuguese background, live in the community (and are therefore exposed to some of the needs of the Portuguese), and are completely fluent in both English and Portuguese. This has proven to be a very valuable asset since the methodology involves a great deal of teacher/student interaction such as: explaining the difficult points of the language, adapting the curriculum to the class particular needs, and disseminating information, for example, on the Educational [Education] system, labor laws new employment policies and Citizenship laws. That is an overall orientation to this society.

The teachers have been trained by the West End YMCA and Ministry of Culture and Recreation staff through initial training workshops and continuing seminars.

Through our experience in teaching, we have found that those attending the classes have benefitted greatly in two ways: not only have they acquired sufficient English to express their needs but have also become more aware of Canadian society, laws and personal rights. This we feel, helps them to cope in this new country.

I have fond memories of both the training as well as of the teaching itself that took place. My contact with the Portuguese community had been somewhat limited until then. It was mostly restricted to family and friends of the family. At Bloor Collegiate, there had been very few

Portuguese-speaking students and, at the University of Toronto, even fewer. To make a long story short, I taught both in the summertime during the day and at nighttime twice a week between 7 and 9 from September to March. It was the first time that I actually tried teaching something to people that were total strangers. Many years later, when I was already a teacher of French and Spanish at Harbord Collegiate, I had the distinct pleasure of seeing one of my former students, Mr. Manuel Ferreira, who had gotten a job at the school as a hall monitor. He, together with his wife, had been my ESL students at the Niagara Site Office when they had first arrived in Toronto from the Azores where I taught out of a temporary trailer. He remembered me vividly and still spoke with fond memories himself of those evening classes in the middle of the winter in a small trailer.

For me, those ESL classes gave me the opportunity to get my feet wet at teaching a second language. Whether it was English, French, Portuguese or Spanish, it did not matter. What mattered was the competence in the field, the empathy towards the student, the enthusiasm for the subject, the level of energy and, last but not least, the methodology employed. All critical components of what it took to deliver successfully a program.

In the winter of 1978, I was also involved in the teaching of ESL to three adults, one Portuguese and two Italians, who were recovering from life changing accidents at the Lyndhurst Hospital. All had worked in construction and all had had accidents that had left them paraplegic. They were coming to terms with their new reality in different ways and they were not necessarily in the mood for ESL classes all the time. Mostly, they wanted someone to listen, in their broken English, to their relating of the accident that had left them "useless", that's the way they put it. They were all in a state of deep depression. Being Portuguese myself, I became closer to the Portuguese patient than the other two fellows. After classes, we used to spend some time speaking in Portuguese. I met one of his daughters occasionally at the hospital and she used to talk about her dad before the accident and what would happen to him once released from the hospital. The entire family was scared and in the grips of despair. Aside from providing a listening ear and some encouragement, there wasn't much more that could be done. Eventually, the person in charge of rehabilitation at Lyndhurst decided that the teaching of ESL was not the most important concern for all three patients and the once-a-week class came to an abrupt end. When I told my Portuguese student/patient that the classes had been cancelled, the poor guy began to cry, that's how emotionally weak he was. I used to come out of the hospital myself feeling a bit down in the dumps. Here were three men who had had active, useful lives that in the space of just a few seconds had dramatically changed. There was no hope for any of them of ever returning to what they used to do. Life can be cruel and unforgiving for some people.

Aside from teaching ESL classes, I would also be involved in the running of summer camps for Portuguese elementary school children aged 6 to 12. These were fun programs that ran in the summer time from 9 to 4 o'clock Monday to Friday. They were held in elementary schools that would normally be closed in the summer time. The Portuguese language and culture were taught in the morning and, in the afternoon, we went on field trips to local parks, including a special trip to the Toronto Islands. This program was a lot of fun. Again, the experience proved to be invaluable to me, especially when I taught French for one year at the elementary level at Darcy McGee Catholic School. Dealing with youngsters is not at all like dealing with adolescents or adults. A different audience requires and, indeed demands, a different approach, a different methodology.

In all modesty, I can say that both of these programs prepared me well for my future profession as a teacher and for my involvement in all sorts of social justice causes throughout the rest of my life.

While working at the West End YMCA, I had the pleasure of meeting Margarida, São (Conceição), Marcie (Marcelina), Carlos, Alice and so many others who became part and parcel of my daily life simply because we all shared a common goal and purpose. Socially, they were also a lot of fun to be with. All of us, except Alice who was still a teenager at the time, were in our early twenties and had boundless energy and lots of free time at our disposal. Margarida, myself, Carlos and Alice all went on to become teachers. Sadly, many years later I found out that one of the members of the group, Margarida, such a pretty, friendly and energetic colleague at the West End YMCA, had committed suicide. I was shocked by the tragic news. What could have brought about such a personal tragedy?

9

A Long-Distance Relationship, 1976-1978

After having met Filomena in September of 1975, the following year, in the summer of 1976, her parents and brother came to Toronto during a weekend so that they would meet and check me out. In the meantime, the two of us had started a long-distance relationship in early 1976. For the next two years, we would exchange many letters and all sorts of cards for special occasions. And, when I finally got a telephone installed in the flat that my mother and I were renting on Lansdowne Ave., we would spend quite a bit of time chatting on the phone, too. In those days, making long-distance phone calls to Boston was rather expensive. So, it was Filomena, who was already working full time at the East Cambridge Savings Bank, who was the one who used to call the vast majority of the times. Long-distance relationships are never easy and ours was no exception. I was in my third year at St. Mike's and quite busy with studies and working part-time. Furthermore, I was also involved in the French Play. Truly, free time was at a premium. But in spite of all the obstacles, we managed to keep our relationship alive and well.

In the late summer of 1976, my sweetheart flew to Toronto to spend a week with me before university started. She was staying at her cousin's home. During the day we would go to all sorts of places such as the Toronto Islands, Casa Loma, the CN Tower, Ontario Place, etc. I had finished my summer job and was waiting for the academic year to start. Normally, that late in the summer, the weather is kind of iffy in southern Ontario, but not that year. Day after day the weather was perfect and the two of us took full advantage of it. We started talking about the possibility of getting married once my studies were done and I had found a teaching job. Filomena was willing to leave everybody and everything behind to come and live in Canada. That was a tremendous sacrifice and a definite sign of love. Did I deserve it? I only hoped that I would be worthy of it one day. Time would tell.

Once Filomena returned to Somerville, life went back to normal. We kept in touch and talked about the Christmas holidays. I would be going to Boston to spend the holiday season with her and her family. My cousin Carlos was going to get married in May of 1977 to Paula Pimentel, a Portuguese girl from São Miguel who lived in Fall River. They had been long-distance dating ever since they were teenagers. Now they were in the final planning preparations for their wedding. So, a few days before Christmas, on a very snowy day, we drove in my cousin's father's Impala to Somerville where he dropped me off at Filomena's home before proceeding to Fall River. It was agreed that after the Christmas festivities, he would pick me up there before we returned to Canada. When I knocked at the door, Filomena's mother told us that she was still at work at the bank, a short distance away. So, we got back into the car and my cousin dropped me off at the East Cambridge Savings Bank. After a hug and a kiss, Filomena and I slowly walked back to her house. We were ecstatic to see each other.

During the Christmas holidays, we had the opportunity to spend some quality time together. I stayed at her parents' home for a week during which time I had a chance to converse extensively with her parents, too. José Jacinto, her father, and Suzy, her mother, were pleasant and welcomed me warmly. They lived modestly. He was a custodian at Boston University and Suzy was a housewife on account of Filomena's younger sister, Gabriela, who had Down syndrome and had to be looked after around the clock. After his regular job at Boston University, José Jacinto had another part-time job in one of the psychology laboratories there where professors were doing experiments using pigeons and mice. His job was to make sure that all these captive animals were healthy and fed properly. In spite of having inherited a fortune in properties from his parents in the Azores, it never occurred to him to sell them to enjoy a better standard of living for himself and his family in America. At root, he was a true miser. He reminded me of Molière's Harpagon in *L'Avare*, although José Jacinto himself had never heard of him, I am sure. Now, that he is dead and I think of it, I am convinced that he never sold his properties in São Miguel because he was already thinking of using them as an enticement to catch another woman after my mother-in-law's passing. She was seven years older than him and deep down I think that he was convinced that he would survive her which he did. Yes, the guy was that cunning. The man and his life story are material for another book.

Suzy, on the other hand, loved all her four children, especially Gabriela, who needed the most love, and her grandchildren. She was a generous and kind person but, regrettably, was totally dominated by her husband. She lived to please a man who clearly did not deserve all the attention that he got from her.

In the meantime, my cousin Carlos invited me to be his best man and Filomena was invited by Paula to be a bridesmaid at their wedding. To that end, my mother and I drove to Boston the same day that Carlos' parents and sister were driving to attend the wedding which was to take place on May 21st, 1977. After picking up Filomena at home we drove to Fall River where we stayed overnight with friends of the family. On the wedding day itself the sun was shining and there was a pleasant breeze. Perfect weather for a wedding. Both the church ceremony and the reception took place early in the day so that by mid-afternoon we were all free. A lot of us gathered at the bride's parent's house where a few beers were drunk before the return trip to Somerville. Everyone had a pleasant time.

In June of 1977, I graduated with honors from St. Michaels' College. Filomena flew to Toronto for a four-day weekend so that she would be with me for the convocation and the festivities surrounding it. It was, after all, an important milestone for the little guy from São Miguel who was now not only a Canadian citizen but a proud recipient of a university degree, one that would open the door to the Faculty of Education at the University of Toronto (FEUT).

Just a few weeks later, I, in turn, flew to Boston for Emanuel's wedding on July 31st. Emanuel was Filomena's only brother. He was the third child of the Sá Ponte family. He was marrying a girl of Azorean descent from the island of Santa Maria after his first marriage to a Spanish girl had ended in a quick divorce. He had been nineteen years old at the time. Sadly, this second marriage would turn sour a few years later and ended up in another divorce. Emanuel, lamentably, lacked self-assurance, was easily manipulated and, consequently, a good target for the Church of Scientology who made a "slave" out of the vulnerable young man. He must have contributed more than a hundred thousand dollars to the Church of Scientology during his life not to mention, of course, countless hours of his personal time. Just a short time after his divorce from Cidália, his second wife, the guy found an Italian girl and before anybody knew anything about it, he had tied the knot once again. Predictably, this marriage also ended up in another divorce in just a matter of months. Eventually, he would marry for the fourth time a woman of Greek descent, sired five children in quick succession and promptly died at the age of fifty-three of a brain aneurysm. Another very sad story.

Later that summer of 1977 I returned one more time to Boston after I was done with summer work at the West End YMCA. This time I drove the Camaro there. It would be the second of many pleasant car trips to Boston in that car. Filomena and I spent a few glorious days going to several beaches in and around New England. By now we already knew each other quite well and we began speaking seriously about getting married in the near future.

During the Christmas holidays of 1977, I flew again to Boston, proposed to Filomena and gave her a diamond engagement ring. Plans for our wedding were the topic of the day during those holidays. There were people from Portugal to invite for this milestone event as well as a thousand details about the church ceremony, the invitations, the ordering of flowers, the photographer, the venue for the reception, the menu, and the list went on. Aside from all this, there was the honeymoon trip itself to plan. Both of us wanted to return to Portugal for it. We wanted to revisit São Miguel because neither one of us had returned there since emigrating, and we also wanted to visit mainland Portugal and Madeira, two places that we only had heard about. We were planning for a month-long honeymoon. Naturally, both of us were quite excited about the detailed preparations that would make the summer of 1978 a unique event in our future life together. In the meantime, there was not a minute to spare. Filomena would take charge of most of the planning while I attended the Faculty of Education in order to become a qualified teacher. I also had to land a teaching job upon graduating from FEUT at a time when vacancies did not exist.

10

Faculty of Education at the University of Toronto, 1977-1978

My teacher training at FEUT was quite an experience in 1977-1978. In those days, teacher candidates spent time taking courses directly related to the subjects that they intended to teach, in my case French and Spanish, as well as theoretical courses about methodology, classroom management, teenage behavior throughout adolescence, etc. And, every other month we would do a practicum in a high school. For me, although some of the psychology theory courses were useful, the overview and review of the subject related courses and the six hands-on sessions were the most helpful, practical and, frankly, the most fun, too. I practice taught in both public and catholic high schools and was very fortunate to teach under the supervision of very competent, efficient and friendly associates who took the time to show me the ropes. Later on, when I become an associate myself, I tried to emulate them and give my teacher candidates as much as I had received from them. Perhaps even more. All in all, during my long career as a teacher, I had the pleasure and distinct privilege of guiding over sixty teacher candidates as they took their baby steps in a classroom setting.

My first school was Jarvis Collegiate Institute, the oldest school run by the Toronto Board of Education. I practiced under the guidance of Mr. Ian Hay whose specialty was French and Spanish, just like me. He had started his teaching career in Scotland before moving to Toronto. We used to discuss classroom management at lunch time while shooting a game of pool in the staff room. That pool table was extremely popular with the teachers, let me tell you. We had literally to line up to get in a game or two. Afterwards, when I landed a job myself at Harbord Collegiate, we used to see each other frequently at conferences and the topic of the pool table would invariably resurface for our great amusement.

After Jarvis Collegiate, I was off to a catholic high school: Madonna High School. My associate was Mrs. Frances Long; she also taught French and Spanish. It was the first time that I had stepped into a catholic high school exclusively for girls and what surprised me the most was the fact that every single class started with a prayer. Everybody stood up and recited a Hail Mary or an Our Father after which everybody took their seat and the class itself started. By the end of the day, Frances had prayed numerous times and the students too. Another thing that I remember about this particular high school is meeting personally the principal upon arriving at the school the first day, a woman by the name of Sister Philomena. A hell of a coincidence since my fiancée's name was Filomena! One that I already knew quite well. Another fond memory is that at Madonna there was a wonderful Drama Department whose teacher was about to stage a play entitled *The Madwoman of Chaillot*, *La Folle de Chaillot*, a satire by Jean Giraudoux, at some point during the school year. The cast was, needless to say, all female. I had never seen an all-female cast produce a play until that time. The teacher proved that it could be done. You kind of work with the resources, human and others, that are readily available to you and you do what you can to the best of your abilities.

From Madonna High School, I was off to St. Joseph's Morrow Park, on Bayview, another all-female school, this one in a relatively well-to-do Toronto neighborhood. My associate was not only competent but a beautiful woman, Ms. Gerda Ryckaert. The classes, just like at Madonna High School, started with the usual prayer to then proceed to the teaching of the subject itself. Gerda taught both French and

Spanish and I was given lots of opportunities to actually teach with very little interference from her. What I remember best about this particular teacher and some of the staff members who taught there was that on Friday afternoons, after the last class of the day, a group of teachers would get together at a local pub to have a pint or two, and to unwind before going home. It was a great way to socialize and to get to know colleagues outside of the normal work environment.

After the Christmas break, in January of 1978, my first school was Mimico High School. There, Mr. Iain Campbell was the Head of the French Department and my associate. For the first time in my teacher training, I saw with my own eyes what could be done with a novel, in this case *L'Étranger* by Camus, that the grade 13 class was studying. Not only were the students reading and writing about it but they were also doing *saynètes*, sketches, once in a while, bringing to life parts of the novel which they had more or less memorized. I remember in particular the scene at the courthouse as played by the members of that grade 13 class. I was in awe and I promised myself that if in the future I was assigned a grade 13 French class, I would attempt to do the same. I had experienced myself as an undergraduate the intrinsic value of the exercise as a tool to bring about fluency.

At Mimico High School, I got to know Iain quite well. He wanted to be principal one day and, several times during my stay at the school, he took me for lunch at a local restaurant so that we could speak more freely. He was a great mentor.

From Mimico High School, I went to my last high school, Sir John A. MacDonald Collegiate Institute. It was the only school where I actually had two associate teachers: one for French, Ms. Lynne Pollard, and one for Spanish, Mr. John Lavis, an older gentleman. It was a school on the east side of Toronto and not the easiest one to get to in the mornings with heavy traffic on highway 401 but we managed. I said deliberately *we* because my old friend from my days at the West End YMCA, Carlos, was practice teaching at the same school as me. So, I used to give him a ride to the school and back home. I taught French in grades 9 to 12 and Spanish in grades 11, 12 and 13.

By the end of the practicums, I had taught my two teaching subjects in all high school grades. I also had observed attentively how my associates taught and I tried to imitate them to the best of my ability. I figured that there was no point of rocking the boat when I was parachuted into the schools for such short periods of time, only two weeks at a time. After this last teaching assignment, I was ready to wrap things up at the FEUT and start looking for a job.

At the Faculty itself two of my instructors who taught French and Spanish were Mr. Carl Theodore, who was the Head of Modern Languages at Forest Hill Collegiate Institute and who was on loan to FEUT for a couple of years, and Mr. Ross Jones, Professor of Methods in Modern Languages at FEUT. There was also another Head of Modern Languages at the Faculty in 1977-1978. His name was Mr. Dieter Euler. His school was Grand River Collegiate Institute, in Kitchener, Ontario, about an hour's drive to the west of Toronto along highway 401.

It so happened that Dieter's tour of duty at the Faculty of Education was going to be extended by one more year in the spring of 1978. So, he asked Professor Jones to choose two noteworthy candidates to apply for his job at Grand River. He chose me and another guy. So, on Saturday, May 13th, a gorgeous sunny day, I drove to Kitchener with my best friend Mario for moral support for a morning interview with Principal Ross Shaver, Vice-principal N.F. Boyle and Dieter Euler. It was going to be my first job interview for a real teaching position. I needed practical experience when it came to interviews. Also, naturally, like all other teacher candidates, I was curious as to what questions would be asked during a real interview. I was hoping to teach in Toronto but we were being told at FEUT that there would not be many jobs available, especially in French and Modern Languages. Everything went well and none of the questions asked by the three interviewers caught me unprepared. Later that day Principal Shaver called me at home to say that the position was mine. At that point I had the audacity to ask him for some time to think about it. He said: "Young man, you have until tomorrow at noon to think about it." Fortunately, common sense prevailed and I did accept that teaching position. It was a one-year appointment until Dieter would return to Grand River Collegiate. Now I had a job under my belt and Filomena and I could focus on the details of our upcoming marriage which would take place on Saturday, July 29th, 1978, in Somerville.

My parents, António and Elzira, photograph taken by Mr. Gilberto Nóbrega, a professional photographer and the proprietor of Foto Nóbrega, on December 21, 1950, to mark the third wedding anniversary of the couple, a tradition that started in 1947 and that continued until 1960.

With my parents, December 21, 1953. I am 18 months old. Again, Mr. Nóbrega took the shot for posterity.

December 25, 1957. Christmas party at my maternal grandparents' home. Virgínio and Margarida made it a point of celebrating the festivity with a formal dinner for their adult children and their offspring. The two boys in the picture are myself and my cousin Carlos whose father had just returned from Canada.

Eduardo Neves, a neighborhood friend, and me dressed as cowboys for a Carnival party in 1958. The two of us were inseparable for a few years during our childhood until, suddenly, his family emigrated to America.

Elzira and Roberto walking along the pier in Horta, Faial, one of the ports of call during the 1958 week-long cruise of the Azores. One can read in the background the ship's name, Carvalho Araújo. I still remember vividly the lunar-like landscape caused by the eruption of the Capelinhos volcano in that island.

Reciting a poem during a special assembly at Liceu Nacional de Ponta Delgada in 1959. It was the first time that I found myself on stage under the gaze of curious onlookers who were mostly strangers to me with the exception, of course, of my parents.

Ring bearer at my uncle João's wedding on June 21, 1959. He was my favorite uncle on my mother's side of the family because of his friendly and playful disposition. He had just turned 19 years old when I was born. He is the one who took the time years later to show me how to ride a bike.

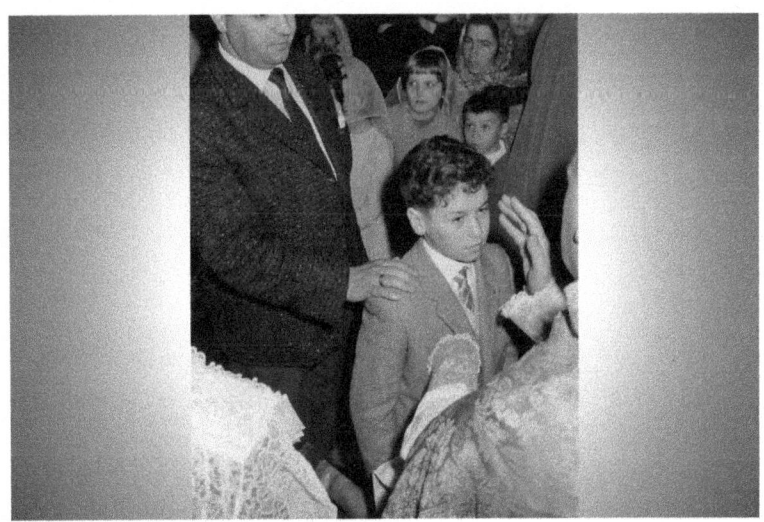

Confirmation in February of 1962. Uncle João sponsored me. After my father's premature passing in 1961, he was always there for me.

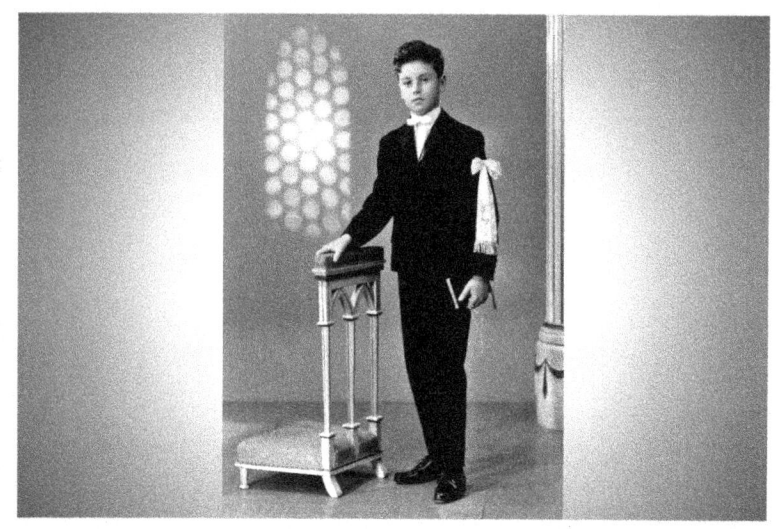

Communion on May 31, 1964. An important milestone for every Catholic boy or girl in São Miguel. The photograph was taken by the talented Mr. Nóbrega.

First role in a play, As Profecias do Bandarra de Almeida Garrett, an important Portuguese playwright and poet, staged on May 6-7, 1969, at Teatro Micaelense, in Ponta Delgada. It was the first time that I was part of an amateur troupe, an experience that stayed with me. I played the modest role of a blind man in it.

Joe Curatola, Mario Amato and me whiling the time away at Joe's home in the summer of 1973. Many subjects of conversation were discussed at length in Joe's room up in the attic of his parents' home that particular summer ranging from politics to sports and, of course, and for good measure, girls.

The cast of Pique-nique en campagne with its playwright Fernando Arrabal who purposely flew in from Paris to attend the performance of February 7, 1977. I am standing immediately to his left. He was kind enough to sign my working copy of the play in which he wrote: "Para Roberto Machado con todo cariño, F. Arrabal, (en recuerdo de tu excelente interpretación de Zapo)." I have treasured that working copy of his play all these years.

YMCA personnel in February of 1977. I worked for the Y, as we used to call it, from 1976 to 1978 in Summer Camps for Portuguese children or teaching ESL classes to adults who were recent immigrants from Portugal and who needed a working knowledge of the language in order to get by independently. My immediate supervisor was a fellow Azorean, Mr. João Medeiros, a true gentleman and a committed defender of workers' rights. I am second from the right on the bottom row.

Filomena at Toronto's waterfront during the summer of 1977. She is standing next to my beloved first car, a 1974 Camaro. She had flown in from Boston to attend my undergraduate Convocation at the University of Toronto. One year later, in August of 1978, we got married.

Standing with my mother on the front porch of the house on Lansdowne Avenue where we rented a two-bedroom flat on the second floor from the Bellissimos, an older Italian couple who were most kind to us.

With Joyce, Toni, Pat and Sal at the University of Toronto Bachelor of Arts – 4YR (ST M) – Honours Convocation, June 17, 1977. We were all undergraduate students at Saint Michael's College, one of the founding colleges at the University of Toronto, and took many French courses together. All of us went on to teach French at either the elementary or secondary panels. Toni, many years later, in 1989, accepted graciously to be my daughter's godmother. Some friendships never die and, on the contrary, with the passage of time, get stronger.

Mario Amato, my best man, toasts the newlyweds at the Lantana Banquet Hall located in Randolph, Massachusetts, on July 29, 1978. My mother, Elzira, is standing next to him.

With Fernando Reis and Lourdes Marchão, two of my many student actors at Harbord Collegiate Institute, on May 14, 1982. They were the main protagonists in a play entitled O Circo Fantasia de Gualberto Gonçalves Silva. The two of them went on to participate in several other plays that I staged at the school.

A chance encounter in Ponta Delgada with Luís França Machado in the summer of 1987. The last time we had seen each other was on December 22, 1969, the day I emigrated to Canada. He was one of my best friends throughout my adolescence and we still exchange emails periodically nowadays.

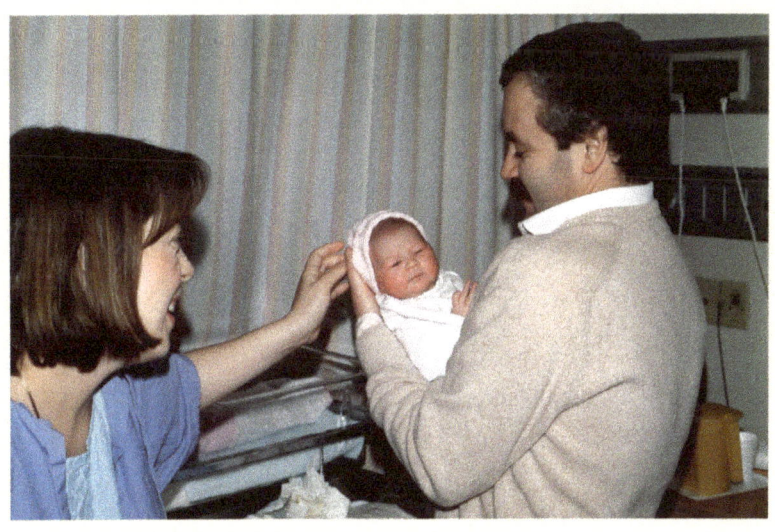

February 11, 1989, the day Natasha, my daughter, was born. It remains one of the happiest days of my married life.

Natasha's baptism, May 21, 1989. My friend Toni, a friend going back to my undergraduate days at Saint Michael's College, and Filomena's cousin, Filipe, were kind enough to serve as godparents.

Summer time in Cape Cod, Massachusetts, one of our favorite holiday destinations as a family for many years in a row. Natasha loved all sorts of water activities, just like her dad.

Reading time, another daily pastime that my daughter and I enjoyed tremendously.

Figaro, our beautiful tabby. He was born in our home on August 22, 1995, a few days after our arrival from vacation in Boston and Cape Cod. The mother cat belonged to our neighbor across the street and Natasha used to let her into our home to play with her which explain why she gave birth to the litter there.

End of the school year party at Jim Rayner's home in the 1990s. Jim had succeeded Jack Harryman as the Head of Modern Languages at Harbord Collegiate Institute and, when he retired in 2000, I succeeded him in the same position at the school until I retired in 2010.

Christmas party at my cousin Paula's home in Oakville, Ontario, not far from Mississauga where we live, a tradition that started in the 1990s and that is still going strong today. Natasha and her cousins were all about the same age. In the picture, from left to right: Paula, Carissa, Filomena, John (Paula's husband), Andrea, Megan and Natasha.

The day that "Madame", Professor Paulette Collet, the artistic director of La Troupe des Anciens, University of Toronto, celebrated her 80th anniversary. My friendship with her goes back to 1975 when she invited me to participate in one of the French plays that she was staging that year: La Cantatrice chauve de Ionesco. I have participated since then in many other plays staged by her.

International trip information evening for parents and students alike at Harbord Collegiate Institute in the winter of 2008, just weeks before departure. Myself and Renata Todros, a fellow teacher at the school and the Head of the Music Department, the two teachers responsible for organizing the trips, used to stage these information evenings followed by a party to explain to everyone involved how the trip would unfold and the rules of behavior for all participants. From 2005 to 2010, the year I retired, we visited many European countries and even Egypt; all trips were memorable and unique experiences.

With Professor Laura Fernanda Bulger in 2013 when she was in Toronto for a conference. Our friendship can be traced back to 1973 when, as an undergraduate, I was one of her students in a Portuguese course that she taught at the University of Toronto. In 1975, she started Portuguese and Spanish at Harbord Collegiate Institute and when she returned to U of T in 1980, I took over from her at the school where I stayed for the bulk of my entire teaching career. Also, from 1985 to 1989, the two of us worked tirelessly for the implementation of a minor program of studies at Glendon College, York University, where she was now teaching. In spite of our best efforts, it was only after she returned to Portugal in 1989 that the program saw the light of day. That said, we had fought the good fight and become great friends in the process.

Natasha and Joel's wedding reception at the Ivy Lea Club, in Lansdowne, Ontario, on October 22, 2016. Another memorable day in the life of our little girl (and her parents' life!) who was now an independent young woman starting another chapter in her life.

Gord Berg and I waiting to be admitted into a cinema in Barrie, Ontario, in 2019, after a day of "matching" Canadian students with their European counterparts. He was in charge of international student exchanges for high schoolers for the Canadian Education Exchange Foundation (CEEF) and, back in 2010, he had invited me to be part and parcel of this amazing not-for-profit organization that offered experiences of a lifetime to adolescents who wanted to improve their knowledge of French, Spanish, Italian or German. Unfortunately, due to COVID-19, the organization ceased to exist. That said, our friendship remains strong.

I am standing next to Lucien Benacem at a summer garden party in 2019. I first met him in 1974 when he had just arrived in Canada from France and was teaching an undergraduate course in French at Saint Michael's College and I was one of his students. We have been friends ever since.

School trip to Egypt in March of 2000. Valley of the Kings; the photograph was taken in front of Queen Hatshepsut's temple in Deir ei-Bahari. It was an incredible trip!

August 13, 2022. I am 70 years old! Standing beside me are my wife, Filomena, my daughter, Natasha and my son-in-law, Joel. I never thought that I would see the day!

La Troupe des Anciens de l'Université de Toronto on April 21, 2023; it was our first production after COVID-19. As in past productions, it was a great success much appreciated by Francophones and Francophiles in and around Toronto.

TWO

The Middle Years

11

The Wedding, July 29th, 1978

    The summer of 1978 was the last one that I worked at the West End YMCA. My job entailed running a summer camp for youngsters, an activity that I was very familiar with given that I had done it the previous year and going back to the Program Ketchup days of 1973-74. That said, I was going to be quitting before the summer camp would be over on account of my forthcoming wedding. For continuity's sake, I asked my friend Mario if he could replace me starting on July 30th. He would be responsible for wrapping things up in my stead. He accepted. At around the same time, I asked him to be my best man. Of course, he accepted the invitation with pleasure. Over the years we had become excellent friends. And, since he was dating Marcie at the time, a coworker of mine at the YMCA, she also got invited. Virgilio, another friend from the Program Ketchup days who had a car, also wanted to attend the happy event and, therefore, got an invitation. He would be the one driving the little group of friends to Boston. Marcie, as it turned out, happened to know someone who worked at the Four Seasons Sheraton in downtown Boston and this person found us a room to stay at the hotel the night before the wedding for a very reasonable rate. All in all, Mario, Marcie, Virgilio and Tony, another friend from the Bloor Collegiate days, ended up driving together for the special occasion. In addition to my friends, there were family members who had arrived from São Miguel and my own family members from Toronto and Mississauga, not to mention Filomena's cousins and family from Toronto, too, who were attending the festivities. So, on Friday, July 28th, the day before the wedding, a caravan of cars set out from southern Ontario to make the long trip to Boston, a trip that normally took about ten hours and was quite boring, especially the portion along the New York Thruway because of the flatness of the landscape. This particular trip, however, was a lot of fun because there were so many people travelling together with the same objective in mind, to attend my wedding.

Upon arriving in Somerville, we left our Portuguese guests at my father-in-law's home; Mario and I picked up our wedding suits and, afterwards, myself and my friends proceeded to the Four Seasons to get refreshed in order to come back to the house for a party in honor of the new couple. At the hotel, we would be sharing a large room with two queen size beds. Mario and Marcie shared one, they were dating after all, and the other one was for the other three of us. At the house, lobster, steak, followed by dessert, accompanied by wine and beer and coffee were served and then it was time to say good night in order to get set for the big day, the wedding day.

On Saturday, July 29th, the church ceremony was going to be at five o'clock followed afterwards by a reception at Lantana, a wedding hall in Randolph, one of Boston's southern suburbs. So, my friends and I would have lots of free time before the main event of the day unfolded. We made good use of it. It was a beautiful day, the sun was shining, the temperature was not too high and, most importantly, there was no possibility of rain in the forecast. Good!

Since I would be taking a limousine from the church to the reception hall, it was decided that after the wedding at St. Joseph's Catholic church in Somerville, Tony would drive my Camaro to the hall so that, once the reception was over, I would have a car to make it to the Sonesta Hotel, in Boston, where Filomena and I would be staying for three nights before taking a Trans World Airlines (TWA) airplane to Terceira, in the Azores, on Tuesday evening.

After getting up at the Four Seasons in the morning of July 29th, everybody took showers and afterwards we went for breakfast and a walk in the immediate vicinity of the hotel. After lunch, we explored downtown Boston for a while and then returned to the Four Seasons to get dressed for the wedding.

The church ceremony went without a glitch. Everybody was happy to be part of a religious ceremony where two beautiful young people were taking their vows and making it known before all assembled that they were committed to one another for better or for worse and that they intended to make their marriage work.

After the church ceremony, Filomena and I took the limousine to the reception hall in the company of Mario and Aura, Filomena's maid of honor. Champagne was served during the ride and by the time we got there we were definitely merry.

At the reception hall, we were introduced to the guests as husband and wife. Mario made a toast and then dinner was served. The only item missing in action was the wine. My dear father-in-law had forgotten to order it and no one working for Lantana, when the reservation had been made and a tour of the facility had taken place, had had the common sense to mention it to him. It didn't matter, people ordered their own bottles of wine anyways.

At some point pictures were taken of the wedding party and of the couple with parents, relatives and friends for the record.

Then, the dancing started. After a while, the cake was cut, coffee was served and Filomena and I went to a reserved room in the hall for the bride and groom to change into their farewell clothes. It was one of our first intimate moments and, as such, it was unforgettable. We danced one more time and said goodbye to all present and drove to the Sonesta Hotel in Boston for a night of fun and games.

After three unforgettable nights at the Sonesta, in room 611, on Tuesday evening we set out to the airport for the beginning of a great honeymoon in three areas of Portugal: the Azores, mainland Portugal and Madeira. We were young, we had money in our wallets to spend and one month at our disposal.

Life was better than ever!

12

A Honeymoon in Portugal, August of 1978

Our honeymoon in Portugal turned out to be a great success in every sense of the word. On Tuesday, August 1st, we took a TWA plane at 11:30 p.m. from Boston that landed in Terceira, the third island of the archipelago to be discovered by the Portuguese, hence its name, early on Wednesday, at 7:05 a.m. Since our connecting flight to São Miguel was going to be in the afternoon, we decided to hire a taxi at the airport to go on a mini tour of the island. Although I had been there as a kid with my parents, I did not remember much about the island at all. As we drove around, what impressed us most was the quaint city of Angra do Heroísmo, a UNESCO World Heritage Site, and Mount Brazil which overlooks the city itself. The taxi driver showed us a few more points of interest but after the overnight trip from Boston to Terceira, we had not slept much during it, and the monotonous drive, we started to nod. Both of us just wanted to sleep for a bit. And that's what we did once back at the airport waiting for our next flight.

When we landed in São Miguel, my Azorean family was waiting for us at the airport. I had not seen my uncle Francisco, one of my mother's brothers, since the mid-1960s. Being an army guy, he had left on tours of duty to the former Portuguese colonies in Africa before I had left the island myself in 1969. It had been more than ten years since we had seen each other. In a decade people change dramatically, physically and otherwise, a fact that is more noticeable because we don't see each other daily. He had changed, his wife had changed, his daughter had changed, she was a young adult now, my other cousins had changed and I had changed too. Irrespective of the changes, we were glad to see one another and to renew friendships that had been put in the back burner for a while on account of separation and immigration. There were lots to talk about starting with Ponta Delgada itself, my birth city, and the island as a whole. Nothing had stood still during my nine-year absence. Progress had come to the Azores.

Even though we had booked a hotel in Furnas, the Hotel Terra Nostra, from August 2-6, the first night we stayed at my uncle's home. He insisted, it was a must, if we did not comply, he would get offended. The very next day, a cousin of mine lent me a Mini Cooper and Filomena and I drove to Furnas. Furnas is located in a valley with a beautiful lake and it is the site of many hot springs, geysers and fumaroles with their very distinct rotten-egg smell. It's at the bottom of a caldera surrounded by a rim of very high mountains. It's an area famous for its natural beauty and its mineral waters. There are around 20 mineral waters in the village. Given these assets, it's no wonder that it is one of the most popular tourist attractions in São Miguel. It was already so as I was growing up. The French, the British, the Germans and some Scandinavians had been coming to Furnas for decades. In those days most of them stayed at the famous Hotel Terra Nostra, first built in 1935, a hotel with the most exquisite garden, really a botanist's paradise, and a huge outdoor thermal swimming pool whose water is lukewarm and yellowish due to the amount of iron in it. One does not go into that pool with a white swim suit! If you do, by the time you come out, your bathing suit will be yellow.

In any case, we had a great time in Furnas. We went to Miradouro do Pico do Ferro, at 537m, a marvelous look-out point overlooking the lake and the village. Miradouro do Salto do Cavalo, another look-out point, from where we can see in the distance the lake, we visited the grounds of the Parque Terra Nostra numerous times where more than 600 varieties of camellias can be found not to mention exotic trees from all over the world. And we took many walks in the quaint tiny village itself. We even found a few minutes to visit the family summer home belonging to Filomena' side of the family. A country home that had been in the family for almost a century and one where my wife as a child had spent many happy summer holidays with her parents and cousins.

On the weekend, my family came up to Furnas to visit us and we had a terrific picnic by the lake. We had *bacalhoada*. This is a local specialty dish. The ingredients are: cod fish, sausages, potatoes, eddoes and lots of olive oil. All these ingredients are put inside a big pot which is wrapped in burlap and buried into the ground where it will simmer, thanks to the volcanic activity, for hours before it is ready to be enjoyed. It is served with corn bread and lots of wine. It is a delicacy. That culinary experience alone is well worth a trip to São Miguel. Another one is Cozido das Furnas, a sort of *pot au feu*; its ingredients are beef, pork, spicy sausage, blood sausage, chicken, potatoes, sweet potatoes, yam, carrots, cabbage and kale. Like *bacalhoada*, it is cooked in a big pot wrapped in burlap which is buried for at least seven hours before it is ready to be served. Its juices are something to die for. After a most delicious lunch, we went for a walk to Ermida de Nossa Senhora das Vitórias, the only Neo-Gothic chapel in the whole island, where one of the greatest Azorean botanists, José do Canto, and his wife are buried.

Before returning to Ponta Delgada, since we were on the east side of the island, we also visited Lagoa do Fogo, one of the most mysterious lakes in the island. It occupies the crater of another extinct volcano. It is surrounded by mountains averaging about 800m high. From there one can see on a clear day to the north the town of Ribeira Grande, the second largest city of São Miguel, and the Atlantic Ocean to the south. What makes the lake so mysterious is that, every once in a while, clouds cover it momentarily. The silence in that area is sublime.

After those days in Furnas, it was time to return to Ponta Delgada before boarding a plane that would take us to Lisbon and the rest of mainland Portugal. To that end, we left Furnas on Sunday afternoon. We stayed one night at Dona Izalda's home. She was the lady, together with her daughter Conceição, who had introduced Filomena to me during their weekend trip to Toronto in 1975. They were therefore directly responsible for my happiness. Conceição was much taller and prettier and was already dating the guy next door, Noé, who eventually became her husband. He was studying to be a lawyer in Lisbon and she would be going to university in Lisbon too in order to become a high school teacher of Geography. The final night was spent back at my uncle's home.

In Ponta Delgada, I absolutely had to see some of my childhood and adolescent hang-outs such as Liceu Nacional de Ponta Delgada, my high school, Palácio da Conceição, a government building where my father used to work, Teatro Micaelense, where I used to go to the movies in my teenage years, Avenida Marginal, where my friends and I used to go to flirt with the local girls, and my favorite coffee shop, O Gil. We also made it a point of driving by the house where I was born and the one where my mother and I went to live after my father's death, my grandparents' home. Filomena did the same. Just walking from place to place brought back thousands of memories, some happier than others, of course, but all important and dear to our hearts.

Before leaving the island, we still had time to drive to its western side, to a place called Sete Cidades, a sight famous for its two adjoining lakes, one blue and the other green, located at the bottom of another volcanic crater. The view from Vista do Rei, the King's View, called thus because in 1901 King Dom Carlos and Dona Amélia, his wife, had stood at that spot to admire the beauty of the two lakes, is simply stunning and over the years has become emblematic of the island of São Miguel. No tourist ever travels to São Miguel without visiting this sight.

The few days spent in our birth place were not enough time to see everything we wanted to see. To our amazement, we found ourselves in the Transportes Aéreos Portugueses (TAP) airplane taking us from Ponta Delgada to Lisbon, a two-hour flight, on Tuesday, August 8th.

One week had not been enough! We promised each other that we would return to São Miguel in the near future.

Our trip to mainland Portugal was divided into three sections: Lisbon and its surroundings, to be followed by a lot of city-hopping going north that eventually would take us to Viana do Castelo, in the province of Minho. Then, we would return south to Lisbon for a day, stay overnight in the capital and the next day take a coach to Albufeira, in the Algarve. Prior to setting out, we had some hotels reserved in key places such as Lisbon, Porto, Viana do Castelo and Albufeira. For the part of our trip going north, we had rented a car. It turned out to be a brand-new red Fiat 124. A cute little car that served us well. It afforded us freedom of movement and thanks to it we saw many sights that otherwise we would not have been able to see. After southern Portugal, we would return to Lisbon for an overnight stay before flying to Funchal, in Madeira.

In Lisbon, we stayed at the very fancy Hotel Ritz. It was pure luxury. It was our treat to each other. However, because we wanted to see as much as possible of the capital and its surroundings, we hardly had time to enjoy the hotel. Our days and evenings were packed with excursions so that by the time we came back to the hotel we barely had enough time for a kiss. Just kidding, of course.

During our stay in Lisbon proper, we visited the Castelo de São Jorge, one of the oldest castles in Portugal from where one gets a bird's eye view of the capital, strolled down and up the Avenida da Liberdade, the most famous boulevard in town, the equivalent of the Champs Élysées, went to Mosteiro dos Jerónimos, a gem of an architectural monument, Torre de Belém, a fortress in the Tagus river that served as a prison at one moment, Sé, Lisbon's oldest cathedral, Alfama, one of the quaintest neighborhoods in the city, Restauradores, Praça do Comércio, Rua Augusta, Chiado and Bairro Alto, before setting out further afield to Palácio de Queluz, the old royal palace dating back to the XVIII century, surrounded by its beautiful gardens. It reminds one of Versailles in miniature.

At some point, we participated in an all-day organized trip by coach and visited Sintra, the playground of the rich and the site of beautiful Palácio da Pena, Cabo da Roca, the western most point of continental Europe, Cascais, a town much admired by the rich and aristocrats in the Tagus' estuary, and Estoril, with its famous Casino. It was a tiring excursion, made much more so by the guide who explained everything in four languages: Portuguese, French, Spanish and English. At first, since I speak all four languages, I found it entertaining but after a while it was just plain monotonous. In front of our hotel, as we got up from our seats, Filomena inadvertently touched one of my eyes and the contact lens popped out. I thought at first that it was still on my eye lid and, therefore, we proceeded to disembark and the bus took off. When I found out that I did not have it on me, we got into a taxi and followed the bus until its final stop. I asked the bus driver if I could go back to my seat and look for it. He agreed and, against all odds, I found it on the seat. What a relief! I could not drive without contact lenses and we had rented a car to visit the north part of Portugal.

That evening we went on another coach tour named Lisbon by Night. Again, the bus covered some of the sights that we were already somewhat familiar with except that there were lights everywhere. That's when we met another Portuguese couple from Toronto on their honeymoon, Frank and Lucy. It included dinner at a typical restaurant called Luso and the singing of *fado*, the national song of Portugal. Thanks to their presence and friendship, the good food and drink and the singing of *fado*, it turned out to be a lovely evening. When the bus dropped us off in front of the Ritz, the tour guide, an older woman, asked us jokingly: "Don't you have better things to do with your money?" It made us feel very privileged indeed to be able to stay in such luxury.

On our last morning at the Ritz, before we picked up our car and left the hotel for good, we asked the concierge to make reservations in a hotel in Leiria and another one in Buçaco, our next two overnight stays. This was a pattern that we adopted at other hotels such as Hotel Infante de Sagres, in Porto, where a reservation was made for us at Hotel do

Parque, in Viana do Castelo, and at the Hotel da Balaia, in Albufeira, where another reservation was made for us at the Hotel Diplomático, back in Lisbon, before our next leg of the trip to Madeira where we already had booked in advance Hotel Savoy.

Once in the possession of the rental car, we headed to Mafra, the site of a convent with its famous 114 bells. From there we moved on to Óbidos, one if not the quaintest of Portuguese towns, a town built within the walls of a castle with, therefore, an important past and history. Onwards to Alcobaça, with its beautiful monastery, where the tombs of Dom Pedro and his unfortunate lover, Dona Inês de Castro, are on display. Next on the itinerary was Nazaré, famous for its beach and its fishing village, and Batalha, with its beautiful basilic. From there we paid a visit to Fátima, the most important religious shrine in Portugal and, finally, we drove to Leiria for a well-deserved night's rest.

The following day we headed to Coimbra, where the oldest Portuguese university, Universidade de Coimbra, established in 1290, and the number one choice for countless generations of Azoreans who could afford higher education is located. Its old library is a sight to behold. From there we headed to Aveiro, with its Ria de Aveiro, and its *salinas*, salt pans, to end up the day in the unique Buçaco Palace Hotel, an ancient convent converted into a royal residence and later into a hotel where my own parents had stayed overnight during their trip to mainland Portugal in 1960. Filomena and I were enjoying ourselves immensely. Stimulated by new sites every day and delicious meals accompanied by wine, it all set the stage for sleepless nights. We were in heaven.

When we got to Porto, we quickly checked into our hotel, the Hotel do Infante de Sagres, another five-star hotel, fairly close to Avenida dos Aliados and City Hall. Porto is a gorgeous city. Much smaller in size than Lisbon, a lot of people prefer it to Portugal's capital. It's the nation's second largest city but it has kept a provincial air to it and the *tripeiros*, as the locals are called, tend to be more friendly and certainly less snobby than their counterparts, the *alfacinhas*, as those who live in Lisbon are referred to. While there, we made it a point to visit such landmarks as Igreja dos Congregados, whose façade is partly covered with white and blue *azulejos*, ceramic tiles, Torre dos Clérigos, the city's "ex libris", Sé Catedral, built by the Romans; we crossed back and forth Ponte Dom Luís, designed by no other than Gustave Eiffel, one that connects Porto to Vila Nova de Gaia, on the other side of the Douro River and where numerous Port wine cellars are located for the delight of all tourists and locals alike, and the list goes on.

Speaking of Port wine, while exploring the streets in the immediate vicinity of our hotel we discovered, by pure accident, a quaint little store specializing in all brands of vintage Port wines. Filomena and I walked in and met its owner, an older gentleman who turned out to be a fountain of knowledge regarding everything that there was to know about the Port wine industry. I told him that I wanted to purchase a good bottle of Port with the intention of keeping it for a few years and crack it open when a milestone occasion came up in our future life as a married couple. He recommended a 1962 bottle of Nieport & Co., Ltd., a company established in 1842. We happened to be in 1978; so, that particular bottle was already 16 years old at the time of purchase. He let us have it for a reasonable price because we were on our honeymoon and visiting Porto, his birth place, for the first time. Well, believe or not I kept that particular bottle until August 13th, 2022, the day that I turned 70 years old, and shared its contents with my family and friends during a wonderful garden party celebration. The bottle was 60 years old and the Port wine inside it was simply divine!

From Porto, we traveled to Guimarães, the birthplace of Portugal, where we visited the ancient Castle. There, it is said, Dom Afonso Henriques, the founder of the nation, lived and we also admired Paço dos Duques, nowadays used as a presidential residence. From Guimarães, it was onwards to Braga, an important site for the catholic religion. Its most important attraction is Bom Jesus, a basilic, and the famous steps leading to it which many Portuguese and tourists alike have climbed over the years. From the churchyard one can enjoy a magnificent view of Braga and the beautiful surrounding countryside.

Finally, we reached our final destination in northern Portugal, Viana do Castelo. The province of Minho resembles in many ways the countryside in the Azores, especially that of São Miguel. It's lush and very green and Viana itself is located by the sea, just like Ponta Delgada. In Viana, we stayed at Hotel do Parque where we enjoyed a delicious fresh fish dinner in the hotel's main dining room. Not being one to appreciate fish that much, that particular meal stands out in my memory as one of the best ever. Of course, no one can visit Viana without visiting the Igreja do Monte de Santa Luzia, now a basilic. It's perched on top of a mountain and offers one of the best views that one can imagine. Looking down at the city below and the coastline is very much like looking at a city from the window of an airplane. It's simply outstanding.

It was time to return to Lisbon again in order to proceed to the Algarve and hit the beaches in the warmest and sunniest province of Portugal. Before we left the hotel in Viana, the concierge made a reservation for us at the Hotel Avenida Parque, in Lisbon, where we would stay overnight before moving on to the Algarve. Upon arriving in Lisbon, the following morning, we got rid of our beloved Fiat 124 and in the early afternoon we were off to Albufeira by coach. It took about four hours to get to the Hotel da Balaia. It was right in front of a lovely beach and for the next few days we enjoyed the warm waters of the Atlantic by swimming several times a day. But in between swims we also found enough time to visit Faro, Algarve's capital, and Sagres, famous on account of Prince Henry the Navigator, responsible for initiating the Age of Discoveries in Portugal, who had a nautical school built in the promontory. We stayed at the Balaia four nights. The last day there, we asked the concierge to reserve another overnight stay in a hotel in Lisbon. He chose the Hotel Diplomático. We trusted him; we knew that he would make a fine choice.

Nice and relaxed, after four days in Albufeira, we took the coach back to Lisbon; the following day we boarded a TAP flight to Funchal, the capital of Madeira, known as "Pearl of the Atlantic", arriving there at around 11 o'clock in the evening. We have travelled countless times by airplane since then but that landing in Madeira stands out in my memory as one of the scariest ever. While on final approach in pitch darkness, the plane suddenly dropped quite a bit only to be pulled back up with the roaring of the engines in our ears. Of course, we could not see anything. Fortunately, there was no mishap. At the airport, located at Machico, there was a taxi driver holding a poster with the words "Hotel Savoy, Mr. and Mrs. Machado" printed on it. On account of the late arrival, he had been dispatched by the hotel to pick us up. It was a wonderful beginning to our stay in the island. The Savoy itself catered to a lot of Brits and French tourists and it had all the amenities that one could wish for. One feature that both of us appreciated very much was the two lovely swimming pools and the jetty in front of them that offered the possibility of swimming in the open sea. The food in the several Savoy restaurants was delicious and tea at 4 o'clock was, it goes without saying, very popular.

As usual, the two of us did not just stay by the hotel. We went on a one-day tour of the island. It was both delightful, on account of its natural beauty and the great variety of vegetation and flowers everywhere, and tiring because the road was so tortuous, with curves and counter curves everywhere. First, we travelled along the southside of the island to Câmara de Lobos, a fishing village much loved by painters, Cabo Girão, a sea cliff standing at 580m and a very popular lookout point, Ribeira Brava, another quaint village, and Ponta do Sol, another lookout point. And then the coach crossed to the north side, to Porto Moniz, on the extreme north-west corner of the island and known for its natural swimming pools. In 1978, there were no major highways on the island linking the south to the north. After Porto Moniz, the coach travelled east along the north coast to São Vicente and to a quaint village called Santana, with its little houses painted white and displaying pitched straw roofs. After Santana, we crossed the island again to Funchal.

On another day, Filomena and I decided to walk the short distance from the hotel to downtown Funchal for a closer look at the capital city. While walking along the road we came to the realization that the charm of the place was definitely related to the natural beauty of its setting: the city sits on the south slope of a mountain facing a beautiful bay. In Funchal proper, we visited the Sé, the cathedral, built in the XVI century, and the Monumento de Zarco, dedicated to Gonçalves Zarco, the Portuguese navigator who discovered the island. We also made a pit stop at a shop that sold Vinho da Madeira, one of the most popular products of the island, and purchased a bottle from Justino Henriques, Filhos, Lda., established 1870. On the label one could read, Fine Madeira Wine, Medium Sweet, and a sentence in French that caught my attention right away: *Ne faire qu'une chose mais la faire bien*. Only do one thing, but do it well. The wine had been bottled the previous year, in 1977, and it was cracked open the same day as the Nieport bottle to the great satisfaction and merriment of all present. The bottle was 44 years old and the quality of the wine did not disappoint anybody.

We had arrived in Madeira on August 21st and now it was already August 25th. The day that we would be returning to Lisbon to board our plane back to Boston. Naturally, we were sad that our carefree honeymoon was coming to an end. We were thinking already as to what lay ahead. We would have to rent a U-Hall trailer to put Filomena's belongings in it, attach it to the Camaro which had been freshly painted during our absence, drive from Boston to Toronto, find an apartment in Kitchener where I was going to start my teaching career at Grand River Collegiate, in September, leave her belongings there, return to Toronto to pick up my furniture, etc. The list of things-to-do was endless. And Filomena wanted to find a job in banking as soon as possible too. The many unknowns made us a bit apprehensive if not nervous.

The TAP flight from Madeira arrived late in Lisbon and, as a result, we missed our connecting flight to Boston. The company put us up in a hotel for the night at its expense and what I remember best about the setback was the discussion in Portuguese between our taxi driver, who was going to drive us from the terminal to the hotel, and a colleague as to what would happen if we did not pay for the fare. The bastard would take off with our luggage. The fool was totally unaware that the two of us spoke Portuguese fluently. Upon arrival at the hotel, I thanked him for the ride in Portuguese and told him that in the future, before speaking his mind, he should watch it. I also told the bellboy at the hotel's door that if the taxi driver wanted to get paid, he should see the hotel's concierge about it.

Luckily, the following day there were no unpleasant surprises and we were on our way to Boston. During the trip we had lots of time to reminisce about our incredible honeymoon and to start making concrete plans about our immediate future and how to face it with confidence.

13

Grand River Collegiate Institute, 1978-1979

On Saturday, August 26th, we rented a trailer in Boston, loaded it with Filomena's belongings and set out on our long trip to Toronto on Sunday morning. At the border, Filomena presented her paperwork as a Landed Immigrant, a customs officer briefly looked at the contents of the trailer and off we continued to Toronto. The following day, Monday, August 28th, we drove to Kitchener, a city to the west of Toronto along highway 401, to find suitable accommodation. We found it at 80 Holborn Dr. It was a two-bedroom apartment on the fourth floor of a modest high rise ideally located a five-minute drive from Grand River Collegiate. It was still being occupied by the current tenants but they allowed us to empty the contents of the trailer in one of the rooms. Without knowing them at all, we trusted them with Filomena's possessions. Officially, we would be taking possession of our first abode on Saturday, September 2nd. On Tuesday, August 29th, we returned to Kitchener with a few of my own belongings: a single bed, a mattress, a student's desk, a night table, and a kitchen table with two chairs temporarily on loan from my uncle José. Afterwards, we drove back to Toronto and got rid of the U-Haul trailer. Finally. In the meantime, I asked my uncle, since he had a car equipped with roof racks, if he could do us the favor of loading it with a few more of my belongings. He agreed. On Saturday, he delivered them to our apartment in Kitchener. For the next month, that was the extent of our furniture. In October, on a weekend, we went to Leon's Furniture and purchased a bedroom set, a sofa, an armchair and a color television. We were all set and ready to entertain family and friends alike. The city had a large German-speaking population and Oktoberfest was one of its big celebrations every year. A great time to invite them.

Grand River Collegiate was an excellent school to start what would be a very long teaching career for me. It was a brand-new high school on the eastern outskirts of Kitchener. In fact, there was an open field immediately to the east of it. It was on the edge of a new subdivision. I quickly met the other members of the Languages Department and it did not take long before we were friends. Mme Thierry was the Acting Head of the department while Dieter Euler was on loan to the Faculty of Education. I was going to be teaching French in grades 9-12 and Spanish in grade 11. Aside from French and Spanish, German and Latin were also part and parcel of the languages' program. Of all the teachers in my department, the one that I got to know the best was Mme Zelda Thomas who taught French and Spanish, just like me. She became my first mentor and came to observe me teach unofficially a couple of times to provide feed-back.

My classroom had windows overlooking a pleasant neighborhood of new bungalows and backsplits, the latter being popular in those days, and the blackboards were not the usual black but rather green and slanted in such a way that prevented glare. The overhead projectors, reel-to-reel Sony tape recorders and the books were all new. The school was also kept spotless by the caretaking staff. I was in heaven. There were a couple of lunch hours to accommodate the large student body and mine was at 10:30 in the morning, something that I never forgot. In my entire life, I had never had lunch that early in the day! But one quickly adapts to such routines. My salary was $16,040.00, the top salary for a starting teacher who had been placed in Group 4 by the Ontario Secondary School Teachers' Federation after taking into account the academic and the professional qualifications of the teacher. It was a good starting salary.

Principal Shaver was an older gentleman, approaching his mid-sixties when I met him, and he was finishing his long career as principal of a brand-new school: Grand River Collegiate. He had accumulated a lot of knowledge, expertise and wisdom along his illustrious career. First as a classroom teacher, next as an assistant head of his department, later as the head, and then as vice-principal and, at long last, principal. In short, he was a no-nonsense type of school administrator who ran a tight ship. He was also generous with his time. He took a liking for me right from the get go, after all he had hired me back in May. So, every once in a while, he used to invite me into his office to chat; he provided free advice which turned out to be sound advice for my budding career in the field of education. He knew that my one-year probationary contract with the Waterloo County Board of Education was probably not going to be renewed. There were not many teaching positions available in 1978, especially in the field of languages but, nevertheless, he saw potential in me and wanted me to be ready to move on successfully at the end of my stint in his school. I, in turn, appreciated very much his professional and "fatherly" advice.

It is said, among teachers, that one always remembers his first and last principal. In a 30-year career span, it's not unusual for most teachers to have taught under the leadership of 6-10 principals. This is certainly true in my case. One afternoon Principal Shaver said to me:

> Roberto, in the next few years try to teach as many courses in your area of expertise as possible and, after about 10 years, ask yourself if you have what it takes to lead a department and serve as a mentor to other teachers in it. If the answer to that question is "yes", then do it for the next 10 years at which point you will ask yourself another important question that will determine the direction of the rest of your career; do you want to be a consultant in your area of expertise or do you want to go into school administration? After 20 years, it's time to face fresh challenges because by then you will have seen it all, so to speak, and if

you took the time to reflect on your experiences along the way, you will have attained expertise and the wisdom that comes with it. Think about your career along this time frame.

On another occasion, he told me:

You Know, Roberto, not every single student of yours will shine in French or Spanish. Sometimes, in spite of all your knowledge, efforts and enthusiasm, they won't put in much effort or even care much about your subjects. Just remember that students are multi-talented people, like all of us, and that they may be very well brilliant in another subject, or in the arts or in sports. It's for you to find out what makes them tick and when you do and see them in action you will be in awe and develop the respect that they deserve even though they don't particularly care for French or Spanish.

Naïve as I was at that early stage of my career, the man opened my eyes to the inevitable reality. I truly think that he made me a more understanding and a better teacher for all his advice during my one-year stint at Grand River Collegiate.

During the Christmas vacation of 1978, Filomena and I drove to Boston to spend the holidays with Filomena's family, a tradition that we maintained until 1988. Sometimes we would also fly in for the holidays. Driving in winter conditions on the New York Thruway or the Mass Pyke were not always the most pleasant and safe on account of snow storms, especially around Buffalo and Albany. This yearly trip to visit her parents, sisters, brother, nephew and nieces pleased Filomena a lot.

In January, I started thinking about my future in education. My contract with the Waterloo County Board of Education would be over in August. I needed to figure out what were my options. I went to see Principal Shaver for advice. He told me to reapply with the Waterloo Board just in case a position would become available in one of the other high schools and, at the same time, to send my résumé to other boards, both public and catholic. He would be most glad if I were to use his name as a reference. Upon contacting Mr. O. L. Day, Superintendent of Personnel at the Waterloo Board, about this matter, he wrote back to me saying:

> When you were appointed to your position in September, 1978, you received a letter indicating the terms of your employment. The Board, at its meeting held on May 17, 1979, officially terminated your contract, effective August 31, 1979.
>
> Thank you for your efforts during the 1978-79 school year. I hope that the experience gained while in our employ will assist you in securing another position.

His reply was more than clear, in fact it was crystal clear; for all intents and purposes, there would not be any future for me with the local Board of Education and in Kitchener.

My qualifications as a teacher entitled me to teach at the intermediate and senior levels, essentially high school. So, during the summer of 1979 I took a course entitled French as a Second Language Part 1, which permitted me to teach the subject at the junior level too. In the spring, the Ministry of Education had sent out a notice to all boards of education announcing the federally funded Teacher's Summer Bursary Program 1979 for "teachers and potential teachers of French to English-speaking students and for teachers in French Language Instructional Units." I took full advantage of the opportunity. It so happened that the summer course took place at Darcy McGee Catholic School, a school that I would become very familiar with in the not-too-distant future.

In the meantime, Filomena had found a job in Toronto with the Royal Bank of Canada in January of 1979. She was placed at the Bloor and Bedford Branch, right across from the University of Toronto's Varsity Stadium. In practical terms, for the two of us, it meant that she stayed from Sunday night to Friday night at my mother's flat while I stayed at the apartment in Kitchener. After work, on Fridays, I used to drive to Toronto to pick her up. It was not an ideal arrangement for a newly-wed couple. We were back into a long-distance relationship. So, I was determined to land my next job in Toronto so that we would not have to live apart. I found it with the Metropolitan Separate School Board. More about it in a moment.

It did not take long for Filomena to make new friends at the bank. Among them was Ana Marcos, married to Eduardo Marcos, one of the first Portuguese lawyers in Toronto. They were both from mainland Portugal. He was from the province of Trás-os-Montes, one of the most remote provinces of northern Portugal, and she was from the province of Alentejo, towards the south. In any case, it was the beginning of a relationship that has lasted until today. Ana was pregnant at the time and after giving birth was not expected to return to work. Her eventual departure did not affect in any way our friendship and we were overjoyed when they invited us to be godparents to their daughter Danielle. In fact, the invitation cemented our friendship. Danielle was followed by Benjamin and Sara and, again, we were invited to be the godparents. Thanks to this friendship, of course, we met their family members as well as their friends, something that enriched our human experience and broadened our horizons. Although all of us were Portuguese, we were *açorianos* and they were *continentais* and, believe me, there are numerous differences in traditions, folklore, every day diet, personal philosophies of life and even language use between the two groups. Over the years we attended numerous parties at their different homes that provided much stimulation, satisfaction and happiness.

Naturally, when we bought our first home in Mississauga, Eduardo was the lawyer in charge of doing the paperwork and closing the deal. It was in 1981 and interest rates for mortgages were skyrocketing. Filomena and I were somewhat worried about the situation. We did not know whether or not we would be able to pay it and the related expenses connected with home ownership. Eduardo took the time to guide us calmly through the entire process for which we were, of course, thankful. He was that kind of a man. Untimely, Eduardo succumbed to pancreatic cancer on October 24th, 2012, much too early, at the age of sixty-two. That said, our friendship with Ana has remained strong.

Kitchener. We invited, while we lived in that city, family and friends to visit us frequently. My mother, sometimes, would come along with us for the weekend, something that made her very happy. Occasionally, our friends Mario and Marcie would come up. Still, on other occasions, it was my family who came for lunch on Saturdays or Sundays. They lived in Mississauga and that meant that Kitchener was just a short drive away. For the two of us, time was passing fast.

Filomena and I also attended Oktoberfest for the first time ever while we lived there. The social committee at Grand River Collegiate was always thinking of fun activities for the staff. So, dinner at a special restaurant followed by a hayride came up around Thanksgiving, a couple of trips to the horseraces at Flamboro Downs, a trip to Stratford to watch a play, etc., were all in the agenda and Filomena and I participated in them all. In 1978, Kitchener was a small city with a limited number of social and cultural activities happening. So, to distract themselves, people were left to their own devices. Families played cards a lot to while the free time away.

All in all, the time that we spent in that city was enjoyable, except for the fact that Filomena could not find a banking job there in spite of all her American banking experience. She spoke English, she had banking experience but she could not land a job in banking in that city because she did not have "Canadian" experience. It was a poor excuse to say the least. One that continues to this day in many parts of Canada. On the other hand, in Toronto, the lack of "Canadian" experience did not pose as many problems. Banking was banking, for heaven's sake!

Personally, and professionally too, I quickly found out that there were advantages and disadvantages to living fairly close to Grand River Collegiate. The obvious advantage was that there was no traffic to speak of going and coming back from school. The biggest disadvantage was, however, that I was constantly running into the students from the school who lived in the neighborhood. Every time that I went to Stanley Mall, the closest one to our apartment, a grocery store, a pharmacy or even church, they were there. The disadvantages clearly outweighed the advantages. For privacy's sake, I made a mental note not to repeat that mistake going forward.

At the end of the last regular staff meeting, Principal Shaver thanked me for my hard work and services to the school; the Acting Head of Modern Languages, Mme Thierry, stood up and said a few words to that effect, too, but referring to my contribution to the Languages Department and gave me a plaque with the school's crest and my name engraved on it. A nice souvenir. Finally, it was my turn to say something; I stood up and thanked the administration and fellow teachers for their friendship and support, especially those in the Languages Department, and that was that. *Au revoir* Grand River Collegiate.

That summer, after much searching in vain, we finally found an apartment to rent in East York, one of Toronto's boroughs. It was at 2 Secord Ave., up on the 10th floor, a short distance to Main and Danforth, a major intersection in Toronto, and a major subway stop on Line 2. After moving in at the end of July, we went on a car trip to the province of Québec. We visited Montréal, Québec City and Ottawa. Our visit to our capital city coincided with the funeral of a former Prime Minister of Canada, John Diefenbaker.

Coming back to the Metropolitan Separate School Board, I applied with it and was interviewed by a Superintendent of Personnel, a certain Mr. Dagenais, who hired me on the spot. I was going to teach French in grades 1-8 in a couple of elementary schools: Darcy McGee Catholic School, yes, the same school where the summer program had taken place, and James Culnan Catholic School. Both schools were so-called open concept schools; an *avant-garde* idea at the time that called for team-teaching. However, in concrete terms at these two schools, it meant that four different classes would be going on simultaneously in a huge open area. Students sat around square or round tables and were distracted easily by the goings-on elsewhere in the other classes. The situation left a lot to be desired in terms of an effective educational approach where team teaching was supposed to be the order of the day but was seldom executed. The teachers taught their subjects as if they were in individual regular classrooms surrounded by four concrete walls. Much before the end of the 1979-1980 school year, I had had enough of this idiotic nonsense. Furthermore, in both schools, the support given to teachers of French was negligible, even insignificant, in short, almost an afterthought. My colleagues who also taught French were all aiming to become regular classroom teachers as soon as possible. Once again, I found myself ready to start looking for another position for September of 1980, hopefully at the high school level. For the time being though and because I was teaching for a catholic board, I had to take Religious Education, Part 1, which I did throughout the fall and winter of 1979-1980.

In early October of 1979, I received a kind invitation from Grand River Collegiate to attend Commencement on Friday evening, October 19th, at eight o'clock. Unhappily, I could not attend for personal reasons. I contacted a fellow teacher, Mr. W.B. Mulligan, who was Director of Student Activities, and asked him if he could send me a copy of *Sequoyah 1979*, the school's yearbook which he promptly mailed to my new address in Toronto with the compliments of the staff. It was with a lot of delight that I leafed through the book finding throughout it pictures of very familiar students and staff alike including one of me as a member of the Languages Department and another one as a participant in a fun sketch put on by the staff for the Christmas Assembly. But what amazed me the most was the breath of the courses offered, the sheer number of the cultural activities, sports, clubs and community involvement events on display. It confirmed my deep held belief of how lucky I had been to have started my teaching career in such an exceptional school. I have kept that school yearbook in pristine condition all these years and, like many teachers who collect school memorabilia, every now and then I have opened it to relive some very good memories of my first year in education.

One fine day, while I was having lunch in the staff room at Darcy McGee Catholic School, I happened to find an advertisement in the *Globe and Mail* for a language teacher at Harbord Collegiate Institute, one of the oldest and most prestigious schools run by the Toronto Board of Education. The school was looking for a teacher of Portuguese and Spanish for grades 11-13. I immediately applied and within a few days was given an interview by Principal Ralph Peters.

When I arrived for the interview, I was greeted by Principal Peters, Vice-principal John Bird, the Head of the Moderns and Classics Department, Mr. Jack Harryman, and my former instructor of Portuguese at the University of Toronto, Mrs. Laura Fernanda Bulger, the teacher responsible for Portuguese and Spanish at the school. The interview went extremely well and I was offered the position. It was the best thing, career wise, that ever happened to me. Harbord Collegiate turned out to be a dream of a school. It had just undergone major renovations between 1978 and 1980, with the exception of its lovely auditorium where two former students, two budding comedians, Johnny Wayne and Frank Shuster, had performed countless times on its stage. They had been active members of the Oola Boola Club, a club dedicated to staging funny and satirical sketches during the school's assemblies. Its official reopening had taken place on November 14th, 1980. For landing that job, I considered myself the luckiest person alive! It was also the beginning of a friendship and a professional collaboration with Laura that lasted until she passed away in 2014.

Nevertheless, before I could accept the position, I had to contact the Metropolitan Separate School Board and let the Superintendent of Personnel, the same Mr. Dagenais, the gentleman who had hired me the previous summer, know that I had accepted a job at the high school level with the Toronto Board of Education, its rival board, even though I had an ongoing contract with his own. The man, rightly so, was not pleased that I was breaking the contract unilaterally because my actions were not very ethical, a point well taken given that both of us were practicing Catholics and people with integrity, but he agreed to let me go when he saw that it did not make any sense retaining someone who had made up his mind to teach elsewhere. I promptly contacted Principal Peters to let him know the good news.

What I remember best about the summer of 1980 are the relaxing afternoons that I spent by the apartment's swimming pool at 2 Secord Ave., or at the waterfront, by the Beaches' Boardwalk, the once-a-week meetings at Laura's home in Etobicoke where we instructed four of her former Harbord Collegiate students in Spanish (they would be in my grade 13 class that September), and Filomena's parents driving up from Boston to visit us, something that made her very happy. But the biggest surprise happened when Filomena won, by the luck of the draw, a lovely one-week trip to Acapulco, all expenses paid, at her branch of the Royal Bank.

Our trip to Acapulco was an eye opener culturally and otherwise for both of us. We stayed at the Ritz Marriott Hotel, a far cry from its namesake in Lisbon in terms of luxury but it was directly on the beach facing the lovely bay of Acapulco, on Costera Miguel Alemán. Needless to say, we did not spend all of our time at the beach sunbathing and swimming in the warm waters of the Pacific. We wanted to see more of Mexico.

On our first Sunday in Acapulco, in the late afternoon, we went to the *Plaza de Toros*, to watch a *corrida*, a bullfight. We had never been to one. We were sitting behind an American couple with two young children. There were four or five bulls to be slain during the event. Within just a few minutes of the *corrida*, the young matador attempted to kill repeatedly the first bull without much success. He kept on missing the mark with every attempt that he was making to dispose of the poor animal. Eventually, another matador had to step in and give the *coup de grâce* for him. It was a bloody mess and the children in front of us were in tears. It was obvious that the experience was traumatizing them. So, the parents got up and left. We stayed to see what fate was in store for the second bull. It was the same story all over again. In disgust, we also got up and left. To this day, in my humble opinion, it remains the most barbaric event that my wife and I have ever witnessed. An experience not to be repeated.

We also participated in an all-day trip to lovely Taxco, the silver capital of the world, where we had the opportunity to visit some of its monuments, such as the Paroquia de Santa Prisca, its most famous church, a baroque jewel, and La casa Humboldt, where Baron von Humboldt stayed on his way from Acapulco to Mexico City in 1815, and, of course, of buying some, you guessed it, silver jewelry. A typical lunch of *tacos* was served at Bar Paco accompanied by tequila refreshments that made the drive back to Acapulco much more pleasant in spite of the incident that occurred half way through the trip. At some point, some very young soldiers with machine guns on hand stopped the coach along the highway and made all of us tourists get off. It was a scary situation that made us realize that we were in a Latin American country where human rights were not always respected. After much arguing with the bus driver, they let us go. To this day, I still do not know who or what they were looking for. The bus driver and tour guide when questioned about it by some of us quickly changed the subject.

On another occasion, we participated on an evening excursion to La Quebrada, one of the most famous tourist attractions in Acapulco. Essentially, it's a cliff from which divers jump off from a height of 12 m or 24 m, especially at night, carrying a torch. These daredevils put on a show that is unforgettable all the more so when one considers that they are putting themselves at risk with every single dive.

And, on yet another outing, we went to a traditional show put on by dancers, singers, acrobats, daredevils, etc., at the Centro de Cultura de Acapulco. As we were purchasing our tickets, we recognized a young couple that both of us knew from Somerville, Joe and Henrieta. They had been Filomena's friends since they had met at Somerville High School in the late 1960s. The four of us were pleasantly surprised and most happy to see one another in such an unexpected place. If we had planned it in advance, probably it would not have worked out so well. For the next couple of days, we hung together at the beach before we went our separate ways.

Finally, while relaxing at the beach, we saw countless tourists go parasailing for a few minutes at a time without any mishaps occurring. Filomena and I decided that we would try it, too. We signed a waiver that absolved the company from any responsibility in case of an accident and off we were. It was both an exhilarating and scary experience. On the plus side, we got a gorgeous view of the entire bay of Acapulco from up there, on the minus side, if the rope snapped, you were left to your own devices to come back down safely. Luckily, nothing tragic happened to either one of us.

Life continued to be good.

14

Harbord Collegiate Institute, A Dream of a School, 1980-1997

I said it before, but I will repeat it, professionally and personally speaking, the twenty-seven years altogether that I spent at Harbord Collegiate were the best of my life. That's where I blossomed as a teacher of languages, a mentor, an associate teacher, a department head, a producer of school plays, a coach, a chaperone of countless local excursions and trips abroad, an avid supporter of the arts programs in the school, and the list goes on. There were countless opportunities to develop professionally and I took advantage of them all. On a personal note, it allowed me to mature as an individual who was not only a teacher but also a husband, a father and a responsible member of the community at large.

I was also lucky to be coming into a well-established Modern Language Department headed by Jack Harryman and assisted by Jim Rayner. It was a well-oiled machine, to use a political term. Other members of the department included Lena Winesanker, a former student at the school, Margherita Manuele, Penny Hustler (now Vincent), Paulette Kuehn and Peter Liu. I was the youngest member of the department and had lots to learn from them all. Fortunately for me, they were generous with their time and advice and, thanks to their encouragement, I blossomed. Of course, the student body played a large part in my own professional successes. Without a motivated, gifted and self-disciplined student body my best efforts would have been in vain.

Harbord Collegiate had first opened its doors in 1892. It is located almost next door to the downtown campus of the University of Toronto, St. George Campus, and it has always attracted a student body coming from a wide variety of ethnic backgrounds. Most of its students, however, share one common characteristic – they are university bound and their number one choice is the University of Toronto. It is, therefore, a highly academic school which means that there are relatively few discipline issues. Consequently, teachers can concentrate on teaching and students on learning. In other words, throughout Harbord Collegiate's illustrious history the students have always used the school as a stepping stone to access higher education.

I arrived in the school in the nick of time. The official reopening of the new Harbord Collegiate took place on November of 1980. Many important dignitaries were on hand for the occasion. In an article for the *Review '81*, the school's yearbook, entitled "Saluting a New Beginning", one can read the following message:

> The opening ceremony was an especially important day for Mr. Peters, also chairman of the ceremony. In his remarks, Mr. Peters talked about the progress of the construction and thanked many of the distinguished guests. These guests, which made up the platform party, consisted of representatives from the Toronto Board of Education, the architects, and the engineers.
>
> Other distinguished guests were Ross McLellan, MPP for the riding of Bellwoods, and Suzie Marr, former SAC (Student Activity Council) president. Trustee Robert G. Spence officially opened the school and Trustee Pat Case had the honour of presenting Mr. Peters with a large key placed on a plaque.
>
> Most of the speeches addressed by the guests referred to the importance of an educational institution such as Harbord and her overall contribution to the community.

Also, in the spring of 1981, Harbord Collegiate was going to celebrate its 90th Anniversary. It was the third oldest high school in Toronto after Jarvis Collegiate and Parkdale Collegiate. It was a very exciting time to be part of its faculty.

Not many faculty positions became available at Harbord Collegiate as the years came and went. Teachers tended to stay and even overstay at the school, including myself. Therefore, when a position opened up, it was usually on account of someone retiring or being promoted to another school in the Toronto Board of Education, a fact that spoke volumes about the school's reputation. I had gotten in because Laura was going to be teaching once again at the University of Toronto. I was one of the few lucky ones. To my surprise, on the first day of school in September of 1980, during the first staff meeting, I recognized a familiar face among the staff; it was that of Mr. Bill Carder who had been a teacher of Geography during my student days at Bloor Collegiate. That October a few more teachers joined the staff: Lisa Caparelli, a fellow Bloorite as well as a friend dating back to the program Ketchup days. She was joining the Physical Education and Typing Departments. I also met Mike Covello, another Bloorite, one that I had not met before. He was going to be part of the Science Department. Finally, another teacher, one who would also become a close friend, Jean-Paul Ginestier, joined the Mathematics Department. He was coming from the Toronto French School, a private school.

During its long history, Harbord Collegiate attracted, decade after decade, a huge Jewish clientele followed by Italian, Portuguese and Chinese ones. Many of the Jewish students went on to accomplish great things in all areas of society bringing continued glory to the school's reputation. In 1980, the Jewish crowd had been replaced by the next wave of immigrants who were just as motivated as the previous ones. According to a formal survey done by the school's office on March 31st, 1984, the school had a total of 1,274 students and the four main ethnic groups were: Chinese, 590, Portuguese, 177, Italian, 157 and Greek,

81. These were followed by smaller groups of Vietnamese, Spanish, Korean, etc.

At Harbord Collegiate, right from the start, I found myself in a privileged position, one that afforded me many advantages and relative few disadvantages. I was the only teacher of Portuguese and Spanish. That meant that I had six different courses to teach which entailed six preparations and a grand total of eighteen exams to prepare. In those days, students used to have three sets of exams per academic year. Jack, my Head of Department, was very supportive and provided as much help as he could even though he did not teach my languages. For me, those first few years were a huge learning curve, one that taught me the value of methodic preparation and hard work in order to achieve as much success as possible.

My predecessor at Harbord Collegiate, Laura, had also come up with the brilliant idea of staging plays in Portuguese in the beautiful school auditorium. So, every spring, on the Friday preceding the Victoria Day long weekend, there was a show for the Portuguese community at large entitled Noite de Teatro. Although I was swamped with work just from the teaching of my six courses, most of my colleagues had only three, I was intent on maintaining this tradition because of its intrinsic academic and cultural values. To that end, my former involvement with the French Play at the University of Toronto paid big dividends. In the spring of 1981, I staged the first of what would become a well-established tradition for the rest of the 1980s. While Laura had only staged classical plays, I combined a classical play with a modern one. When I noticed that my audience definitely preferred modern plays, I dropped the classical ones altogether. It meant choosing two one-act plays for the show, doubling the work because my attention was divided between two groups of students who were performing in the plays. That said, this innovation proved to be a great success. I staged, from 1981 to 1989, a total of fourteen one-act plays in seven shows. For some of them, before each play, I also had students recite poetry. For others, I invited *Ranchos Folclóricos*, groups of folk dancers and singers, from the social clubs that my students belonged to within the Portuguese community, to open the show. They themselves were part and parcel of these groups and were keen to display their talents. At the end of each show a reception took place in the school cafeteria for the audience. Coffee, tea and juice were served together with all sorts of mouth-watering desserts supplied by my students' parents.

I had learned from Professor Collet that staging a play meant relying on many different people to pull it off. So, I tried to involve all my students of Portuguese in the production. There were the actors, of course, but also stage managers, prompters, set decorators, a stage crew, publicity directors, ticket collectors, program distributors, etc. To this day, it remains one of the most satisfying extra-curricular activities that I did during my career. And, to this day, whenever I happen to bump into my former students of Portuguese, they seldom mention the "beautiful things" that I taught them in class, but remember vividly the plays in which they participated in one way or another. It became a highlight of their high school experience. Of course, I also relied on some of my colleagues at Harbord Collegiate to lend a hand with every production. Some of them helped with make-up such as Jack Harryman, John Hilbish and Ron Bottaro. Fernanda Santos, one of the school's secretaries, always pleasant and helpful, typed and retyped (on account of last-minute changes) and photocopied every single program to my great relief and gratitude. And my first two principals at the school, Mr. Ralph Peters and Mr. Doug Lougheed, made it a point of attending the performances although they did not speak a word of Portuguese, the latter always accompanied by his wife, to show their support for this unique community event. And as I write these last words, I remember with gratitude and fondness the support given by Mr. Hugh MacDonald, the Head of Guidance, who insisted on paying for his own ticket, although he was entitled to a free one as a member of the staff, just to demonstrate how much he believed in the project. To all of them, *je tire ma révérence*.

Regarding Noite de Teatro, one of my greatest pleasures was to have my own mother attend that first production on May 8th, 1981. The show consisted of two plays: *Ressonar sem dormir* (To Snore Without Sleeping), a modern play, and *Quem tem farelos?* (Who Has Bran?), a classical Gil Vicente satire. I could see how proud she was that her son not only taught in one of the oldest and best-known high schools in Toronto but that he could put on a show that was enjoyed by so many people in the community at large. It was the first and last production that she ever witnessed. She passed away on November 19th of that year while on a trip to the Azores in order to attend the wedding of a cousin of ours. That day remains one of the saddest days of my life.

I was sitting at the back of the classroom watching a friend from my St. Mike's days, Barbara Santamaria, who was now a student at FEUT (she was my first teacher candidate), teach a Spanish class when the head secretary, Ana Chachula, called me on the internal phone and asked me if I could take an important phone call, something highly unusual, in the Guidance Department which was located close to my classroom. When I picked up the phone, I heard my aunt's tearful voice on the other side. She gave me the terrible news. My mother had passed away. I was devastated. I quickly went back to the classroom and told Barbara that I needed to see Principal Peters immediately. I needed to absent myself from school for a few days in order to fly to São Miguel and attend my mother's funeral. After offering his condolences, Principal Peters told me to take as much time as I needed. Briefly, we discussed the fact that Barbara was my student teacher and that there was nobody else available in the Modern Language Department to supervise her during my absence. I assured Mr. Peters that she did not need much supervision. She had already been with me for a few days and I knew that she was quite competent and responsible and that she had the situation under control. So, it was agreed that Jack, my Head of Department, would lend a hand if she needed help with anything. Also, a supply teacher had to be found in a hurry to cover my Portuguese classes. He assured me that he would take care of that. I took my leave of him and quickly went upstairs to have a quick conversation with Barbara. She was sorry to hear about the sad news and told me that she would manage all right and for me not to worry about anything. Next, I informed Jack himself about the news. Being the gentleman that he was, not only did he offer his sincere condolences, but he also offered to lend me money to pay for the last minute and totally unforeseen trip to the Azores, something that touched me profoundly. He knew that Filomena and I had purchased our first home just recently, in the summer of 1981, and that perhaps we were short of cash, hence his offer. I thanked him very much for his kind and generous gesture but declined the offer and left the school to meet my wife at the bank where she was working in order to give her the news. She was equally devastated. She had had the opportunity in 1980 to get to know my mother well when she had stayed with her and knew that she was a good woman. That night, in our new home in Mississauga, we shed many tears.

After picking her up, we drove to my uncle's house in Mississauga. When we got there, of course, everybody else in my family already knew the news. We needed to figure out how to make it to Ponta Delgada in short notice to attend the funeral. Luckily, my cousin Paula's boyfriend, John, happened to be there and he knew a Portuguese travel agent. There was no direct flight from Toronto to the Azores for the next few days. However, there would be a TAP flight from New York to Lisbon the following day in the evening. So, Tibério, the travel agent, booked us on a trip to New York in the afternoon. We would be on standby for the trip to Lisbon. Fortunately, we were able to get on that flight. Upon arriving in Lisbon, we would be taking another flight to Ponta Delgada later in the afternoon. In the meantime, our family in Ponta Delgada was made aware of all these travel arrangements. It so happened that Dona Izalda and her daughter Conceição were in Lisbon at the time. Conceição was attending the Universidade de Lisboa. Dona Izalda had been alerted of our arrival in Lisbon by her brother Eduardo. When we landed, mother and daughter were there to welcome us. We were all sad to be reunited in such somber circumstances. The last time we had seen one another had been during our honeymoon in 1978. In any case, they had been invited for lunch by a couple who were friends of theirs, Mr. and Mrs. José Inácio do Couto who, when they were informed of the particulars of what had brought us unexpectedly to Lisbon, quickly invited the two of us for lunch too. Their generosity, warmness and, especially, their company were much appreciated by Filomena and me. It was a temporary distraction from what lay ahead when we would get to our final destination in Ponta Delgada.

Much too soon it was time to return to the airport for our flight to Ponta Delgada. We got there in the early evening of November 21st. All our close family members were at the airport waiting for us. There were hugs and many tears shed and we were briefly informed about the funeral arrangements. The funeral itself was going to take place the following day in the morning. So, Filomena and I retired to my uncle's house and soon went to bed. We were both exhausted, physically and emotionally. We had not slept for more than a couple of days.

When we woke up the next morning, the sky was covered up and soon it began to rain heavily. Such a sad looking day, one that matched so very well our heavy hearts. There was an open coffin at the cemetery's chapel. Filomena and I stood next to it and said our farewell to a mother and mother-in-law who had done the impossible for me ever since my father's death and who had welcomed her with open arms as a daughter-in-law. I had not been present at my father's funeral. He had died in New York and had been buried in Boston while on a personal business trip to America. We lived in Ponta Delgada at the time. I was 9 years old when it had happened and, because it had taken place so far away, it had seemed unreal. He had simply vanished from our lives. Now, it was only too real. My cold mother's body lay in a coffin right before my eyes. A million memories flooded into my brain in those brief minutes before the coffin's cover was nailed shut and transported to the grave never to be seen again. She was interred in the same grave as her own mother Margarida, in Ponta Delgada's Cemetery, known to the locals as Cemitério de São Joaquim, in grave number P-N-24. It was the worst day of my life!

We returned to Canada on Thursday, November 26th, via Terceira and Montréal before arriving in Toronto. I was in school the following morning to meet Barbara whose stint at Harbord Collegiate as a teacher candidate was ending that very day. I was dead tired and I remember that in the morning there was an assembly in the auditorium and that I could not keep my eyes open. In any case, that afternoon I wrote Barbara's Appraisal of Practice Teaching, a good one, although I had only been present for the first few days of her assignment, and we said *¡Hasta la próxima!* See you around!

As you can see, there are a lot of important life memories associated with my long stay at Harbord Collegiate. Fortunately, most of them were not as sorrowful and tragic as the one I just described. In fact, most of them were very happy ones which brings me to the 90th Anniversary of the school in 1981. It was quite an event. All staff, many students, local trustees, superintendents, some politicians and, of course, past generations of Harbordites showed up for the extravaganza. In the same issue of the *Review '81*, one can find the following note written by a Harbord Club member who attended the proceedings. It was addressed to Principal Peters:

> To the letters of appreciation that have reached you, and which will be reaching you in the next few days, I must add a few words.
>
> The Harbord Club and the Reunion Committee have received superlative cooperation from you, your staff and your students. I am writing because this cooperation was so outstanding that I wish to express it personally.
>
> The many comments from our older members on the courtesy and friendly helpfulness of the students are still reaching us every day. The staff and students of our Harbord Collegiate contributed in great measure to the success of the reunion.
>
> The tangible appreciation of the Harbord Club, ever-increasing, should manifest itself.

My own classroom, room 217, was chosen as one of the many theme rooms: Pre-20s Room, 1920s Room, 1930s Room, all the way up to the 1970s Room. Furthermore, there were also other themed rooms such as: Harbord Review Room, Teachers' Room, Music Room, Sports Room, Scholarship Room, Harbord Club Room and the list went on. There were plenty of refreshments to keep the guests happy, too. It was a tremendous success. June 5th and 6th, 1981, would be remembered by all who attended the 90th Anniversary Reunion for many years to come because of the effort put into it by so many and the unique opportunity to renew old friendships and fraternize with people who had attended the same school during adolescence, the so-called "best years of your life".

With my first year at Harbord Collegiate under my belt, it was time to relax a little bit. Just a little bit, though. We had purchased our first home in the early spring to take possession of it in the final days of summer. In the meantime, we were watching interest rates for mortgages go up literally every day. We were a bit worried. Since Filomena was going to be working most of the summer, except for her two-week vacation, I decided to apply with my Board for a position to teach a grade 13 French course at night school. It was a new credit course for the students which meant that it was quite intense. A lot of material had to be covered in less than three months and the course culminated with a final exam. Fortunately, it was going to be held at Monarch Park Secondary School, a school not too far from our apartment. It was the first and last night course that I ever taught in the summertime. Aside from the keen students, some of them young adults already, who attended the course, what I remember most about it was looking through the window at a lovely summer evening on display and all of us imprisoned in a classroom without air conditioning. It was hard for all concerned.

That said, starting with the summer of 1982, during the month of July, I became involved in day-time Summer School. The Head of Science at Harbord Collegiate, Mr. Hank Stratton, who was also the principal of Summer School, invited me to join the team. I was going to teach French to students who had failed the subject during the regular school year. The students needed to upgrade their mark in order to obtain the credit. Classes were held from 8:30 a.m. to about 1:00 p.m. I taught Summer School for essentially three reasons: first of all, I was teaching a full timetable of Portuguese and Spanish with no room for the teaching of any French courses. I needed to use the language in order to maintain a high level of fluency; second of all, my wife was working during that period of time anyways and, therefore, would not be home with me; thirdly, as all people who have purchased a home know, there are many expected and some unexpected financial obligations and responsibilities that come with home ownership. Although the two of us had good salaries, if we wanted to go on vacation, we would have to touch our savings, something that we did not want to do because we were intent on paying down our mortgage as quickly as possible. So, whatever money I made teaching Summer School, eventually most of it went towards a well-deserved summer vacation abroad.

That is not to say that in the meantime we were just living to work. Between 1982 and 1988 we visited Montréal (1982), Cuba (1983), Spain (1984), Venezuela (1985), France (1986), São Miguel (1987) and the Dominican Republic (1988). The arrival of our daughter in February of 1989 put a momentary stop to our travels. Babies do bring drastic change to one's daily routines and lifestyle habits whether one wants it or not. But it was a small price to pay for the countless pleasures and joy with which she showered the two of us who happened to be already in our late thirties when she decided to surprise us with her presence.

In the meantime, before I knew it, it was September again. The school year 1981-1982 was going to be a critical one for me. I had signed a probationary contract with the Board back in 1980 and in 1982 I would either become a permanent teacher or I would be terminated. Principal Peters came to observe a couple of my classes and was pleased with what he saw. I was given a permanent contract and from that moment onwards my most important priority was to keep the two programs that I taught viable and meaningful to the student body. So, aside from making sure that the courses were up-to-date, that the material was relevant and that the students were engaged and happy, I looked for opportunities to invite people from the community to visit my classes and demonstrate in concrete terms how their knowledge of Portuguese or Spanish had enriched their personal and professional lives. I also took my classes on local field trips to keep them motivated and focused on the big picture. I used to repeat to them at nauseum that knowledge of languages was an invaluable tool in their tool box, something that would set them apart from the next candidate provided that everything else was the same.

In the case of Portuguese, the traditional Noite de Teatro kept a good many of them involved in an activity that was successful and, therefore, a source of pride to all involved. In the case of Spanish, there was the yearly OMLTA (Ontario Modern Languages Teachers' Association) Spanish Contest, a trip to a restaurant at least once a year, outings to cinemas to view movies in Spanish and a steady stream of invited guests from a variety of Spanish-speaking countries.

Another feature that kept my students interested in languages was the fact that I was an associate teacher with FEUT and that at least four teacher candidates per school year came into my classes for a two-week practicum at a time. I considered myself fortunate to work with future teachers of Spanish, and the odd Portuguese ones, too, who came from a variety of countries, many of them native speakers of the languages involved, and this, believe it or not, made a huge difference for my students. They could see concrete examples of other people aside from me who not only spoke those languages but also wanted to teach them as a viable career option. By the time that I wrapped up my teaching career in 2010 with the now named Toronto District School Board, I had had the opportunity to have worked with over sixty teacher candidates. I felt that I had made a small contribution to the future of my profession. It was also a small token of my appreciation for those wonderful associates who had welcomed me with open arms and showed me the ropes when I had been a student teacher myself back in 1978-1979.

In the fall of 1981, Principal Peters asked me to introduce at Commencement the valedictorian, Alice Peixoto. She had been president of SAC, my student in grade 13 Portuguese, and one of the actresses in my first production of Noite de Teatro. I was thrilled by the opportunity. Alice was not only very popular with her fellow students and the staff but also a brilliant student who was contemplating medicine as a career. There were many good things to say about her, and I did say them. She was pleased.

Also, starting in 1980, my wife and I began to be invited to all sorts of weddings. Some of Filomena's colleagues at the Royal Bank, Helga, Rea and Shirley tied the knot. My own cousin Paula also tied hers in 1982. She married a heck of a nice guy originally from Ponta Delgada, John. And then one of my first students from Harbord Collegiate, and one of my best actresses for three years in a row, Lourdes, got married too. It was the first of many former students' weddings that we attended with great pleasure. Some were more memorable that others, of course, because the former student in question had given so much to the Noite de Teatro. A case in point is the wedding of Tony and Suzanne. Suzanne was not only my student in Portuguese, but also in Spanish for three consecutive years. I saw her daily. Tony was my student in Portuguese for an equal length of time. Both participated in the theatre productions for three years in a row. Consequently, I came to know both of them very well. They tied the knot in 1986. A few years later, I was invited to their first-born's baptism party and they, in turn, were invited to my daughter's baptism party in 1989. We are still friends to this day and see each other occasionally. So, life was not just work. Thanks to seasonal parties, birthday parties, weddings and special occasions, we were enjoying ourselves.

As the 1980s unfolded, I kept on teaching Portuguese and Spanish, producing the Noite de Teatro. (Except in 1984 when some of my students preferred to replace it with a Movie Night that required very little student participation because there were no roles to learn by heart, no stage managers, no prompters, etc. It turned out to be a major flop in that it attracted very few members of the Portuguese-speaking community. The Portuguese community had come to expect much more from its students at Harbord Collegiate.) I was also organizing field trips, inviting guests into my classes, supervising many school activities such as Friday evening dances in the cafeteria and, afterwards, in the main gym, assisting with the coaching of the junior boys' soccer team, etc., and teaching French in Upgrading Summer School.

That summer of 1982, Summer School took place at Humberside Collegiate, a school close to High Park, one of the loveliest and the biggest park in Toronto proper. After school, I used to drive to the park, park my Camaro, and go for a lovely walk. It was most relaxing. Starting in the summer of 1983, however, Summer School took place in my own school which meant, in practical terms, that I could use the Languages Office, since I had the key, before, in-between and after classes to unwind with the other two teachers of French. At first, we were total strangers but, as the years came and went, we became good friends and many wonderful discussions took place during the break between the first and the second class. Upgrading consisted of only two classes per day. Because Filomena was working until five o'clock I would, many times, stay in the office after school correcting tests and preparing for the next day until she finished her day and it was time to pick her up before our drive home.

My in-laws had started the tradition in 1980 of driving up to Canada to spend a couple of weeks with us. The summer of 1982 was not an exception to this rule. Since they did not know Montréal, we made the decision to take them there for a few days. I made reservations at the Hôtel de L'Institut, on rue St-Denis, in a lovely area of Montréal called Plateau Mont-Royal. The hotel is also a training school for future hoteliers. It meant that the service was impeccable. Suzy, being quite a religious woman, wanted to visit Saint Joseph's Oratory on Mount Royal, on account of Frère André's reputation, Mary Queen of the

Earth Cathedral, inspired by St. Peter's Basilica in Rome, and, it goes without saying, Notre-Dame Basilica, a must sight for anyone who visits Montréal on account of its beautiful interior. Lastly, we paid also a visit to Notre-Dame-de-Bon-Secours, in the heart of Old Montreal, a church associated with Saint Marguerite Bourgeoys who is buried in the church's sanctuary. She was the colony's first teacher, too, something that appealed to me. It was for all intents and purposes a sort of Québec religious pilgrimage that we did to make Suzy happy. She loved it.

In 1983, after the traditional Noite de Teatro was over and the regular school year came to an end in June, I taught Summer School in the month of July and then it was time to travel somewhere to unwind. A change of scenery is always most refreshing. The highlight of the summer of 1983 came with an exceptional trip that my wife and I took to Cuba. We flew to Varadero, where perhaps one of the loveliest beaches in the entire Caribbean is to be found, for a week. We stayed at Club Kawama. But, as usual, we did not stay put at the resort for the entire vacation; we had a chance to visit La Habana, Cuba's capital, twice. Firstly, to visit its most important points of interest and, secondly, to attend an evening show at the famous Tropicana cabaret. "*Tropicana, un paraiso bajo las estrellas*". An open-air cabaret under the stars. I was most interested in retracing Ernest Hemingway's steps in the old city and visit his cherished hang outs to taste his favorite Cuban drinks in La Bodeguita del Medio, *mojito*, and in El Floridita, *daiquirí*. Unfortunately, I did not have a chance to visit La Finca Vigía, Hemingway's main abode in Cuba, a place where he wrote some of his most famous novels. Hopefully, there will be a next time.

While in La Habana, se were interested in seeing: La Plaza de la Catedral with its old adjoining palaces, El Castillo de la Real Fuerza, the oldest fortress in Cuba, El Capitolio Nacional, the house where José Martí, an Independence hero, an intellectual, a poet, saw first the light of day, La Plaza de la Revolución with its unusual *obelisco*, a place where Fidel Castro delivered many a speech to his fellow countrymen over the years, La Universidad de la Habana, the oldest in the country and its famous staircase, the sight of numerous student protests, El Malecón, the seaside boulevard, etc. There was no shortage of places of interest. During our visit, my wife and I had the distinct impression that we had stepped back in time and that we were in the 1950s, mostly because many of the cars and buses, kept in pristine condition, dated that far back. Be that as it may, everywhere we went, we found Cubans to be extremely friendly and warm towards us. They came across as a proud people who were pleased with what they had been able to accomplish socially, culturally and economically without any help from the US. Fidel Castro was still firmly in control of the country and he counted on communist countries for help when needed.

On March 6th, 1984, Toronto celebrated its Sesquicentennial. The former city of York, back in 1834, had adopted its original Indian name of Toronto. To commemorate the special event, City Council presented all students and staff with a lapel pin. It represented the City's Coat of Arms as well as two symbols from the Arms: Canadian beaver and waves representing Lake Ontario. Many teachers had provided help to the Youth Committee's Sesquicentennial programs which included a Science Fair, Video Dance, Music Fest, a Youth Parade, etc.

The 1980s also saw important changes in Ontario's education system. Grade 13 was replaced by OAC (Ontario Academic Credits) for all students who started high school in 1984. The OACs were meant for students who would go on to post-secondary education. There were different courses for students who were university or college bound. Eventually, many years later, in 2003, this fifth year of high school would be eliminated creating the so-called double cohort which meant that students who were finishing grade 12 and OAC all graduated at the same time creating a nightmare for universities and colleges alike who were not ready to receive such a large number of students all at once. But that is another story. In practical terms, the elimination of OAC meant that Ontario's education system would be aligned with that of all the other English-speaking provinces.

1984 was also an important date for me for another reason: Professor Collet asked me to play the role of Géronte in the staging of *Le Légataire universel* by Jean-François Regnard. The play is written in verse and this feature poses problems of its own for many actors who are trying to memorize their parts. It means that faithfulness to word order is critical, otherwise one's fellow actors may be left stranded waiting for their cue to intervene in the dialogue. In other words, there is very little room for improvisation and words cannot be arbitrarily changed at the last second without negative consequences. It would be the first time that I would be participating in a play written in verse. The show would be staged on Friday and Saturday, June 15th and 16th, to mark the official opening of the brand-new Saint Michael's Theatre located at Alumni Hall. It would be a fundraiser for the theatre. For the price of $30 one would be entitled to two tickets and also be invited to a reception at intermission.

Naturally, I accepted the new challenge with pleasure. How could I refuse? My association with Madame dated back to the mi-1970s. Although I had been coming to see her yearly productions in the meantime, and after the show dropping by to congratulate her and say hello, her invitation marked officially the renewal of our collaboration in the staging of a play in French. Since I was not tied up with my own production at Harbord Collegiate which would take place in May, I had lots of time to memorize my role and to attend the numerous rehearsals that staging a play under the artistic direction of Madame entailed. This I knew only too well from my previous two experiences.

1984 marked as well the year that my good friend and best man Mario got married. He had met Cheryl at Bell Canada where he worked and they had been dating for a while. Filomena and I were invited to be part of the wedding party as bridesmaid and groomsman. It was a very happy occasion which, woefully, many years later ended in tragedy. As I said before, life is a mixture of happy and sad events.

Later that summer Filomena and I went on a two-week organized trip of Spain. We took the Iberia flight from Toronto to Madrid.

Afterwards, by coach, we slowly but surely made our way from Madrid to the southern part of Spain and even went across the Mediterranean to Morocco for an unforgettable day there. In Spain, we visited such places as Toledo, Córdoba, Granada, Seville, Málaga, and the famous Costa del Sol where we stayed for a few days at Hotel Las Palomas, in Torremolinos, to unwind. It was a glorious vacation in many ways starting with the superb Spanish summer weather.

There are many pluses and minuses associated with an organized trip. On the plus side, one does not worry about transportation, hotels, meals, guided visits, etc. On the minus side, one has to put up with one's fellow tourists and their little peculiarities and routines. Aside from my wife and me, and a couple of other people, most of the other excursionists were in their sixties or even seventies. Generally speaking, at places of interest where there was walking to be done, the older ones were not interested and stayed behind killing time. It seems that the only thing that they were looking forward to was being pampered at the next hotel on the list, and overindulging at meal times in the food and drink that was served. Fortunately, we befriended two young women and the four of us sort of stuck together for the duration of the trip. Also, our little group befriended the tour guide and the bus driver who would join us for some fun wherever we were when everybody else had gone to bed. It is my firm conviction, corroborated by experience on the field over the years, that when one speaks the language of the host country, inevitably one's interactions with the locals tend to be very fruitful. The natives will go out of their way to please you and make sure that you have a good time simply because you made the effort to converse with them in their language. Consequently, their efforts will enrich your personal experience while in their country.

Madrid, the capital of Spain, is a city with so many outstanding places to see starting with an unforgettable tour of the Museo del Prado. After the Louvre, it's perhaps the second greatest museum in the world. El Palacio Real, La Catedral Santa María la Real, Plaza de España, where one will find the two statues of Don Quijote and Sancho Panza side by side, calle de Alcalá, calle de Atocha, and so many other places of interest that make Madrid, Madrid.

Upon arriving at Madrid-Barajas International Airport, nowadays called Adolfo Suárez Madrid-Barajas, we were transported to our hotel. We went up to our room to freshen up and decided to go for a walk in the immediate vicinity of the hotel. It was a very hot day and after walking aimlessly here and there we returned to the hotel and went straight to the bar and ordered a jug of *sangría* which was served with a side dish of delicious olives. It was the best sangria that we ever tasted in Spain. All we know is that after finishing the jug, the two of us were kind of tipsy. We went up to our room and straight to bed only waking up around supper time. Sleepless overnight flights to Europe can bring about this kind of outcome, especially if you find yourself in Spain in the summer time and you happen to have ordered a jug of delicious *sangría*!

Toledo, the home of El Greco, was our first stop on our way south. After it, came Córdoba *"lejana y sola"*, according to the haunting poem by Federico García Lorca, *Canción de Jinete*. Granada came next with its exquisite *Palacio de Alhambra*, a prime example of Islamic architecture in Spain, a UNESCO World Heritage Site, surrounded by its beautiful gardens. Afterwards, we visited Sevilla and its glorious Catedral de Santa María de la Sede, another UNESCO site. Basically, the trip consisted of one wonder after another. It was also in Sevilla that we attended an exquisite Flamenco show in a local restaurant. Although I had attended, in my undergraduate days and thanks to the Spanish Department at the University of Toronto, a Flamenco show on College St. in a restaurant called Don Quijote, this particular one simply blew me away. The dancers, guitarists and singers were simply outstanding. As we discovered slowly Andalucía, I was coming to the conviction that this region of Spain was the best that the country had to offer. Unfortunately, the northern part was not included on the itinerary and it was only after other trips that my eyes were opened to the beauty of the north, the north-east, Cataluña, site of the second biggest Spanish city, Barcelona, and the home of important artists such as Gaudí and Picasso. So, Spain has much more to offer than just the south.

In 1985, I applied for a program available to Board employees called the Four Over Five Plan. It ran under the banner of Leaves of Absence with Pay. It was for Permanent Teachers. I chose to be absent on my fifth year, that is to say in 1989-1990. In a publication entitled Collective Agreement between The Toronto Board of Education and OSSTF (Ontario Secondary Teacher's Federation) one can read the following: "The Teacher shall agree to forego 20% of the Teacher's Total Salary for each of the four years of the contract during which the Teacher is not on leave of absence." And "the period for such leaves of absence with pay granted to a Teacher shall be credited to Teaching Experience." It was a great program in that it was self-financed and there were no penalties of any kind attached to it; the free time allowed the teacher to take stock of one's life, rejuvenate, discover in a leisurely manner what else was going on in the world, travel, etc., etc. We started dreaming about what we would like to do during 1989-1990.

15

School of Graduate Studies at the University of Toronto, 1985-1989

Also, in 1985, I was accepted into the M.A. program in French Language and Literature at the University of Toronto with the understanding that "you must complete the requirement in Medieval French". (As an aside, thanks to this requirement, I came across one of my best former students in Spanish at Harbord Collegiate, David Heap, who was working on an M.A. in French himself. Now, both of us were students in Professor Peter Grillo's Medieval French class. We were thrilled to be together again. David would go on to earn a Ph.D. in French Linguistics followed by a teaching career at the University of Western Ontario. As for Professor Grillo, he had been the instructor in one of my French undergraduate courses, FRE271Y. He had hardly changed; he was as pleasant as ever.) Professors Jean-Claude Susini and Paulette Collet, two former professors of mine who knew me well were kind enough to write recommendation letters praising my academic achievements, my determination to « mener à bon port le projet de maîtrise », my involvement in both La Troupe des Anciens and the Cercle Français and, last but not least, my own professional experience as a teacher of French, Portuguese and Spanish at the high school level for the last eight years. Their wonderful letters literally sealed the deal for me. In a letter from Registrar R.H. Fisher dated August 23rd, he stated:

Dear Mr. Machado

On behalf of the School of Graduate Studies, I am pleased to inform you that you have been offered admission for a program of study as described below.

Session: Winter 1985-86   Program Commences: Sept. 3, 1986

Department: French Lang & Lit   Program: Master of Arts

Program: Length One Session   Status: Part-time

In order to embark on this academic adventure, the Graduate Department of French had established the following Program requirements for all incoming students:

1. Four full courses (or equivalent) as follows:
2. The M.A. seminar in literature or in linguistics. Part-time students will normally take this course in the first year of their programs.
3. Five half courses (or equivalent) from the regular graduate offerings. Up to one course may be taken outside the Department.
4. FRE 5000H, L M.A. Essay.
5. Prerequisite work, if necessary, as follows:
6. Old French if not included in the undergraduate program.
7. Language requirement: one of Latin, German, or a second Romance language.
8. Students must maintain a B average in order to be recommended for the degree and must obtain a minimum of B in the M.A. seminar and the M.A. Essay.

Description of the M.A. Essay

The M.A. Essay is a separate half-course – FRE 5000H, L "M.A. Essay" – in which all M.A. students will enroll. The L suffix means that the grade will be due at the end of the Summer (September 10); the H means that the course is weighted as a half course. A copy of the M.A. Essay is to be filed with the Co-ordinator of Graduate Studies.

Since I had a full-time teaching job at Harbord Collegiate which I was not about to relinquish, I would be working on the M.A. on a part-time basis. Luckily for me, my high school was located almost next door to the St. George Campus where the graduate classes were held in the office and classroom spaces allocated to the Department of French Studies. This set up was most suitable to me because it meant that I could easily get to my destination after the end of the school day to attend some of the classes that usually started at four o'clock. In practical terms, it also meant that for the next few years I would be busy teaching full-time and studying part-time. This kind of lifestyle suited me perfectly in that I had always been a firm believer in lifelong learning. Furthermore, Filomena and I had no children and were not expecting any anytime soon, a fact of life that facilitated tremendously my new academic endeavour.

So, it was with much trepidation that I waited for September 3rd and the start of classes in the Département d'Études françaises. Eight years had passed since my graduation in 1977 from Saint Michael's College and my direct dealings with the local chapter of the Department. In the meantime, the Department of French Studies had been centralized across the University of Toronto's St. George campus and now was located temporarily at King's College Circle where Mme Monique Lecerf, the Graduate Counsellor and Administrative Assistant, reigned supreme over all of us graduate students. And, as expected, some faculty members and staff had retired and new ones had been added to the roster. Naturally, time had moved on for everybody, including me.

As required by the Department, all graduate students were obliged to take FRE1200Y entitled Séminaire Littérature as an introduction to graduate studies. That year, Professor Peter Fitting had been assigned the course. He was a competent and friendly man who kept all of us extremely busy with a heavy reading list and seminar presentations.

As I looked around the classroom during that first class, I realized that out of the seventeen students or so I was the oldest. The vast majority had enrolled in the program right after completing the BA. I was already thirty-three years old, approximately ten years older than most of them. However, as time passed, the difference in age became more and more meaningless. We were all colleagues pursuing further studies in French, a language that we all loved and cherished.

On account of my long relationship with Professor Collet and my involvement in the French Play, I chose FRE1704F, a half-course on Molière taught by Professor David Trott, a specialist in everything Molière. It further consolidated what I knew about Molière's plays. It was in this course that I first heard of Anne Ubersfeld, the great theatre theorist, and the « modèle actantiel en tant qu'outil qui permet au chercheur d'accéder à la structure profonde de l'action d'une pièce ». It was one of the tools that I would use many years later in the analysis of the deep action in some of Marcel Dubé's plays in my own Ph.D. thesis. Who would have known it at the time?

In 1986, the Examination in Medieval French Language and Literature took place and, luckily for me, everything went well because Medieval French was not my cup of tea, so to speak. The first two courses that I had taken in year one would be followed by FRE1807Y, a full-year course entitled Histoire des Idées/XVIII Siècle, a course that dealt quite a bit with the works of Jean-Jacques Rousseau, sometimes referred to as Jean-Jacques Superstar, Diderot and Voltaire. The professor in charge of delivering it was Aubrey Rosenberg, a fine gentleman and even a finer scholar. In the fall of 1987, I took FRE1707F, a half-course on Racine taught by Professor Ross Curtis, a 17th Century specialist, especially in the area of drama, a course in which I scored my highest mark ever, an A+. In his comments, Professor Curtis noted the following: « La dissertation se lit très bien. Bon rythme. Excellentes proportions. [...] Clarté exemplaire; méthode rigoureuse; d'une lecture agréable et instructive; français de premier ordre. »

In the spring, I took FRE1805S, a half-course on Beaumarchais led by Professor Peter Moes, an inspiring scholar who had had the privilege of playing, when he was a student at university, the fantastic role of Figaro. After writing an essay entitled « Beaumarchais, inventeur de la comédie d'intrigue » as part of the course work and gotten an A on it, I decided to ask him if he would be interested in supervising my M.A. Essay which would be titled « Beaumarchais, disciple de Diderot ». After reading the details of my proposal, to my relief, he kindly accepted to do it. In the proposal, I stated that:

Le but de cette dissertation sera de montrer que Beaumarchais a été le disciple de Diderot en ce qui concerne les idées que celui-ci avait élaborées sur le « drame sérieux » et que celui-là a acceptées et démontrées dans trois de ses pièces – à savoir, *Eugénie*, *Les Deux Amis* et *La Mère coupable*.

Dans la première partie de cette étude, on étudiera les idées de Diderot telles qu'exprimées dans *Les Entretiens sur Le Fils naturel* et dans *De la Poésie dramatique*. Après, on analysera *Le Père de famille* afin de vérifier jusqu'à quel point Diderot a réussi à mettre en valeur ses idées dur le théâtre. Dans la deuxième partie notre travail, on analysera les idées de Beaumarchais dans *Essai sur le genre dramatique humain*.

Ensuite, on se penchera sur ses trois drames bourgeois mentionnés ci-dessus. Finalement, on en tirera quelques conséquences pertinentes.

By the time I got around to write the M.A. Essay in the spring and summer of 1988, time, it seemed to me, had just flown by ever since that first day of my M.A. classes back in September of 1985. I had been super busy during those years. Professor Moes approved my dissertation with minor corrections here and there and, therefore, I would be receiving my degree in the spring Convocation of 1989. At that time, the thought of one day in the future returning to the university and attempting to do a Ph.D. in French was not on my radar screen at all, especially when my wife found out that she was pregnant. Our priority number one would be the child that was going to share our daily life for the foreseeable future. I, in particular, would not have at my disposal the free time absolutely necessary to devote to such a long-term academic commitment as a Ph.D. That said, one can never tell what the future holds for oneself because it brings all sorts of unexpected surprises, some of them more pleasant than others.

To conclude, all in all, pursuing an M.A. had been a most gratifying personal and intellectual experience for me, one that perhaps would open new doors should I want to do something with my free time once fully retired from teaching and delivered of parenting obligations.

16

Harbord Collegiate Institute, 1980-1997 (continued)

The winter of 1985 also marked the beginning of a movement within the Portuguese community in Toronto that would occupy a lot of my time, talents, dedication and energy until the fall of 1989. I became Co-chairperson of the Working Group for Portuguese Studies at Glendon College, York University. We had in mind the creation of a Minor in Portuguese Studies at the college. In order to see this worthwhile project to fruition, we had to mobilize the Portuguese community to get its support. That called for numerous organizational meetings of the Working Group itself, led by my friend Laura Bulger who taught at the college, followed by meetings that involved the community at large which were followed, in turn, by deputations made by members of the group at the university level. The *raison d'être* of the Working Group was to convince the university administrators, starting with the principal of Glendon College and, afterwards, the President and Senate of York University, of the need for such a program within the confines of the second largest university in Toronto.

In the meantime, my personal friendship and professional association with Laura was augmenting by the day. She had left the University of Toronto and was now teaching Spanish at Glendon College, the bilingual college associated with York University. The fight for the implementation of a Minor Program in Portuguese Studies had just started. Countless meetings and phone calls between the two of us ensued. Many of them involved Principal Philippe Garrigue who was then in charge of Glendon College.

I am sad to report that in spite of our best efforts over the five years of meetings and more meetings, nothing came of it. By the time that Laura left Canada in 1989, the Minor Program was still not in existence. That said, we had fought the good fight and, in the process, made many new friends. In fact, in my modest opinion, we made it possible for the next group to see the original plan become a reality not at Glendon College but rather at York's main campus.

That year, for the Noite de Teatro, I had the idea of having some of my students who were not directly involved in the two plays recite poetry before each one of the plays as a warm-up to the show. Some of the poems were classics in that they were well-known to most members of the public, others, less so. The result? The public loved this new feature of the Noite de Teatro. I kept this innovation in the back of my mind for future reference.

In the summer of 1985, we travelled to lovely Venezuela for two weeks. We flew into Simón Bolívar International Airport located at Maiquetía, just north of Caracas, not far from the Caribbean Sea. For the first week we stayed in a resort hotel in Caraballeda, the Meliá Caribe, close to Caracas itself. For the second one, we flew to Barcelona, located towards the eastern part of the country, also on the Caribbean shoreline, and from there we went to our hotel in Puerto la Cruz, the Meliá Puerto la Cruz. While in Venezuela, we took another two flights: one to Margarita Island, a duty-free zone very popular with Venezuelans, and the second one to Angel Fall, the highest water fall in the world with a drop of 972m, and named after the American pilot, Jimmy Angel, who discovered it accidentally on October 9th, 1937. The trip to Angel Fall remains engraved in my memory as one of the most exotic trips that I ever took. Two small Beechcraft Bonanza A36 airplanes flew ten of us tourists, five per plane, to this remote area of the country situated in the state of Bolívar. My wife and I volunteered to separate for the flights because the other couples would not. It was a two-and-a-half-hour trip just to get to Angel Fall. Unfortunately, within the first hour of the flight, my plane encountered turbulence and the woman seated right across from me began to vomit. The smell was nauseating and before long her husband was also bringing up. Eventually, I could not hold it anymore myself, I joined the two of them. But the two aspects that I recall most vividly are the spectacular and dangerous dive of the plane into the huge crater where the fall is located and looking at the top of the water fall from almost the bottom of the crater itself. It was quite an impressive sight. We landed on a strip that looked like a narrow dirt road in the middle of the jungle by a village, Uruyen, inhabited by the natives Karamatas. When I disembarked, I was as pale as a ghost. My wife, upon seeing me, asked what had happened. After relating the scene in my plane, she told me that her flight had been super smooth, with no turbulence at all. She had flown with the older of the two pilots. Afterwards, we all went for a refreshing swim in a lake nearby. On the other margin, there were two indigenous young couples totally naked frolicking in the water. It was a beautiful sight to behold. Fortunately for me, on the return trip, I chose the plane piloted by the older gentleman and the trip was uneventful.

The one-day trip to Margarita Island was very enjoyable. The weather was magnificent and the beaches lovely and, at one point, we went on a motorboat ride through the mangrove canals of La Restinga lagoon where we watched in amazement the Ibis Escarlata, a red-plumaged heron, a rare sight, and saw mussels clinging to the roots and lower branches of trees.

As for Caracas, the organized excursion that we took there covered most of the city's highlights and then some. Our tour guide was a lovely *caraqueña* who kept referring to all of us as *"mi amor"*. She was friendly and very generous with the amount of information about her city and country that she showered on us. Her friendliness turned out to be a personality trait that was displayed by Venezuelans everywhere we went.

The all-day excursion included: National Pantheon, Natal House of the Liberator, Plaza Bolívar circled by the Cathedral, the Episcopal Palace, the Yellow House, etc. It also included a ride on the *teleférico* to the top of El Ávila National Park from where one can enjoy a panoramic view of Caracas as well as of the coastline. Finally, it included a side trip to the Arte Murano factory, the only one established in South America, in San Antonio de los Altos, not far from Caracas, followed by a barbecue dinner in a typical restaurant. It was a wonderful day.

The only souvenir that we brought back from lovely Venezuela was a precious vase from the visit to the Arte Murano factory and, of course, the lovely memories of a beautiful country that lately has gone through very tough political, economic and social times.

In 1986, due to difficult contract negotiations between OSSTF and the Toronto Board of Education, all extra-curricular activities were cancelled. Noite de Teatro was part of the collateral damage that resulted from that dispute together with many other events that made life interesting for students. On the plus side for me, my M.A. studies were progressing well. My good friend from St. Mike's and also a participant in the French Plays in the 1970s, Antoinette (Toni) Liscio, joined the M.A. program in 1986 too. For the two of us, it was like being undergrads all over again except, of course, that both of us were now full-time teachers. It was fun discussing with her the challenges that we were both facing at school and as graduate students.

In the summertime, we travelled for the first time to France with a friend that we had met during the Spanish trip, Lydia, who also had never been to France. *La belle et douce France.* Not only, so it seemed, I had been studying French for a good many years, but I had read some of the works of many of its authors as a result of my undergraduate and graduate courses. I had read about its history, culture and traditions, too. Now it was time to be there in person and to enjoy the moment. The first few days were spent in and around Paris. Many a person, including this one, makes the mistake of wanting to see too much all at once during a first trip to La Ville Lumière. Please don't make that mistake. Since there is so much to see and do, it's preferable to choose judiciously what you really want to see and do during that first visit to one of the greatest cities on Earth. Instead, it's a better idea to start planning a second, a third and many other visits while you are there. Irrespective of my previous advice, we wanted to see: La Tour Eiffel, Le Palais de Chaillot, Les Invalides, L'Arc de Triomphe, Les Champs Élysées, Place de la Concorde, Le Louvre, La Cathédrale Notre-Dame, La Sainte Chapelle, La Sorbonne, Le Panthéon, Le Jardin du Luxembourg, Place de l'Opéra, La Comédie-Française, Le Sacré-Cœur, La Défense and, further afield, Versailles.

To get to the other regions of France, we had rented a car, a Renault, and basically did a mini-variation of the Tour de France.

Even if we wanted to, there was no more time for Paris. We had other places to visit such as Reims, the winery Moët et Chandon, at Épernay, one of the world's largest and most famous producers of champagne worldwide. Next on the itinerary were the following cities, towns and villages: Dijon, where we stayed overnight at the *campus universitaire*, in one of the student residences, quite an experience, Lyon, Grenoble, Nice, Monaco, Marseille and Le Château d'If, Aix-en-Provence, Avignon, Pont du Gard, Nîmes, Montpellier, Le Vigan, Carcassonne, Saint-Émilion, La Rochelle, Chartres, Le Château de Chenonceau, for a "*spectacle son et lumière*", Le Château de Azay-le-Rideau, and back to Paris where we attended a farewell to France show at the Folies-Bergère. We were enriched by so many sights and sounds but, at the same time, exhausted by the pace of our French adventure. Frankly, we needed another vacation just to relax and recover from it. It felt good to be young and foolish, though, and to have done it.

One of the highlights came when we paid a former professor of mine at St. Mike's, Jean-Claude Susini, in Le Vigan, in the southern part of France, where he spent his summers, a visit. We stayed overnight at his quaint country home and the next day he was kind enough to show us the lovely mountainous countryside in the area.

In 1986, Laura published a book of short stories entitled *Vaivém* (*Back and Forth*). It dealt with the everyday trials and tribulations of the Portuguese in Canada. It tackled head on such topics as discrimination, exploitation and the general malaise of a people who did not quite fit in, who were struggling in their new country. For many of them, emigrating to Canada had turned out to be a bittersweet dream. Ten years or so after João Medeiros, whom I had met at the West End YMCA had published his study about the Portuguese immigrant situation in Toronto, it seemed that very little progress had been made by the community as a whole.

Noite de Teatro in 1987 resumed with another smashing success. It took place on Friday, May 15th. I invited the folkloric group from the community club Amor da Pátria to open the show. This feature was appreciated by the public. Many Portuguese families belong to all sorts of social clubs having to do with the part of Portugal they came from and many of these clubs have folkloric groups that compete with one another in a friendly way. Then, followed two one-act plays. One of them had been written by my colleague at Central Commerce High School, a funny guy, Luís Moniz. Its title was *Uma Casa Portuguesa Sem Certeza*, A Portuguese House with Some Doubt. It's a satire. In it the playwright deals with a lot of social issues present in the Luso-Canadian community such as alcoholism, physical and emotional abuse, stereotyping, etc. The following year I would stage another play written by Luís, a light-hearted comedy whose setting took place in a classroom, *Os Repetentes do Sr. Becas*, Mr. Becas' Repeating Class.

Also, Madame called on me once again to participate in the staging of *Tartuffe*, by Molière. Another play in verse. She gave me the role of Damis. The experience from *Le Légataire universel* proved to be very useful when it came to memorizing my role. The shows were scheduled to take place on April 23rd, 24th, and 25th. Since my own production was happening on May 15th, it would not interfere with it, a good thing.

In the summer of 1987, Filomena and I returned to São Miguel on vacation. Another six years had flown by since we had been there and, once again, we noticed remarkable changes in the island itself and its people, especially in our family members. The island looked prettier than ever and our family members were aging gracefully. More children had been born and they, together with their parents, seemed to be relatively happy. During our stay, I had the greatest pleasure of seeing one of my best friends when I was a teenager, Luís, who was spending part of his vacation in the island, just like me. Now he lived in mainland Portugal and only occasionally returned to his native São Miguel. He taught Visual Arts in a school and had become a fairly well-known artist. Needless to say, we reminisced a lot about the past and brought each other up-to-date on what we had done ever since 1969. We also talked about what had become of our common friends. He had lost track of most of them, just like me. He was glad to meet my wife and surprised that I had married someone from the island.

The school year 1987-1988 was one of my busiest ever. Aside from teaching my six courses at school, taking myself courses towards my M.A., working with teacher candidates, choosing the plays and the actors for the Noite de Teatro and spending time doing rehearsals with the troupe, attending school functions, and fighting for the establishment of the Portuguese Program at Glendon with Laura, at some point in the spring my good friend Antoinette invited me to be part of an exciting opportunity that would take place in the southern part of France, close to Villefranche-sur-Mer, in July. It would entail teaching French to high schoolers as part of an enrichment summer program at Université Canadienne en France. The program was run by Blythe and Company in association with Laurentian University. The campus was up on Mont Leuze which offered a wonderful bird's eye view of the Mediterranean coast and in particular of Saint-Jean-Cap-Ferrat. How could anybody in his right mind refuse such an offer? I could not and did not.

Most of the students enrolled in the program were from the US, especially from the New York City area, but there were others from Florida, Texas, etc. Many of them attended private schools and their parents were too busy in the summer time to take care of their offspring.

So, they shipped them off to southern France for a good time. Although the primary focus of the summer course was the further development of linguistic skills in French, the students were mostly interested in the social, cultural and sports activities that were planned for them. So, I flew from Toronto to New York where I met many of the students and their parents at the airport before we boarded a flight to Zurich. In Zurich, we had enough time between flights to go sightseeing downtown before proceeding to Nice.

Most of the summer went fairly well although the students did not like the remoteness of the campus. Every time they wanted to go to Nice, it was a major complication in that a special bus had to be booked to take them there and bring them back. There were also the odd cases of some students getting drunk which, of course, was not allowed. But, between morning and early afternoon classes, swimming and tennis and outings in the evening to Nice, most students were quite happy. I remember in particular many of us going to an evening concert in Nice where Carlos Santana was the main attraction. We also were there for the celebrations of the 14th of July, Bastille Day, a national holiday in France, and witnessed the stunning display of fireworks just above the Promenade des Anglais.

The last couple of days were spent in Paris before returning to North America. We took the train from Nice to the capital, an experience which is always a challenge when students are travelling with lots of luggage because people have only a few precious moments to get themselves aboard and settled in. In Paris, we went to see the local usual attractions without any problems. However, when it was time to go to the airport, a female student from Texas reported to the principal of Summer School that she had lost her passport. He pleaded with the ground personnel of Air France at Charles de Gaulle and, amazingly, she was allowed to board the plane on the leg of the flight to Geneva. This turned out to be a bad decision because her final destination was Texas. Inevitably, in Geneva she was denied a boarding pass on the Swissair flight to New York. Since I was the only teacher flying with all the students, the decision was made that I would continue with them to New York and that she would stay behind alone until she could get a temporary passport form the American Consulate the following Monday with the help of the Swissair personnel who were complete strangers to the girl. She should have stayed in Paris in the company of the Summer School's administrators instead of being put in this unfortunate position for a young teenager. In spite of this last-minute glitch, teaching at Université Canadienne en France was a most pleasant way to spend part of the summer.

The summer of 1988 also marked an important milestone for Filomena and me: it marked the 10th anniversary of our wedding. We wanted to celebrate the occasion in a special way. To that end, we had booked a trip to the Dominican Republic. We would be staying at Casa de Campo, a gated resort community about an hour's drive from Santo Domingo, its capital city. In those days Casa de Campo used to call itself "The Caribbean's Most Complete Resort". It probably was.

When I got back from my trip to France, Filomena told me that she was now quite certain that she was pregnant. The baby would be due in mid-February. We were ecstatic and at the same time a bit worried because she would be thirty-eight years old when she would give birth and because there was a history of Down syndrome in the family. Suzy had given birth to Filomena's youngest sister late in life. We quickly made the decision to accept our child with open arms no matter the problems that she may or may not bring with her. She would be a precious gift to both of us.

Our day of departure on vacation to the Dominican Republic was fast approaching and we were looking forward to a relaxing time at Casa de Campo, its surrounding areas as well as a trip to Santo Domingo. It was an all-inclusive vacation. It turned out to be a lovely, relaxing trip for both of us. Just what we needed in order to recharge and face the future with confidence and optimism.

We stayed in a beautiful villa, one of many within the resort, the back of which faced the ocean. There was a spa in the backyard too. The grounds were kept impeccable. We were issued a golf cart which allowed us to drive freely within the gated compound. We soon discovered that there was an air strip attached to the resort itself that accommodated private jets to land. It turned out that rich Americans used to fly in and out for a day of golf at Casa de Campo. Meals at the resort's restaurants were delicious, it goes without saying. Apparently, the famous Oscar de la Renta, a native of the island, had a hand in designing this outstanding resort.

This time, because Filomena was pregnant, we did not venture out to too many places. That said, we still managed to go on an all-day trip, in a class-bottomed boat, to a local island with a lovely beach where a barbecue and drinks were served for lunch and where we took a dip in the sea from time to time all day long. We also visited a small village constructed with artists in mind and for the display of their talents, Los Altos de Chavón, at the top of a mountain from where one had a bird's eye view of the countryside and the Chavón river. The last couple of days were spent at the Hotel and Casino Jaragua, in Santo Domingo. During a dinner, we had the pleasure of meeting personally the chef of the main restaurant who sat at our table to chat with us about a variety of subjects. A most friendly guy, not to mention a talented chef, too.

Santo Domingo is one of the oldest cities in the Americas. It was founded in 1496. As such, it has much to offer in terms of monuments and history. Given that the two of us were refreshed by our stay at Casa de Campo, we were ready to explore a little bit the most important monuments before our departure to Canada. Specifically, we wanted very much to take a look at El Alcázar de Colón, El Museo de las Casas Reales, El Panteón Nacional, and La Catedral de Santo Domingo, where the tomb with the ashes of Cristóbal Colón is to be found. The second last monument in our list was El Palacio Nacional, the official office of the President of the Dominican Republic. Finally, it was time to take a look at the Plaza de la Independencia with its high, yet beautifully simple arch and the huge statue of the Piety right underneath it.

After all the sightseeing, it was time to spend a few dollars at the casino Jaragua before departing for Canada.

The school year 1988-1989 was out of the ordinary for several reasons. It marked the end of my first decade at Harbord Collegiate. In 1989-1990 I would be off on the Four Over Five Program and I had made up my mind that upon returning to the school the following September I would be teaching mostly French and Spanish courses leaving the teaching of the Portuguese program in the hands of Alice Freitas who had been hired to replace me in the meantime by Principal Lougheed.

In the fall of 1988, while driving to attend a scheduled meeting of the Working Group for Portuguese Studies at Glendon College with the President of York University, Dr. Harry W. Arthurs, at York University main campus, I had a car accident at the intersection of Keele and Sheppard Streets. I was going through an amber light when an older gentleman decided to make a left turn before I could clear the intersection. I did not have time to brake in time to avoid the crash. Luckily for me, the force of the impact was absorbed by my car's left front wheel and the drivers' door and no one was seriously hurt in the mishap. Except for a sore leg and neck that lasted for a few weeks, I was fine. I had now first-hand knowledge that even at fairly low speeds the sudden, totally unexpected stop of a car on impact is a most scary experience. Needless to say, I never made it to that meeting. I asked my wife to call the President's office at the university to let him know what had happened. Laura and the other members of the Working Group for Portuguese Studies at Glendon College were stunned by the news and disappointed that I could not be there to present the point of view from a teacher's perspective, one who actually taught Portuguese at the secondary level and who knew that many students furthering their studies at the university level wanted to continue their studies of Portuguese. Regrettably, as is the case in many discussions between university administrators and members of the public, nothing concrete resulted from this particular meeting. Progress moves slowly in the world of education, at all levels.

My Head of Department, the friendly and generous Jack Harryman, retired at the end of 1988 and Jim Rayner, his Assistant Head, took over his role. A few weeks after Natasha's birth, Jim surprised all of us language teachers by calling a lunchtime meeting. When I arrived at the office, all the members of the Moderns Department were present and the reason for the unexpected meeting became obvious to me: they wanted to congratulate me formally for the arrival of my daughter, something that touched me deeply. Jim had brought some bubbly to celebrate the occasion, although, of course, it was illegal given that we were in a school setting, and after the celebrations were over, the gifts for my daughter acknowledged and thanked together with the congratulatory cards of which I was the happy recipient, we all went back to our respective classes to teach until the end of the school day. Throughout life, one is sometimes the happy recipient of gestures of thoughtfulness and kindness, gestures that are impossible to forget.

Natasha, my daughter, was born at 9:30 p.m. on Saturday, February 11th, 1989, at Saint Joseph's Hospital in Toronto. She was a beautiful baby. For the next few months, we lived in awe and, like most parents, we worried about all sorts of things that can go wrong with a baby. Little did we know in those first few months that before she would be one-year-old we would have good reasons to be truly worried.

Filomena and I made the decision that she would quit her job at the Royal Bank in order to raise Natasha. She stayed home with her from 1989 to 1995. Our daughter was growing beautifully when, all of a sudden, in the summer of 1989, she was diagnosed with McCune-Albright Syndrome, also referred to as "precocious puberty". In other words, at the ripe age of six months, she started having her period. The good doctors at Sick Kids did a lot of tests and decided to operate on her to remove the cysts in her ovaries, the cause of the problem. We were devastated by the news, especially my wife who feared the worst would happen to our precious little girl. We went through some sleepless nights just mulling over and processing the diagnosis and, when the day of the operation finally came, the two of us were super nervous, stressed and worried while we waited for the doctors to report back on the outcome of the operation. Parents always fear the worst for their children. The surgery itself went well and, since Natasha had to be interned for a few days in the hospital after it, Filomena requested to stay overnight with her, a request that was easily granted. She slept in a cot next to Natasha's hospital bed.

Unfortunately, the therapy recommended by the doctors at Sick Kids following the operation to prevent the recurrence of cysts from developing and attaching themselves to the ovaries, which were causing too much estrogen to be released into the bloodstream, brought about all sorts of negative side effects. Natasha, who had been to that point a good-natured and calm baby, became almost overnight a restless one with sudden mood swings. Furthermore, when the follow-up tests were done, the cysts had returned and the only solution proposed was more surgery to remove them. It was obvious that this state of affairs could not go on for the next few years. Consequently, my wife decided to seek an alternative way of dealing with Natasha's chronic problem. She sought the advice of a homeopathic doctor, Dr. Alexander Wood, who until Natasha's teenage years kept her in good health and out of the operating room.

One of the many side effects of McCune-Albright Syndrome is the rapid growth associated with too much estrogen in a child's body. As a consequence, until the end of grade 5 Natasha was the tallest in her class but, by the time that she was in grade 8, she was the shortest of all the pupils. This was not only inevitable but predictable for children with her condition. It was a small price to pay for maintaining Natasha healthy. Under Dr. Wood's guidance, her good disposition returned almost immediately and to this day she remains a friendly, happy, caring, optimistic and accomplished human being who has managed to live as normal a life as possible in spite of being the victim of a freaky act of nature. It could have been worse, much worse.

Raising a child under the conditions that I just described takes perseverance, resilience and an act of faith on the part of the parents that everything will turn out OK. In our family, Filomena was that pillar of strength. Although it took a lot out of her emotionally, and physically, too, she never gave up hope that everything would turn out just fine for our daughter.

In 1989, Noite de Teatro took place on Friday, April 19th, and it met with its usual success. The youngest audience member in attendance was my own daughter, who was just a few months old and who slept peacefully throughout the performances. Little did I know at the time that that particular performance would be the last one under my artistic directorship. My successor in this capacity attempted to replicate the many successes of the Noite de Teatro but soon found out that to put on a show takes expertise, dedication, perseverance and boundless energy, not to mention a wonderful relationship with dozens of students and colleagues. After one attempt, she gave up the tradition. At this point, I would like to pay tribute to the many committed and talented students who made this unique event one of the most memorable and meaningful educational experiences of my entire career. They were actors, presenters, stage directors, prompters, make-up artists, set designers, sound and light technicians, ticket collectors, etc. Among the dozens who participated, were the following: Antero Rebelo, Alice Peixoto, Ilda Silva, Conceição Bettencourt, Fernando Reis, Lourdes Marchão, John Cardoso, Eulália Pereira, Rui Moita, Tony Medeiros, Suzanne Neves, Maria João Teves, Ricardo Duarte, Ana Manão, Tony Pinarreta, Ana da Rosa, Jorge Filipe, Carlos Cunha, Lucília Igreja, Bernadete Gomes, Ricardo Inácio, António Pinto, Cristina Brum, Manny da Silva, Octávio do Padre, Emília Machado, Maria da Cruz and countless others who will forgive me in advance for not mentioning them by name here. You made yourselves proud by entertaining audiences with a dazzling display of talent and humour. You made the public laugh but, on occasion, you also made people think about some of the most serious social issues facing Toronto's Portuguese community.

In connection with the staging of Noite de Teatro, a word of thanks goes as well to these esteemed former colleagues of mine who supported the endeavour throughout the 1980s in a variety of capacities: Laura Bulger, Jack Harryman, Ron Bottaro, John Hilbish, Penny Vincent, Hugh MacDonald, Julia Bjarnasson, Ron Brown, Ced Hope, Ken Mucha, Luís Moniz and the indispensable Fernanda Santos at the office who typed and retyped the programs and countless letters of invitation to VIPs.

As I said before, I was scheduled to be off on the Four Over Five Program for the school year 1989-1990. It was a pure coincidence that Natasha was born in February of 1989. So, starting in September of 1989, we were available twenty-four hours a day, seven days a week, to take care of her. After the trials and tribulations of that summer, we were thankful to have all the time in the world to devote to our daughter.

In the meantime, starting in the fall of 1989, Filomena decided to enroll in courses at Sheridan College dealing with young children which proved to be most beneficial in her daily interactions with Natasha. She was determined to do the right thing as a parent and used to say that the only thing in life that people don't prepare for adequately is parenthood. In 1991, she finished the program and graduated with a diploma in Family Daycare.

In the spring of 1989, we celebrated Natasha's Christening with a huge party for our family and friends. Her grandparents, her aunt and husband and their three kids came up from Boston for this important occasion. My side of the family was also present. For godparents, we invited Filomena's cousin, Manuel Filipe, together with my good friend from St. Mike's, Antoinette. The idea behind inviting these two very fine people to be her godparents was very simple: we knew that if we could not be there for our daughter for whatever reason, they would step in and take good care of her until she would be old enough to fend for herself. Furthermore, we knew both of them to be responsible adults and, therefore, worthy of our total trust.

As for me, starting in the winter of 1990, I decided, with the help of my cousin's husband, John, and my best man, Mario, to finish part of the basement in our home. The idea was to prepare the huge family room for Natasha's first birthday party. We had already staged in it her Christening party although none of the walls were drywalled and the floor was unfinished. But with the many decorations we had put up for the occasion, lots of good food and much wine to celebrate the event, our numerous guests paid very little attention to the bare surroundings. When the birthday day came, in spite of the trio's best intentions, the party room was far from being finished. When one relies on friends to lend a hand after they come from work, the inevitable result is that projects just linger on and on and on. Irrespective, the birthday day came and we had no choice – we staged it once again in the partly finished but well decorated recreation room. As it turned out, it was just months before the house was sold that finally the party room and the washroom were finally completed to our entire satisfaction. So, Filomena and I really never enjoyed much the fruits of our labors. Such is life.

In the summer of 1991, we returned to São Miguel to show off our toddler to the rest of our families. We went for four weeks. It was the first time that we actually stayed at my wife's side of the family summer house in Furnas. It was a home that had been in the family ever since the beginning of the century, one that brought back many happy memories for her as she had spent many happy summer days there as a child. One of my cousins lent me a car for the duration of our stay and we made good use of it. Aside from the little trips to visit family members and attend lunches or dinners, most of the time we stayed in the beautiful village of Furnas or we went to the beach at Ribeira Quente, just a short distance from Furnas. A good many hours were spent at the peaceful Parque Terra Nostra and on walks around the village. It was most relaxing and enjoyable which is precisely what my wife and I needed in terms of a vacation.

When September of 1990 came along, I was ready to return to Harbord Collegiate. I was refreshed and recharged and looking forward to a change in my timetable that up to that point had entailed teaching three courses of Portuguese and three courses of Spanish. Six different preparations! I was given the opportunity to teach French and Spanish. It meant fewer preparations and the chance to get into the teaching of French on a regular basis, something that I truly missed. For the last ten years I had only taught French in Summer School. By taking this opportunity, Alice Freitas, who had taken over the teaching of Portuguese during my one-year absence, was given a chance to stay at the school and continue to teach the subject on a part-time basis. The change proved to be a wise decision on my part because it allowed me eventually to get involved with both the Extended and Immersion French programs which became more and more popular as the new decade unfolded. I was, in many ways, just following Principal Shaver's sound advice about teaching as many courses as possible within my area of expertise.

In turn, this additional experience prompted Principal Don Creighton, in 1994, to nominate me Assistant Head of the Moderns Department while my colleague Margherita Manuele was on a leave of absence. Thanks to this opportunity, in 1997, I applied for a promotion outside of my own school as the Head of Moderns at Malvern Collegiate and got it. By now, I had been at Harbord Collegiate for seventeen years already and needed another challenge to grow professionally. I would spend the next three years at Malvern Collegiate before returning, once again, to my former school, in 2010, as the new Head of Modern Languages and Classics, and thus replacing Jim Rayner who was retiring.

Now, when I think of Principal Creighton, I think of Education Week. He picked me to represent and promote the school at Dufferin Mall, the closest mall to the school. There were displays of students' work in a variety of courses and when people stopped by to look at them and had questions, one had to be prepared to answer them. I was proud of Harbord Collegiate and promoting it was the easiest job in town. I loved that opportunity.

In our small family of three that fall and for the first time ever, I was the only one going to work. Filomena was at home taking care of

Natasha and having a great time of it. Until 1995 we were reduced to one salary. In order to make up for the reduced income and to pay for all sorts of expenses associated with parenthood and home ownership, I kept on teaching Summer School.

In the spring of 1992, we decided to put up our raised bungalow for sale located on Crystalburn Ave., in Mississauga, our first home, and look for another house close to a school that had a fine reputation for its Immersion French Program, a program in which we wanted Natasha to be enrolled. We figured that by the time she would be old enough to attend junior kindergarten, she would be quite familiar with the new neighborhood and its streets. We found a house within walking distance to the school and so we packed up our belongings and moved to Turney Dr., in Streetsville, in that late summer. One's first home is always special. So, leaving it was a bittersweet moment for the two of us and, I think, for our daughter, too, who was lost for the first few weeks in the new house. The poor child had lost her bearings.

Also, I started taking the GO train from Streetsville to Kipling Station, the first subway station on Toronto's west side because Filomena, who was at home taking care of Natasha, might need our only car during the day. It turned out to be a welcome change to the routine which up to that point had meant driving to Toronto and returning to Mississauga during rush hour, never a pleasant thing to do. Waiting for the train on the platform at Streetsville GO, I used to meet up with John, who lived in my neighborhood and who had a couple of kids of Natasha's age. He worked for the Ministry of Education and for the twenty minutes or so that the ride lasted to Kipling, we used to talk about all sorts of topics, mostly related to education. There was never a shortage of items to discuss. Eventually, we also met other passengers with whom we used to engage in animated conversations. Thus, there is some good that can come out of commuting if one takes the train. It can be a therapeutic, relaxing and, at the same time, an intellectually stimulating experience if one is lucky enough to find willing partners to engage in it.

Because Natasha was an only child, she was definitely spoiled in many ways by the two of us. I had been an only child myself. One of the drawbacks is that there is no one to play with. In my case, I had grown up with cousins who were my age and who lived in the same house. So, I had never missed not having brothers or sisters to play with. In Natasha's case, although she did have three cousins with whom she got together from time to time, usually for birthdays, Christmas, Easter, etc., most of the time she was alone at home with her mother. To make up for the lack of siblings, she was enrolled in many community-organized programs such as music, visual arts, story time at the local public library, swimming and skating lessons, etc., where she would be in contact with other children her own age and be able to interact with them, all this before she was old enough to attend regular school.

The first school that our daughter attended was the small Credit Valley Montessori School, a school fairly close to our home on Turney Dr. We enrolled her at the school in the fall of 1992. She was three and a half years old. There, kids learned everything hands-on and she was excited about doing all sorts of little projects that required the development of early thinking skills and perseverance to see them to fruition. Good skills for any future student attending public school. Furthermore, she was thrilled to be in the company of children her own age.

Sadly, there were two deaths in my family right at the beginning of the 1990s. The first one was totally unexpected. It happened on August 20th, 1990. My favorite uncle from my childhood days, and the man who had sponsored my mother and me to come to Canada, my uncle João, now addressed by all of us as uncle John, died suddenly of a massive heart attack. He was only fifty-seven, the same age as my own mother when she had passed away in 1981. We were on vacation in Boston when it happened. Consequently, we cut it short in order to come back for the funeral. I was sorry to see him disappear so suddenly from my life. He was the man who had shown me how to ride a bicycle when I was a boy, the man who had invited me to be a ring bearer at his wedding, the man who, after my father died, made the time to drop by my grandparents' house once a week to play with me, in short, the man who had made it possible for me to have a bright future in Canada. I owed him a lot. He was buried in Saint Mary's Catholic Cemetery, at 2099 Dickson Rd., Mississauga,

The second one took place the following year and it was not a huge surprise. My uncle José was living on borrowed time ever since his open-heart surgery and died on November 6th, 1991. At my aunt's request, I had taken the time to speak with the surgeon who had operated on him a few months earlier and he had told me the bad news. Many years of heavy smoking had caused irreparable damage to his heart. Unhappily, he was not on speaking terms with me and my wife when he passed away. All of a sudden, in the mid-1980s, he and my aunt just stopped speaking with the two of us without a word of explanation for their conduct. When my daughter was born in 1989, my aunt unexpectedly offered congratulations and resumed socializing with us as if nothing had occurred in the intervening years. No explanation was ever given for their long silence and absence from our lives and, although I pressed her on this issue several times, she never had the courage to supply one. Courage is not her forte, so it seems. Maybe she has forgotten the silly reason that could have led to such drastic action to be taken by both of them. I have alluded to my uncle José before; this is the same man who kicked out of the Machado's home in Ponta Delgada my mother and me after my father's death. I am convinced that deep down he was a good man, a generous man but, alas, a bit unstable and easily manipulated by others around him. Given his erratic behavior over the years, I am led to believe that he had some sort of personality disorder that was never properly diagnosed, a condition that was aggravated by his heavy drinking habits. Also, the fact that he was only three years old when his father passed away in 1930 must have negatively impacted him. I am sure that this tragedy affected profoundly all four children left fatherless who ranged in age at the time between three and thirteen, him being the youngest and my father the oldest. Also, his married life was a disaster from the very beginning, a huge source of his frustration which, in turn, led to his aggressive and abusive behavior towards those closest to him. Filomena and I paid our final respects at the funeral parlor. He is also buried in Saint Mary's Catholic Cemetery.

We started going, during the summers of the 1990s, to Boston and Cape Cod for two weeks. So, we used to spend a week at my in-laws' followed by a week at the Cape in a rented cottage. The cost was equally divided between ourselves, my in-laws and one of Filomena's sisters. Ah, the pleasures of family time combined with the great swimming at Cape Cod! This experience also enabled Natasha to get to know better her grandparents and the rest of her American family members. We used to drive to Boston. For Filomena and me the road was super familiar because we had done the trip dozens of times in the late 1970s and throughout the 1980s. But for Natasha the trip was a new experience and one that she enjoyed tremendously in spite of the long drive to get to her grandparents' home. There were lots of things to talk about during the endless hours on the New York Thruway and the Mass Pike. And, upon arrival at our destination, her grandmother Suzy, being a warm, caring and kind woman, was ecstatic to see her. This kind of reception, in turn, made Natasha very happy to see her grandmother. Suzy knew how to please a child. She always had a special treat prepared for Natasha, her bean cupcakes, my daughter's favorite and one of Suzy's many delightful baked specialties. Among many personal attributes, Natasha's grandmother was a great cook, no doubt about it.

Woefully, Suzy had a brain aneurysm in the mid-1990s that left her quite incapacitated. It was so sad to see a woman who had been so alert all her life suddenly not being able to recognize at times her own husband, daughters and grandchildren. Many days, she lived in a distant past, in a time zone when she was much younger, still living in Ponta Delgada and was, consequently, totally disoriented by her present surroundings. She needed constant care and supervision now. Her husband, seven years younger than she was, many times did not have the necessary patience to deal with the situation at hand in spite of having been pampered by her all of his adult life. He found Suzy a burden. He refused to hire outside help for the everyday household chores although he had the financial means to do it. He did nothing to provide a minimum of comfort in her moment of need. It was now up to her daughter Eduarda, who lived nearby, to keep an eye on the goings-on at her parents' home. Filomena also lent a hand, especially during our vacation in the summertime, to give her sister a well-deserved little break. In spite of this *contretemps*, we still continued to rent a cottage for one week at Cape Cod for the next few years. The continuity of this yearly tradition gave Suzy some degree of happiness, I am inclined to think. Although she was not her former self, she never complained about anything. She took her new reality in stride, so to speak. The biggest change in her was that overnight, from being a super active person, she had become totally passive. Inevitably, a few years later she had a stroke and had to be hospitalized for it for the long haul. She slowly let go of everything that had been important in her life, even of her daughter Gabriela, her Down syndrome child, who had been her biggest worry and concern from the day that she had been born. Suzy eventually passed away peacefully at the hospital, alone, on January 27th, 2002. By the time that her husband and daughter Eduarda got a call from the hospital informing them that the end was near and to make it there fast if they wanted to be present when the moment came, it was too late. Some people just fade away as time marches on, regretfully. She was a good and decent woman who did her very best to please everyone around her during her passage on Earth.

We drove to Boston to attend Suzy's funeral. It was the least that we could do for someone who had given so much of herself to her entire family and all three of us in particular. During the church service, Filomena read a passage from the Bible and, at the end of the service, when the priest asked if someone from the family wanted to say a few words about the deceased, I got up to read a eulogy in her honor. From the church we went to the nearby cemetery, Pine Haven Cemetery, in Burlington, where she was interred. Afterwards, all of us went to Eduarda's house where we celebrated Suzy's life with lots of good food and drink and recalled some of her pet peeves and most memorable moments. But, in spite of the delicious food, the drinks, and the many anecdotes about Suzy, all in all, it was a very sad day for all of us.

Slowly but surely, one by one, our closest family members were vanishing from our everyday life leaving us more and more alone and lonely. All of these people had had a direct impact, for better or for worse, and whether we liked it or not, on the kind of people that we had become.

After Credit Valley Montessori, Natasha, in 1994, started attending a francophone catholic elementary school – Saint-Jean-Baptiste, close to the intersection of The College Way and Mississauga Rd., in Mississauga. Her kindergarten teacher was Mme Lise Wiseman who was assisted by Francine. So much for our intentions of enrolling her in our local French Immersion elementary school which had prompted our move to Turney Dr. in the first place. When it came time to enroll her in kindergarten, we found out that there would be thirty pupils in the classroom and no teacher's aide. On the other hand, in spite of the distance, the francophone school was offering a class with twenty pupils and a teacher's aide. My wife and I had no trouble making the right choice although it involved either driving our daughter to school or her taking the school bus. For a while, my wife drove her to school and picked her up at lunch time.

Natasha was disappointed at first with our choice of school. She used to say that the kids there did nothing but play. A criticism that is perfectly understandable given that at Credit Valley Montessori she was into small projects. However, by the time that Christmas came along, she was speaking French fluently on the phone with her new friends. It was astounding to see how much progress she had made in such a short period of time. All the more so when one considers that when she had started back in September, she had only had a scarce knowledge of the French language. Whatever they were doing with the kids at Saint-Jean-Baptiste was paying big dividends.

So that I could find out more about what was going on in Natasha's school, I volunteered to be part of the Parent-Teacher Association, a group of devoted parents who worked in close collaboration with the school administration to make the school the best that it could be for the benefit of all students. For me, of course, this proved to be a great opportunity to meet other parents who were very much engaged in their children's education and to get to know the principal, a few staff members, and some of the issues that were being discussed internally on an on-going basis.

Life was quite busy for all three of us throughout the 1990s. I kept on teaching regular school as well as Summer School. Natasha was attending all sorts of enrichment programs after school on weekdays and on Saturdays too: piano, ballet, soccer, swimming, skating, Portuguese lessons, just to mention a few. Not to mention, of course, the inevitable piano and ballet recitals at the end of each season. There was no shortage of physical and intellectual stimulation at her finger tips.

On August 22nd, 1995, we also welcomed into our family another member – Figaro, our beloved Tabby. That summer my six-year-old daughter befriended our neighbors' female cat from across the street, Fifi, and we used to let her into our house every once in a while. She was a rather small dark brown and black queen cat. None of us knew that she was pregnant, including our neighbor, its owner. So, one fine afternoon we found her in the process of giving birth to four kittens behind the living room sofa. Three were either dark brown or black or a mixture, like their mother, but one of them was light in colour and immediately became Natasha's favorite. It was a male cat. A couple of days later, to our surprise and dismay, one of the dark-furred kittens died. We gave it a proper burial in our backyard. The rest of that summer was spent observing how the mother cat interacted with her litter. It was most entertaining and, really, a basic introduction to feline behaviour. All three of us went through a huge learning curve as none of us knew much about cats. Consequently, a few trips to the local library were in order to bring us up to speed on all cat matters. A few weeks later, it was time to part with the mother cat and the three surviving kittens. Needless to say, the queen cat returned to my neighbor's home with one of the kittens. The other black one was given to my aunt who wanted a cat for company and, surprise, surprise, the golden-furred one stayed with us. It was given Figaro as a name. Figaro was not only a physically gorgeous cat, but he was also smart, confident, adventurous and a hunter. He accompanied us in our life adventures and misadventures until April of 2009 when he had to be euthanized on account of being too sick with cancer. We were extremely saddened with his passing. He enriched our lives with wonderful memories by his very existence. Fortunately for us, when he passed away, Lulu, his sister, was already living with us as my aunt was not capable of looking after her anymore. Lulu lived with us until 2015. Unfortunately, as a kitten she had not been stimulated and, in fact, had been mostly ignored, if not mistreated and, by the time she came to live with us, she was fearful of everything and everybody. A clear sign of abuse. It took a while before she could trust us not to harm her in any way shape or form. In any case, she was the total opposite of our beloved Figaro. He had been playful, sociable and smart; she had become mistrustful, a trait that never left her entirely in spite of our best efforts. Animals cannot speak and vouch for themselves but their actions and reactions speak volumes about the kind of life that they have experienced.

In the fall of 1995, Madame surprised me once again by asking me to participate in the French Play that would take place in January of 1996. She asked me to reinterpret the role of Capitaine des pompiers in *La Cantatrice chauve*, a role that I had played in 1976, twenty years earlier. It had been the first role that I had ever played under her direction. It is a dream of a role. I could not say no. That said, the last time that I had participated as an actor in her productions had been 1987. I was a bit rusty, to say the least. Nevertheless, when I started memorizing the replies, I found that the words were just coming effortlessly to me in spite of the passage of time. The *Soirée Molière-Ionesco* that year consisted of *Le Médecin malgré lui* and *La Cantatrice chauve*. It was, as usual, a tremendous success. Some of my closest friends in the Moderns Department at Harbord surprised me by coming to attend one of the evening performances and, afterwards, congratulated me for my interpretation of the role. It's most pleasurable when one's colleagues support and appreciate one's activities outside of the classroom.

Towards the end of 1996, I started seriously thinking about applying for a headship position as they would become available across the now Toronto District School Board (TDSB) system throughout the winter of 1997. With that in mind, I kept a close eye on the advertisements that were posted in the Main Office of my school. Eventually, I noticed one that appealed to me in spite of the distance from my home to the school. It was the position of Head of Moderns at Malvern Collegiate Institute. After a few inquiring phone calls, I found out that the current Head of Moderns at Malvern Collegiate was leaving to take a similar position at North Toronto Collegiate Institute. A good sign. I discussed my intentions with my new principal at Harbord Collegiate, Mr. James McCarron, who had just arrived at the school in September. He encouraged me to apply. Consequently, I prepared carefully a cover letter and my résumé, asked Principal McCarron, Jim Rayner, my Head of Department, and my colleague Penny Vincent if I could use their names as references and forwarded the package to Principal David Wells at Malvern Collegiate. In due time I was given a date and a time for an interview which went really well. When I got to the school the day of the interview, I went straight to the Main Office. I was a bit early. Principal Wells greeted me and walked with me to the staff room. On the way there, he explained to me that he had excused himself from the interview process because he knew personally one of the candidates who had applied for the job. Once at the staff room, he offered me a cup of coffee and took the time to chat for a while. Back in the Main Office, I was interviewed by Ms. Elisabeth Mowat, the current Head of Moderns, Ms. Susan Freeman, the Head of Extended/Immersion, and one of the Vice-principals, Mrs. Jane Wingate, whom I knew from Harbord Collegiate as the Head of Library. The interview went really well. Upon leaving, as I was closing the door, I heard one of the interviewers say "wow". I knew right then and there that I had gotten the job. A couple of days later, Principal Wells called me at school to welcome me officially to the staff of Malvern Collegiate. It had been my first attempt at applying for a position of responsibility anywhere. I was thrilled and, at the same time, apprehensive about the challenges that lay ahead and, of course, sorry to have to leave Harbord Collegiate, a school where I had been so successful and happy.

In the spring of 1997, Natasha celebrated her First Communion. In the Portuguese tradition, after the church ceremony, such an occasion called for a memorable party at our new home on Turney Dr. And we made sure that it was. Family and friends were invited to celebrate with us this important milestone in Natasha's life. Faithfulness to rites is critical for, otherwise, one day just resembles another day. Close family members from Boston made the effort, just like they had done for her baptism, to be with us and that was much appreciated. The other guests were family members and friends who were part of our day-to-day lives. Typical dishes and desserts were ordered from Europa Catering and the choice of wines and spirits were, including the ever-present Port wine to toast such occasions, left to my discretion. As for Natasha, she looked beautiful in her white dress which perfectly symbolized her innocence. It was a memorable day!

On Friday, May 2nd, my colleagues in the Moderns Department gave me a farewell party at Madison, a favorite pub for us teachers at Harbord Collegiate. On June 4th, there was the Farewell Assembly during which I said goodbye to the students and staff of my beloved school. I did not know at the time that a mere three years later I would be back at Harbord Collegiate to stay for another ten years, until my retirement from the TDSB. Life is full of pleasant surprises. In my speech, I said to the students:

> So, I want to encourage you to get involved in all sorts of extra-curricular activities. It does not matter whether it is music, drama or sports. By participating you will develop and refine some of your many talents and you will have lots of fun while doing it." And further on I stated: "I have spent seventeen lovely years in this great school. I learned

a lot from you, the students, as well as from my colleagues, the hardworking and dedicated member of the Moderns Department. I hope that I have taught you a thing or two about French, Spanish and Portuguese and, specially, about the importance of Modern languages in a world that is becoming more and more interdependent and competitive.

I concluded the above remarks by saying a few brief words in Spanish, Portuguese and French. I wanted to take advantage of the uniqueness of the opportunity to encourage as many students as possible to pursue the study of those three languages in particular on account of the many personal and professional benefits associated with such a lifelong adventure.

17

Malvern Collegiate Institute, 1997-2000

As stated before, the first promotion opportunity that came my way took place in 1994 when Principal Creighton chose me to be the temporary Assistant Head of the Moderns Department at Harbord Collegiate. This experience paved the way for my eventual promotion to Head of Moderns at Malvern Collegiate Institute in 1997, a high school in the east end of Toronto, in the Main St. and Kingston Rd. area. Principal David Wells was in charge of the school, one of the very finest principals that I had the pleasure to be associated with during my long career. He reminded me very much of my first principal, Mr. Ross Shaver, back in my days in Kitchener. He was a very competent administrator and a warm individual who was extremely popular with both staff and students alike. Sadly, he became sick with cancer during my second year there and was replaced by Principal John Fraser, also a very fine principal. The position for which I applied had become available because the Head of the Moderns Department, Ms. Elisabeth Mowat, was moving on to be the new Head of Moderns at North Toronto Collegiate.

Leaving Harbord Collegiate proved to be much harder than I had anticipated. I had spent seventeen years of my life teaching at the school. It had given me all sorts of opportunities to grow professionally and to mature as a person. My esteemed colleagues, especially the members of the Moderns Department, were now good friends. I also had made numerous friends with teachers in all the other departments. Furthermore, the student body was outstanding when measured by any academic standard. It was a dream of a school. I was leaving of my own accord to become the Head of Moderns somewhere else in the TDSB. I was going to have the chance of actually running my own department. It was an opportunity that I was well-prepared for on account of the time that I had spent at Harbord Collegiate. I felt that I had all the prerequisites to do a very good job in my new position of responsibility.

Also, as an educator, by 1997 I had accumulated a lot of classroom experience which, in my opinion, is paramount to carrying out successfully the duties associated with a position of responsibility. It takes more than leading by example. It requires a certain degree of assertiveness that can only come from reflecting frequently on what one is doing well, and not so well, and the reasons for it with the intent of improving one's pedagogy as one goes along. As a teacher of Modern Languages, I never subscribed to any one particular approach to the delivery of the different language programs. Throughout my teaching career I had seen approaches come and go. Methodologies that were fashionable in the 1980s became more or less obsolete a decade later. So, my particular approach to language teaching and learning has always been eclectic. At one moment, for instance, the so-called "communicative approach" was the rave. High schoolers who were exposed to this approach became much more proficient in their oral and aural skills but, lamentably, their writing skills were mediocre. I believe that an equal amount of time should be devoted to the four language skills: listening, speaking, reading and writing. I never hesitated for a moment, in spite of my best efforts to explain something in French, Portuguese or Spanish, to use English sparingly if I saw puzzled looks on my students' faces in an effort to avoid unnecessary frustration on their part so that they would pursue the study of the language in question in the future.

In 1997, I came across a couple of book reviews in the *Queen's Quarterly* by W. J. Keith, Emeritus Professor of English at the University of Toronto, entitled "The Crisis in Contemporary Education". In it, he highlighted two works by David Solway, a poet and an educator – he taught English at the community college level in the Montréal area: *Education Lost* and *Lying about the Wolf*. In essence, Solway decries in both books the lowering of standards at all levels of education to the detriment of accuracy and comprehension. He goes so far as to assert that most of the time the output in English from the vast majority of his students tended to be pure gibberish. He blames it on educational approaches put forth by academic theorists who are not in daily contact with students and, quite frankly, are dreamers. In the name of not wanting to damage the students' self-image, praise is given for mediocre work. As for Keith himself, he states that: "All thinking North Americans are conscious of the crisis in education today, of shocking revelations of the collapse of intellectual standards." I, for one, concurred totally with this statement of his. I can vouch for the steady decline of standards in both my students and my teacher candidates over my thirty-two years as a teacher. I worked with thousands of high school students in two academic high schools in Toronto and what was possible to demand out of them in the 1980s was next to impossible when I wrapped up my career in 2010. As for the competence of some of my teacher candidates, it had deteriorated over time, too. At times, I had to resort to teaching them some basic grammar, correcting their pronunciation and filling them in on the details of the plot of a play, or of a novel, that the students were reading because they did not "have the time" to read the entire work themselves. Consequently, I developed the reputation among my students and teacher candidates of being a demanding but fair educator that expected the best that they could offer at all times. In any case, after reading Professor Keith's synopsis of Solway's two books, I proceeded to read them myself. Although I cannot say that I agreed with everything that he was putting forth in the realm of education, I sympathized with his predicament as an educator because what he was witnessing and experiencing first-hand in the teaching of English literature at the college level, I was experiencing myself in the teaching of French, Portuguese and Spanish at the high school level. Professor Keith could not have summarized Solway's major premise better than when he states:

> His argument, it should be noted, is saying something that cutback or clawback-obsessed governments and no-frills bureaucrats do not wish to hear: that literature, arts, the humanities – those subjects currently looked upon as unnecessary luxuries to be sacrificed for the protection of obviously important subjects like engineering, practical sciences, and business administration – are essential after all. This is not to play down the contributions of other disciplines (including computer technology) but it does insist that scientifically unmeasurable qualities like literateness, articulate speech, and a capacity for sustained thought are necessities rather than luxuries for the maintenance of a flourishing civilization.

I could not have agreed more with his assessment of what was going on in the field of education in the late 1990s and I regret to say that the situation has only deteriorated further, to my chagrin and to that of many other educators.

I arrived at Malvern Collegiate in the nick of time to introduce the Spanish program. It was a privilege to choose the textbooks for it, almost a once in a lifetime chance during most teachers' careers. My colleague, Ms. Janine Geddes, shared the teaching of the Spanish classes with me. She also taught French and Computer Science. The other members of my department were: Mr. Richard Mehringer, who taught German and French, Mr. Danny Lamontagne, French and Géographie, Ms. Joanne Cortes, French and History and, sometimes, depending on the number of French classes available, Mr. Bill Mighton, who taught mostly music classes. It was a fine group of individuals to have in my Moderns Department; they made my job a breeze.

In those days, Department Heads taught one less period than other teachers. The "free" period was reserved for departmental duties such as researching new publications about programs of study, ordering materials, contacting other Department Heads to find out about innovations in their departments, helping out members of one's own department if requested, etc. I was used to teaching at Harbord Collegiate six different classes. By comparison, most teachers had only three. Consequently, I found my first year at Malvern Collegiate to be the easiest of my entire career. Regrettably, this state of affairs did not last long because of Premier Mike Harris' budget cuts in all domains but, particularly, in the field of public education.

I stayed at the school for three turbulent years in Ontario's education system. Premier Mike Harris, a conservative, and his "fearless" Minister of Education, John Snobelen, a high school drop-out, were creating a lot of unnecessary turmoil in the field of public education. They effectively created a crisis because of the cuts that the passage of Bill 160, the Education Quality Improvement Act, caused. Consequently, there were major demonstrations at Queen's Park in 1997-1998, the seat of the provincial government, and throughout the entire province that pitted the various teacher unions against the government. It culminated with a province-wide strike that left all concerned bitter, especially the teachers and the public at large. One of the consequences of the "new" vision in education was that principals and vice-principals were removed from the different teachers' unions creating, going forward, an invisible barrier between the former and the latter to the overall detriment of school atmosphere. No reasonable teacher could count anymore on them for support because now they were perceived as the "enemy". It brought about a sorry state of affairs that divided needlessly former colleagues and friends who had worked for years for the benefit of all students. In typical conservative fashion, "none of the savings from the Bill were reinvested into education."

By 1998, on the home front, we were already well-established on Turney Dr. and belonged to St. Joseph Parish. It was there that we became familiar with the charity work that one of the priests, Fr. Andrew Cuschieri, JCD, also a professor at the University of Toronto, was doing with the underprivileged in Bolivia. He had come up with a charitable organization called the Human Family in Christ whose objective was, and remains to this day, in spite of his passing, "to help the most vulnerable to escape poverty through better health and an education". To that end, he created the Child Sponsorship Program. We decided to help out by sponsoring a child, preferably a girl, something that we will do for the rest of our lives. Father Cuschieri used to say that "individually we can achieve little. If we join forces however, we can accomplish much to alleviate the suffering of many". He was a kind man, someone who had a practical goal in mind and who did much good for many people but, in particular, to dispossessed Bolivians.

During my second year at Malvern Collegiate, my friend and former colleague from Harbord Collegiate, Penny Vincent, joined the staff as the new Head of Extended/Immersion French. For the next couple of years, it was a pleasure working with someone that I knew so well and for whom I had a lot of professional respect. I was in charge of the core program of French and the two international languages taught at the school: German and Spanish, and she was in charge of the Extended/Immersion French programs. Working side by side with her was like old times at Harbord Collegiate. That said, in the winter of 1999, I started looking for a headship in Toronto's west end, much closer to my home in Mississauga, to cut down on the commuting time and spend more time with my family. I had learned lots as department head at Malvern Collegiate, had made new friends, had met some outstanding students such as Jane who has remained a friend to this day. But, when everything is said and done, what I remember most about those three turbulent years at the school is the amount of time that I spent on the picket line and political demonstrations on account of Mr. Harris' conservative government's ill-advised cuts in the field of public education. As I said before, a country's most important resource is its people and a well-educated populace is critical for any country to move forward for the good of all its citizens. This, however, never seems to be the conservative credo.

Although I enjoyed the student body, the staff and the administration, there was a major inconvenience associated with teaching at the school – the distance from my home in Mississauga to the school was just too great and it took too much of my personal time. In order to get there, I had to take the GO train from Streetsville to Kipling Station, from there take the subway to Main Station, along Line 2 and, once there, take a bus to the school. In winter, this proved to be too much for me, especially after a huge snow storm in 1998 that forced the mayor of Toronto at the time, Mel Lastman, to call in the army to clear the city's streets. The amount of time that I was spending commuting was not tenable. It was impacting negatively on my obligations as a parent. It's difficult finding a proper balance between work and family life in ideal conditions, never mind when so much time was being spent on the road.

On a more pleasant note, still connected with Malvern Collegiate, I have to confess that one of my most treasured memories is related to my daughter. During her own school's PD (Professional Development) days, now that her mother was back at work, she used to come to school with me and attend, just like any other student, my classes. It did not take long for the students, upon seeing someone so young in their midst, to figure out that she must be my own daughter. They were always impressed by Natasha's mature ways and took the time at the end of the class to ask her all sorts of questions about herself and me. Students will always be students and they will always remain curious about their teachers' personal life.

18

Back at Harbord Collegiate Institute, 2000-2010

Fortunately for me, my previous Head of Moderns at Harbord Collegiate, Jim Rayner, decided to retire in 2000. I applied for his position and Principal Frances Parkin, the first female principal in the school's long history, hired me as his successor. I would stay at Harbord Collegiate for the next ten years, until 2010, when I retired from teaching high school, but not from education, at the ripe old age of 57. I was extremely glad to return to the school for another tour of duty but, of course, very sorry that I was abandoning Penny and my department members at Malvern Collegiate. That said, Penny and I have remained excellent friends and continue to see each other occasionally to this day.

The year 2000 started with a bang. There was so much uncertainty about the possible turmoil that the transition to a new century would bring. Needless to say, nothing drastic happened. "The universe was only unfolding as it should." The next ten years at Harbord Collegiate were certainly the most important ones of my entire professional life as a high school teacher. I gave one hundred percent and then some to many aspects of school life. Consequently, they were the most rewarding too. I was coming back to a school that was known as the "international language school" within the TDSB. Aside from the Core French program, there were many other languages taught such as Portuguese, Spanish,

Cantonese, Mandarin and even Latin, not to mention the Extended and Immersion French programs. I felt in my own element once again. I was in paradise.

My number one priority was to make sure that all languages in my department did well and that the programs remained vibrant and, therefore, viable; by that I mean that the individual language courses retained as many students as possible from grades 10 to 12. Not an easy task by any means when students have so many competing choices. They have to find the language courses interesting and relevant otherwise, at the first opportune moment, they will drop the study of a particular language in favor of another subject. And, God forbid if a particular language course did not attract a sufficient number of students, a minimum of fifteen. This eventuality would mean that a split-level class would be the result of the unfortunate circumstance, not an attractive scenario for any teacher who would have to teach in one classroom period two different grades and, it goes without saying, even much less so for the poor student who would have to exhibit the maturity and self-discipline to do a lot of work independently. Like many compromises in life, it brings about a reality that, essentially, does not please anybody. So, course relevance became the operative word in the Moderns Department at Harbord Collegiate.

As the newly-minted Head of the Moderns Department, one of my fiercest battles with the other Heads and Assistant Heads came about as a result of a motion that I proposed during the monthly Heads and Assistant Heads' meetings. It had to do with the introduction of all International Language courses in grade 9, something that had already happened in many other high schools, including at Malvern Collegiate. Unexpectedly, all my colleagues, including my own Assistant Head, when asked by Principal Parkin how they felt about it, opposed the motion. They were all defending their own little turfs and saw my proposal as a direct threat to their survival. Principal Parkin decided to give the matter some thought and the final decision on it was postponed until every Department Head could figure out exactly why and how my motion was going to impact negatively on their respective departments. The debate went on for a few more meetings during which I repeatedly brought to everybody's attention that in the schools where a similar proposal had been implemented the sky had not fallen and that students still took other subjects aside from International Languages. To no avail. Months later, when the final vote was taken by a show of hands, all my esteemed colleagues voted against the idea.

I am happy to report that this state of affairs was promptly rectified by Principal Mary-Jane McNamara, who succeeded Principal Parkin when she retired. During my first meeting with her, I suggested the idea of offering the International Languages from grade 9 onwards and, on the spot, she just said "let's do it". *Voilà, fait accompli.* Her decisive action put an end to countless hours of fruitless discussions. This time around nobody complained and all departments survived intact. What had been perceived as a threat by my esteemed colleagues turned out to be nothing more than a figment of their imagination, a clear display of trying to protect their own turf without any regard for the students' best interests.

One of my greatest pleasures as a teacher of French and Spanish was to register some of my most academically gifted students in competitions such as the Concours d'Art Oratoire, the French Contest, and the Spanish Contest. I would pick specific students and explain to them what they would be up against – that is to say strong competition from many other students coming from a variety of both public and private schools as well as inform them that there would be several coaching sessions with me after school and, sometimes, even during lunch in order to prepare adequately for the challenge ahead. I am happy to report that in 2002, Miranda, one of my grade 12 French Immersion students, placed first in her category and that in 2004 Melanie placed third in the same category. My involvement with these contests dated back to the 1980s. Some of my earliest prize winners were Lina, who went on to become a teacher of French herself and someone who has remained a friend, and Jane, of whom I have already spoken.

But I also wanted to get involved in other areas of school life that I felt I had not explored in the past. To that end, I started coaching the Junior Boys Soccer Team, an activity that gave me a lot of satisfaction. Since our field at Harbord Collegiate was too small, all games were played at other schools' soccer fields. This, of course, called for taking the subway and buses to get to our destination. Travelling in public transit with a bunch of teenage boys can be a challenge. In my case, however, it was quite pleasurable simply because my soccer players were so well-behaved. Boys' soccer is played in the fall. As anybody who has lived in Canada knows, in the fall, we can have both glorious days as well as miserable ones. September and all the way to mid-October can be pleasant, but in late October and throughout November the weather is often rainy, cold and plain miserable. Regardless, it was rewarding to bring together a group of boys who sometimes did not know one another at all and witness, through the training sessions and the games themselves, the group gel as a unit. There were incredible victories and crushing defeats. Luckily, over the years, the number of victories outnumbered the number of losses.

Another aspect of school life that had always attracted my attention was music and the arts, especially dramatic arts. During my first stint at the school, I had staged plays in Portuguese, an extra-curricular activity that had given me a lot of personal and professional satisfaction as pointed out elsewhere. Therefore, I volunteered my services in both areas, especially in music. The Head of Music, Ms. Renata Todros, was new to the school and our mutual respect and friendship grew fast. For many years I attended most school concerts and, at spring time, at Massey Hall, the Sounds of Toronto concert in support of our students, a wonderful evening of music which was open to all the music department in the TDSB high schools. Also, I attended every single play and musical that was staged at Harbord Collegiate during that decade. Ms. Barbara Martin, one of the music teachers, was into staging musicals and even went so far as to give me a small part in one of them. It was such fun to participate in a production where most of the cast was made up of students and the audience consisted of our students, their brothers and sisters, and their parents and friends.

Still, another facet of school life in which I wanted to be involved was the presidency of the monthly staff meetings, something that I had already had the pleasure of doing at Malvern Collegiate. So, during the last few years at Harbord Collegiate, I had the duty of maintaining the agenda moving at a brisk pace all the while making sure that anybody who wanted to contribute to the discussion was given an opportunity to do so. This job was made easier for me when my colleague, Ms. Shirley Sue, who became the Curriculum Leader of Students Services, volunteered to be the secretary and take notes during the said meetings.

Finally, starting in 2005, myself and Renata started taking students on international trips during the March break to Europe and even as far as Egypt. We chose an experienced company in student travel, Education First (EF), to be the provider of these wonderful adventures for the students and the staff who accompanied them. We started with a trip to France in 2005 which was followed by others to the following countries: Italy and Greece in 2006, Spain and France in 2007, Germany, Switzerland, Austria and Italy in 2008, England, France and Italy in 2009 and Egypt in 2010, the year that I retired. We had already planned our next trip to Turkey and Greece for 2011 but, alas, I could not take part in it as I was already doing a Ph.D. at the University of Toronto and the TDSB spring break did not coincide with Reading Week at the university. Principal Rodrigo Fuentes, Harbord Collegiate's newest principal, the lucky guy, took my place.

All these trips were excellent in their own way. However, there are three that stand out for me as being truly exceptional: the 2006 trip to Italy and Greece, the 2008 to Germany, Switzerland, Austria and Italy, and the 2010 to Egypt. Therefore, I cannot pass this opportunity without saying a few words about each one of them.

Italy and Greece. After arriving at Charles de Gaulle International Airport from Pearson International, we boarded a plane to Rome's Leonardo da Vinci (Fiumicino) International Airport. The first part of the trip took us to Rome proper, Vatican City, Florence, Sorrento, the Isle of Capri, Pompeii and Bari from where we boarded an overnight ferry to Patras (an experience that our students simply adored), and onwards to mysterious Delphi and, finally, Athens. It was the first time that I was visiting both of these fascinating countries. We were blessed with a tour director, a beautiful Italian young woman, Anna D'Agostino, who knew her stuff and who had great interpersonal skills. We were also blessed in another way: two colleagues of ours from the TDSB, from Leaside High School, Helen and Nat, who happened to have a Greek background, were also travelling with their students on the same EF trip. Consequently, once in Greece, we got so much more out of the experience thanks to the fact that they spoke the national language. As I said before, it has been my experience that if one happens to speak the language of the country that one is visiting, the locals will bend over backwards to make sure that you will get the most out of the experience. This is a clear pitch from a dedicated language teacher, me, for the intrinsic value of learning international languages at the high school level and beyond.

In *Bella Roma*, the Eternal City, we visited such landmarks as the Colosseo, where gladiators would fight to the death, the Pantheon, one of the best-preserved ancient buildings in the city, where Raphael is buried, the elegant Piazza Navona with its numerous cafés, a former hippodrome in Roman times, Trevi Fountain, where natives and tourists alike make a wish by tossing a coin backwards, Foro Romano, where old stones tell a story about Rome's grandiose past, Castel Sant'Angelo, where many prisoners perished, quaint Isla Tiberina, Piazza Venezia, from whose rooftop one can enjoy a wonderful view of the city, beautiful Piazza di Spagna, with its flower-adorned staircase where Romans and tourists alike will sit for a while to enjoy seeing the passers-by and, finally, the Basilica di San Pietro, where the world's largest dome is to be found, a must for anybody that happens to visit Rome. Of course, a few of our students insisted on taking a picture with the Swiss Guards dressed in their brightly-colored uniforms. Once inside the basilica, one never ceases to be amazed by such priceless pieces of art as Michelangelo's Pietà, the *baldacchino*, the canopy above the tomb of Saint Peter, by Bernini, the Papal Altar itself, the Monument of Pope Alexander VII, another Bernini masterpiece, etc. From there one absolutely has to spend some time admiring the art work at the Vatican Museum and from there proceed to the famous Sistine Chapel whose ceiling was painted by no other than Michelangelo himself, an outstanding artistic achievement worthy of a great artist. It's impossible to visit Rome without succumbing to the delicious pleasure of having a few *gelati*, it's part and parcel of *la dolce vita*. With more than 100 flavours to choose from, it's impossible to run out of possibilities.

It was time to go north to visit the beautiful city of Florence, the birthplace of the Renaissance, the Italian language and opera. We had the opportunity to visit Piazza della Signoria, Santa Maria del Fiore Cathedral, also known simply as the Duomo, a structure that dominates the entire skyline and from where one can enjoy a magnificent view of the city, the bronzed doors, right across from the entrance to the cathedral, in the Baptistery, which depict the Gates of Paradise according to Ghiberti, its creator. Ponte Vecchio, the only bridge in the city that survived the bombardments during WWII and, finally, a quick visit to Chiesa di Santa Croce, where Michelangelo, Machiavelli and Galileo are buried. It was a glorious day spent in Florence!

Afterwards, from Rome, we went south to Naples and straight to its port where we boarded a ferry to the island of Capri. Once there, we got into a smaller boat to go on a little cruise along the coast in order to see the Arco Naturale and the Faraglioni, the three limestone colossi that emerge from the sea. Back in dry land, we took the funicular to the town of Capri where we enjoyed a tasty lunch served in a restaurant high up on the coast overlooking the port and the Amalfi coast. The view was simply magnificent. After a few hours spent on Capri, it was time to board the boat headed to lovely Sorrento where we stayed overnight. That evening we attended a most entertaining show called *Tarantella* at the Fauno Notte Club. According to the program, the show was described as "an incredible journey through the ages from 1558 until today. The performance revolves around the most important stories of Sorrento and the Kingdom of Naples in the last 500 years." The music, accompanied by the acting, dancing and the beautiful costumes were a delight to the audience. The next day, on the itinerary, there was the much-anticipated visit to Pompeii, one of the most important archeological sites in the world in that it portrays daily life as it was in A.D. 79 when Mt. Vesuvius erupted and buried the town under ashes. The least that can be said is that it is an eye opener. We proceeded, from Pompeii, to the port of Bari where we boarded a brand-new ferry for an overnight trip to Patras. After dinner, there was dancing in the ship's disco which lasted past midnight. Our students thought that they had died and gone to heaven. We arrived in Patras early in the morning and from there we went to Delphi, the home of the famous Oracle, where we stayed overnight. The next morning, we visited the sights: Temple of Apollo where, it is said, the god communicated with humans, and the Delphi Museum whose priceless artifacts date back to 550 B.C. Then, we were on our way to Athens, the cradle of democracy, for a couple of days. We went up to the Acropolis to see the Parthenon, an incredible sight, and paid a visit to the Temple of Athena Nike, whose city is named after her. We admired, for a few moments, the Presidential Guard dressed in traditional regalia in front of the National Assembly. We passed by the Olympic Stadium, where the first modern-day Olympics were held in 1896. From there, we went through the Agora Site, passing by Adrian's Arch, the Temple of Hephaistos, the Temple of Zeus, the most important of the Greek gods, the Akademos, where Plato founded the academy, and so many other places of historical interest. Also, during our first night in Athens, we attended a so-called Greek Evening in a *taverna* in the famous Plaka district of the city where traditional cuisine was served followed by entertainment that featured belly-dancing and fancy footwork by twirling dancers to the sound of bouzoukis, ageless stringed instruments that are part and parcel of Greek music. On our last evening in Athens, we took our students to a café overlooking Athens where we began reminiscing about our incredible journey through Italy and Greece. Early the next day, after thanking profusely Anna, our lovely tour director, we boarded a plane back to Toronto via Paris.

The 2008 European trip started in Frankfurt and, upon meeting our tour director for the duration of the trip, Mr. Alexander Petersen, a very knowledgeable and friendly guy from Heidelberg, we went on a grand tour of four countries that took us as far as Venice and then back to Frankfurt. From Frankfurt, the birthplace of Goethe and the coronation site for Holy Roman Emperors from 1562 to 1806, we went to Rothenburg-ob-der-Tauber, Germany's best preserved medieval town, via the Romantic Road. Rothenburg is definitely a quaint and quiet little town with its half-timbered houses, cobbled and windy streets and the ramparts overlooking the Tauber River. From there we continued to Munich, the home of the famous yearly Oktoberfest Beer Festival that attracts thousands of tourists from all over the world in search of a good pint, but also the site of the infamous 1972 Munich Olympic Games on account of the massacre of the 11 Israeli athletes killed by Palestinian terrorists at the Olympic Village, the BMW headquarters, the maker of one of the most popular cars in the world, the Deutsches Museum, Marienplatz, Munich's medieval centre, where the famous Glockenspiel is to be found, the Frauenkirch with its twin copper domes and so much more. Using Munich as our base camp, we went on two side trips, one to Dachau, a WWII concentration camp and now a memorial museum, and the other to Neuschwanstein Castle, "Mad" King Ludwig's fairy-tale castle and a model for Disneyland's Sleeping Beauty Castle. Out of the aforementioned two side trips, the one to The Dachau Concentration Camp Memorial Site was the most educational and the most riveting of the two in that it forces the visitor to confront head on the terrible things that humans can do to each other. From the official guide to the Camp one can read the following information:

> On March 22, 1933, a few weeks after Adolf Hitler had been appointed Reich Chancellor, a concentration camp for political prisoners was set up in Dachau. This camp served as a model for all

later concentration camps and as a "school of violence" for the SS men under whose command it stood. In the twelve years of its existence over 200,000 persons from all over Europe were imprisoned here and in the numerous subsidiary camps. More than 43,000 of them died. On April 29, 1945, American troops liberated the survivors.

No visitor to The Dachau Concentration Camp Memorial Site can possibly exit the grounds without having reflected on the atrocities committed by the Nazis on the prisoners of war imprisoned there. The Memorial is designed in such a way as to compel the visitor to face the reality of what took place in it from 1933 to 1945. Noteworthy is the bunker, the so-called camp prison, where torture and executions were conducted routinely, the two blocks of seventeen barracks where the prisoners lived in overcrowded and unhealthy conditions, the camp road that runs through the middle of the two rows of barracks and that served as a meeting point for the prisoners and the crematorium itself, where the sick and weak were put to death in a most degrading and undignified manner. The entire Memorial leads one to the inevitable conclusion that what occurred there was nothing short of a deliberate genocide of the Jewish people at the hands of the Nazis.

While in Munich, Alexander also took us to the Augustiner Bräu München for a taste of local beer. Of course, the students were not allowed to drink alcoholic beverages on account of their age. It was one of the stipulations for going on the trip. So, all of us had to settle for a non-alcoholic drink accompanied by pretzels and delicious sausages. The visit was intended to highlight the importance of beer halls in the daily life of Germans. Later that evening, however, Alexander and I returned to the beer hall where I treated him to a pint of the famous *Müncher Bier*. Onwards to Innsbruck, the beautiful capital of Austria's Tyrol province and the site of two Winter Olympics and from there to Venice, *La Serenissima*, with visits to St. Mark's Square, the Grand Canal, the Doges' Palace, the Bridge of Sighs which connects the Palace to a prison, and even to the Murano store to observe a glass making demonstration. We stayed in a hotel in Lido for two nights and that meant that we took a *vaporetto* to Venice proper in the morning and in the late afternoon. Of course, like thousands of tourists, we also took the mandatory gondola ride through some of Venice's canals and a few more rides on the *vaporetto* just for the fun of it and to see the exquisite buildings along the main canal. After Venice, it was onwards to Verona and its beautifully preserved Roman Arena and the famous statue of Juliet. From Verona, to the Lucerne region of Switzerland where Richard Wagner composed several major works, and a ride by cable car to the top of Mount Pilatus from whose summit, at 2,132 m above sea level, one can enjoy a stunning view of Lucerne, its lake, and the snow-capped Alps. From Lucerne to Heidelberg via the Rhine Falls, the largest waterfall in Europe, measuring almost 150 m wide and 23 m high, and through the Black Forest, where the brothers Grimm placed some of their most classic tales, such as *Hansel and Gretel*. In Heidelberg, our guide Alexander was in his element. He showed us Germany's oldest university, his own, the 700-year-old *Schloss* with its famous *Fass* (wine barrel), the biggest in the world, followed afterwards by a slow-paced walk through Markplatz, the city's medieval streets. Finally, from lovely Heidelberg back to Frankfurt for a return flight to Toronto. What an inspiring trip led by a very competent Tour Director, Alexander!

The third EF trip that I am highlighting in this book, however, was certainly the most exotic of all the trips that I did with Harbord Collegiate students. We were in Africa! After arriving in Cairo from Frankfurt, we were met by our tour director, Adel, an older gentleman who had travelled the world and knew much about his beloved Egypt. We flew, the following day, early in the morning, to Luxor and from there we went on a four-night Nile cruise to Aswan. Cruising on the Nile, one of the greatest rivers of the world, was an outstanding and unique experience. The weather was gorgeous, the food abord the ship was delicious, including *koshari*, Egypt's national dish, and the frequent stops along the way to visit architectural relevant sites such as the Valley of the Kings, where sixty-four tombs belonging to Egypt's rulers have been discovered so far, including the most famous, the one of Tut

Ankh Amun, discovered in 1922. Miraculously, among the 5,000 artifacts in the tomb chambers, the famous gold mask of the young king was located, a treasure that has stunned the world ever since. From the Valley of the Kings, we proceeded to the very unique Al-Deir Al-Bahari Temple where Queen Hatshepsut tomb is found. We finished the day's explorations at the site of the Colossi of Memnon. We were literally in awe at the marvels that our guide was revealing to us one at a time. But he was not finished, on the contrary, he had just started; there were many more marvels to admire in the following days such as the Temple of Luxor, the Temple of Karnak, and the Avenue of the Sphinxes connecting the two temples, and onwards to Edfu via the Esna locks to view the Greek-built Temple of Horus, dedicated to the Sky god and Protector god, the second-largest in the country and the best-preserved. In Edfu, Adel gave our group some free time to go and explore the city's market where we experienced a bit of what everyday life is like for the locals while shopping, an experience that was repeated in Aswan for the delight of our students who visited several Bazars looking for souvenirs for their families and friends back in Canada. We also stopped at the Kom-Ombo Temple, famous for its twin temple dedicated to Sobek, the crocodile-headed god, and Haroeris, the falcon-headed god. Finally, we reached Aswan where Elephantine Island is located and is called thus on account of the dark granite rocks that can be seen on the Nile which resemble a herd of elephants bathing. Once there, we engaged in a variety of activities in and around the city. We visited the Aswan High Dam, one of the greatest engineering feats of the last century; it was built to harness the Nile's waters. It is 3,800-meters-long. We also had a chance to take a look at the granite quarries of Aswan from where the raw material for temples, sarcophagi and obelisks was extracted and transported all over the country. It was most interesting to note that the so-called Unfinished Obelisk had been carved in the granite bedrock itself. However, it was never finished and displayed elsewhere because it developed cracks before it was totally carved out. Another outing took us to the Nubian Museum, an outstanding place to check out for anyone interested in Egyptian artifacts of all sorts. It was in Aswan that we also visited our first mosque in Egypt, the Badre Mosque at El Tabya and its lovely surrounding gardens. We were most impressed by the beauty and solemnity of its interior. Finally, worthy of note was the fact that we also experienced overnight in Aswan a sandstorm, an awful experience. There was sand in the air everywhere, including indoors, that stung the eyes and made them itchy and red. What a difference a day made. We were staying at the Basma Hotel and the previous late afternoon we had enjoyed the swimming pool and its beautiful surrounding gardens. The next morning, the hotel's employees were busy cleaning up all the sand that had accumulated overnight everywhere in just the space of a few hours. But, what's a trip to Egypt without a sandstorm? The answer is obvious, it's an incomplete visit to a major African country where the desert plays such a vital role.

Somewhere along the Nile, we were given the unique opportunity to travel by camel to a small village and once there we dropped by an elementary school to witness the goings-on and to benefit from a quick lesson in spoken Arabic. All of us had lots of fun not only riding a camel for an hour or so but also practicing a few spoken words and expressions in Arabic that we could put to use while interacting with the local population.

From Aswan, we took an overnight train back to Cairo arriving there in the early morning. Finally, our Egyptologist, Adel, was going to show us the biggest African city and some of its most impressive monuments, as well as those to be found in the vicinity, that is to say in Memphis, Sakkara and Giza. The ancient city of Memphis is where Egyptian history began thousands of years ago. It was also the first capital of modern-day Egypt. Sakkara is where one finds the oldest pyramids in the country, including the Step Pyramid. In the Sakkara area, we visited the Mit Rahina Museum, the Imhotep Museum & Saqqara and El Sultan Carpet School where we witnessed relatively young people, of both sexes, work diligently and with amazing dexterity and confidence, given their age, on intricate geometric patterns on carpets. It was an eye opener for all of us, especially for our students, to witness young people such as themselves already working hard for a living.

Giza is, of course, where the Great Pyramid of Cheops is to be found. It is one of the Seven Wonders of the Ancient World and deservedly so. I still remember vividly climbing through narrow corridors to the king's chamber, not recommended for the faint of heart and certainly not for someone suffering from claustrophobia. That said, it was a unique experience. In the general area of the pyramid is also the 4,500-year-old enigmatic Sphinx. Also, while in Giza, we paid a visit to the Sondos Papyrus shop where "all the pictures are hand painted on real papyrus" and, consequently, one is given a Guarantee Certificate should anybody decide to purchase one. In Cairo proper, we visited the amazing Egyptian Museum; it contains the most Pharaonic art in the world including, of course, the mesmerizing treasures found in the tomb of King Tutankhamen and, in particular, his gold mask, the XII century Citadel of Salah Al-Din and the Muhammad Ali Mosque which was built in 1830 and quickly became the emblem of Cairo. The interior of the Mosque is magnificent. It was designed by the Greek architect Youssef Bochna, who lived in Istanbul and who took Hagia Sophia as his model. It is square in shape and features a dome 52 meters high and 21 meters in diameter. It rests on four square columns. There is alabaster everywhere one looks and several concentric crystal chandeliers hung on chains. The court features the lovely ablutions fountain. The entire complex is awe inspiring. As in Edfu, Aswan, and now in Cairo, we were taken by our guide to a couple of stores: the Funky Brothers and David Leather to get some last-minute souvenirs for family and friends back in Canada. The following day our kind, knowledgeable and generous tour director, took us to the airport and we were off to Frankfurt and from there to Toronto. As a departure gift, he offered myself and Renata a book entitled *Art and History Egypt – 5000 Years of Civilization*. It's a book that I open every so often to reminisce about a trip of a lifetime. As a personal souvenir, I purchased, at an Al Rifaie Jewelery store, a cartouche with my given name inscribed in gold hieroglyphic characters officially certified by the Government of Egypt. It would have been impossible for anyone to have been disappointed with a trip such as this one. Simply put, the entire trip was nothing short of awe-inspiring.

In conclusion, what made these particular three trips stand out were a combination of factors starting with the exceptional tour guides, followed by the mostly pleasant weather, accompanied by the amazing towns and cities we visited, the sounds of the different languages that we came across and last, but certainly not least, the friendly natives we met along the way and our fantastic group of students who were part and parcel of each excursion. They made excellent young ambassadors for Harbord Collegiate, the city of Toronto, the province of Ontario and Canada. They made myself and Renata proud to be associated with them.

At the community level, in 2005, Lucien Benacem, a French instructor from my undergraduate days at St. Michael's College in the early 1970s, now an esteemed colleague and Head of Modern Languages, like myself, at R. H. King Academy, had become President of the Union des Français de l'Étranger (UFE) and he asked me not only to join the group, but also run in the upcoming elections for the position of *conseiller*. He knew that I was committed to everything French, a good organizer, a guy who enjoyed the company of people and who, therefore, looked forward to opportunities to have a good time. That spring I became part of the Conseil d'Administration de l'Union des Français de l'Étranger de Toronto, Section Ontario. For the next ten years, under his leadership, we had a most enjoyable time organizing and participating in all sorts of social events and information sessions for the pleasure of the membership at large. It was a wonderful way of extending my own circle of friends and acquaintances. I met, thanks to his invitation, Timothée Li, Marie-Thérèse Saladin, Colette Owen, Jean-Paul Martyniuk, Sonya Urbanc, an old friend from my undergraduate days at St. Mike's, and so many other wonderful people who wanted to get together to speak French, enjoy each other's company, and have a great time in the process. With that in mind, the Conseil planned and organized set events throughout the year such as: Beaujolais Celebration, Christmas Lunch, Galette des Rois, Twelfth-night cake, Theatre Performance, Cruise on Lake Ontario, etc. These regular events culminated with a magnificent Garden Party at the Benacem's abode before the summer pause. There were also special celebrations for which the Conseil was invited such as Célébration de la Fête Nationale Française on July 14th at Glendon College, a wonderful event in a gorgeous setting that, sadly, fell victim to budgetary cuts and ceased to exist. Another one was the 2006 version of the Festival Beaujolais that took place at The Ontario Club, an unforgettable evening of food, wine and prizes, including Air France tickets for two to Paris! And then there was the special invitation from the Consul Général de France, M. Philippe Delacroix at the time, for bestowing on our leader, the médaille de Chevalier dans l'Ordre des Palmes Académiques, at a delightful reception at the Consul's official residence in Toronto. Truly, the UFE under the leadership of Président Lucien Benacem was a lot of fun.

While my professional life was progressing along, Natasha graduated from Saint-Jean-Baptiste on June 20th, 2003. She was chosen by the other members of the grade 8 graduating class to be the valedictorian and she did us proud in her address to her fellow students, the staff and members of the public at large gathered in the school gymnasium for the special occasion. It was a great accomplishment. She had made a lot of progress academically as well as socially ever since kindergarten at that school. She had made many friends with whom she is still in close contact to this day, among them Marina, who was her maid of honor at her wedding a few years later. Towards the end of elementary school, she was even turning her attention to the boys around her without us knowing anything about it. One Sunday afternoon I remember getting an unusual call from one of her teachers saying that she had been caught several times hand in hand with some boy, especially during a recent school trip to Ottawa. Like most parents when it comes to such matters, it was the first time that my wife and I had heard anything about boys in Natasha's life. We were speechless. After a little "chat" with Natasha, we found out that the teacher was exaggerating the nature of the friendship that existed between her and the boy in question. I guess he was concerned just in case the relationship got out of hand.

From elementary school, Natasha moved on to École secondaire Sainte-Famille from which, in turn, she graduated on June 27th, 2007, with first class honors, and a few more certificates of achievement. Naturally, her mother and I were ecstatic. The spring of 2007 also marked, believe it or not, the 30th anniversary already of my own graduation from Saint Michael's College. I had missed the 10th and the 20th anniversary celebrations but was determined to attend at least one of the events this time around. After conferring with Antoinette, a fellow graduate and Natasha's godmother, we decided to attend the All Alumni Reception, held at Odette Hall, in Brennan Hall, on Friday, June 1st, starting at 8 p.m. We had agreed to go for dinner before attending the festivities. In retrospect, it was a mistake going for a bite before the get together because there was lots of delicious food, wine and beer available at the reception itself. There was also live music, a nice touch. For whatever reason, I was expecting to see more graduates from 1977 than there were in attendance. Irrespective, it was wonderful touching base with the ones who actually had taken the time to be there. If nothing else, reunions serve to remind people that time is precious and that one's lifespan is limited. A devastating reminder. I made a mental note to be there, if still alive, for the 40th reunion. And I did, in the company of my wife.

During the summer of 2006, just like I had myself in 1972, Natasha participated in the Summer Language Bursary Program, nowadays called MyExplore. She went to Jonquière where she had a wonderful time and where she improved significantly her French language skills. Filomena and I drove her to Montréal and, after an overnight stay in beautiful Montréal, we put her on a bus to Québec City from where she would take another one to her final destination. It was a long trip but she did it anyway without complaining. She has always been the adventurous type.

By the summer of 2007 Natasha had found her first summer job; it was at the Ontario Travel Information Centre located then at the Atrium, at the corner of Bay and Edward Streets, across the road from the Toronto Bus Terminal. Thanks to two former high school students of mine who had worked at Ontario Travel themselves and who put in a good word for Natasha, she was hired on the spot. Aside from being fluent in English, she was also fluent in French and could make herself understood in Portuguese if need be; it was a tremendous asset for the office because the job involved dealing with Canadian and international tourists who wanted to discover Ontario. She loved her summer job and kept it for the next six years without ever missing a day's work. An incredible *tour de force*.

After high school, she was on her way to university. She chose Saint Michael's College, at the University of Toronto, a college from which I had graduated myself back in 1977, a mere thirty years earlier. She wanted to live in residence and we granted her that wish so that she could experience a part of university life that I had been too poor to experience myself. She was sharing a room with another girl from Alberta and the two of them just did not match. It was a total disaster and, on many weekends, instead of staying on campus to benefit from the countless social, cultural and athletic opportunities available, she used to come home. Consequently, Filomena and I gave her an ultimatum before the second year started: if you want to live in residence again, pay for it yourself. Common sense prevailed and for the next three years she commuted back and forth with us.

Four years later she graduated from Saint Michael's College with High Honors. Her next goal was to pursue her studies at the Master's level. To that end, she applied with the Faculty of Forestry at the University of Toronto to do a Masters in Forest Conservation. She was accepted into the program and graduated in 2013. The highlights of the MFC program came when the entire group went on a field trip to Malaysia, accompanied by a couple of professors from the Faculty of Forestry in the spring of 2012 and when, a few months later, on

December 14th, she defended, in front of her fellow students, professors and a few parents, her Major Project. The title of her project was "Management Plan for Red Oak Regeneration".

In connection with her Masters' studies, she became a Resource Conservation Intern, in the summer of 2012, at the office of the St. Lawrence Islands National Park located at Mallorytown Landing. Fortunately for her, she was able to stay in a student residence at St. Lawrence College, located in Brockville, a mere twenty kilometers away from her place of work. Given that she did not have a car, we lent her our trusted Toyota Tercel so that she could commute back and forth between the residence and the Parks Canada Agency office and, in this way, enable her to do this indispensable internship in view of her future career.

A side benefit from the internship was that she got to know Joel Martineau, a fellow student at the Faculty of Forestry, much better. Previously, Natasha, and a couple of other female friends in the forestry program, had shared a rented house on Robert St., very close to the Faculty of Forestry, with him. He was staying for the summer in Cornwall with his mother, just down the road on Highway 401 from Brockville. Having the Tercel at her disposal meant that she could visit him occasionally and, thus, remain in close touch.

By the time her Convocation occurred in June of 2013, she was already working in Prince George, British Columbia, where she had gone with Joel who would become three years later her husband. So, immediately upon finishing their studies, the two of them had driven from our home in Mississauga all the way to Prince George in January of 2013, in the middle of the winter! The foolish things that young people do and get away with it. Joel had gotten a job there in the field of forestry but Natasha had yet to find one. Luckily, she did find one almost right away in the field of education. They were living an adventure. As a graduation gift, we paid for her trip to Toronto so that she could be with us for a week, receive personally her degree and, at the same time, reunite with university friends in that spring of 2013. We have always been generous with our daughter.

Now that her studies were done, she was trying to establish herself in her field of expertise, forestry. Before that was accomplished, however, her life took several unexpected twists and turns, as most lives do.

Natasha's first job in Prince George was Environmental Educator. She found it with Recycling and Environmental Action Planning Society (REAPS). Basically, she had to drive to different elementary schools and sensitize kids to environmental issues as well as do some community presentations. The worst part of the job was that she was given the use of a standard car which made her nervous every time she went on assignment. She started on February 12th. By May, she had landed another job, this time as Field Technician with Pathfinder Endeavours Ltd. It entailed working with a male co-worker, someone with field experience, and see to it that invasive species were promptly and properly obliterated by means of the spraying of herbicides, always a dangerous occupation. It required a lot of travelling by pick-up truck from city to city. As a result, she discovered quite a bit of British Columbia's countryside. She went to Fort Saint John and Terrace on several occasions, cities that were at least a good six hours away by car from Prince George. Her timetable was unusual in that she was on for nine days and off for the next four. The company had apartments in the different cities where its personnel could stay while on duty there. During the four days off, they would return to Prince George. Obviously, it was not an ideal job for her going forward. Nevertheless, in connection with this particular job, she was obliged to take a course entitled Environmental Monitoring for Construction Projects at the Vancouver Island University, a useful course to take when someone is dealing with mother nature and the human impact on it.

Their brief stay in Prince George lasted until December of 2013. Natasha and Joel did not particularly enjoy their respective jobs and even less their living conditions. Both of them, by Christmas, were back in Ontario after having driven to Vancouver to pay some friends a visit.

Then, they crossed Canada once again by car at a time of the year that is always dicey to do so because of winter hazard conditions. That said, they still managed to take advantage of the spas in Banff before facing countless hours of driving across the prairies before reaching Ontario. All in all, they were lucky in that they only got caught in a snowstorm fairly close to their final destination, our home.

Anticipating my future retirement, in February of 2009, the Asociación de Profesores Hispano-Canadienses honored my years of service as a high school teacher and as an Associate Teacher connected with FEUT/OISE with a Placa al Mérito. It had been the initiative of one of my former teacher candidates herself who, many years later had come to Harbord Collegiate to serve in the capacity of Vice-principal, Susana Arnott. In it, one can find the following description that summarized my contribution to the profession:

> Hace treinta años que enseña lenguas modernas a estudiantes y a profesores de español. Hizo todos sus estudios en la Universidad de Toronto. Empezó su carrera en 1978, en una escuela secundaria de Kitchener, Grand River Collegiate. Ahí enseñaba francés y español. Se trasladó a Toronto en 1980 porque consiguió un puesto en la escuela secundaria Harbord Collegiate donde enseñó francés, español y portugués hasta 1997. En ese año obtuvo una promoción como jefe de departamento de lenguas modernas en Malvern Collegiate. El director de esa escuela buscaba entonces a alguien para comenzar la enseñanza del español. Había mucho interés por la parte de los estudiantes, mayoritariamente anglosajones, en aprender esta lengua maravillosa y, para él, fue un placer escoger los libros del programa e iniciar un intercambio de estudiantes con Costa Rica. Finalmente, en 2000, su antiguo jefe de departamento de Harbord se jubiló y lo reemplazó como jefe de departamento. Les dice a menudo a sus estudiantes que aprender lenguas es una fuente de placer personal u profesional que dura toda la vida.

As you can tell form the previous quote, people who knew me well were already anticipating as early as 2009 my forthcoming retirement.

They had already put neatly in a couple of paragraphs my professional contribution to education. As for me, I had decided, by the winter of 2010, that it was time to pursue a Ph.D. in French Literature. To that end, I let Mr. Rodrigo Fuentes, my principal at Harbord Collegiate, and the TDSB administration know that I would be retiring at the end of the school year. I was 57 years old and wanted, before it would be too late, to do something that I had always envisioned doing, a Ph.D. Financially, my wife and I were doing just fine. Our house was mortgage free and we had saved some money for retirement. So, I asked myself the following question: What else do I want to do in education? It was the same question that Principal Shaver, back in Kitchener, in 1978, had suggested I ask from time to time. My answer to that question was that there was nothing else. Career-wise, there was nothing else for me to accomplish at the high school level. I had done everything that I had set out to do and I had enjoyed myself tremendously in the process. After teaching all the courses in my field of expertise: French, Portuguese and Spanish, after being a Department Head for the last thirteen years, after much travelling with my students in Canada and abroad, after staging plays and coaching soccer and preparing students for contests, it was time to move on and face new challenges.

During the winter of 2010, I applied at the School of Graduate Studies at the University of Toronto to initiate a Ph.D. program in French and was accepted. Although I was mentally and academically prepared for it, I thought, I was about to start one of the most challenging periods of my life and one of the most rewarding too. But more about that later.

In the meantime, the School-University Partnership Office (SUPO) organized an Associate Teacher Appreciation Event on Tuesday, May 25th, at the OISE Library, featuring a Wine and Appetizers and a special presentation by Dr. Larry Swartz entitled "Silver Screen Teachers". During the course of the evening a number of us were singled out for our contribution to teacher training. I was the only one in attendance having worked with over sixty teacher candidates.

A couple of days later, Harbord Collegiate's 2009/2010 Athletic Awards Banquet and Dance took place at Revival Restaurant, on College St. On account of being the Junior Boys Soccer coach, as usual, I was invited to hand out the MIP and MVP Awards to the two most outstanding members of my squad and, of course, to justify my choice by means of a brief speech. It was with mixed feelings that I said good-bye to my Harbord Collegiate coaching career. I had come in contact with such gifted players within the last ten years of coaching, players who had provided unforgettable moments during hard-fought games.

On June 3rd, it was the TDSB's turn to stage a Retirement Reception at The Old Mill to thank its retiring teachers for their "dedication, hard work and contribution to education". As usual, there were several speeches by senior Board administrators and a few retirees themselves. Music was provided by a trio from Western Technical-Commercial School. Every retiree was given a special gift, a bronze school bell, which was used by all in the so-called Bell Ringing Ceremony at the end of the concluding remarks by Penny Mustin, Deputy Director - Operations. Given that the reception was at The Old Mill, the food was delicious, as always.

On Wednesday, June 9th, Harbord Collegiate held the Farewell Assembly. As one of the retiring teachers, I was seated on stage between Paul Channing and Alex McIntyre, two teachers whom I knew well, especially Alex, who staged at his home in Etobicoke for the longest time an end of the school year barbecue that became in due time an annual ritual. He had arrived at the school in 1979 and had never left. There I was, on stage, looking at the students and teachers seating in the auditorium, one that I knew like my own hands because of the many school functions held there as well as the countless hours that I had spent in it rehearsing with my students for the Portuguese plays. Laura and Mugaya, two of my students who had travelled most recently to Egypt with me during the March break, said a few kind words about yours truly and then it was my turn to say good-bye to all present. In it, at one moment, I declared: "I could not have expected or asked for, back in 1978, a more fulfilling career. It has been a privilege to have worked for twenty-seven years in a great school such as Harbord Collegiate, the best high school in Toronto." I meant every single word of what I said.

As the school year was coming to a close, a few of my closest teacher friends: Renata, Penny, Lydia, Linda and Kayla, and one of the school's secretaries, Fernanda, who had started working at the school at the same time as me, began talking about a farewell party in my honor. Before I knew it, close to 125 present and former colleagues, administrators, secretaries, present and former students, custodians, personal friends and family members were on the list of attendees. I was overwhelmed and honored by such a display of appreciation and friendship. It was decided that the party would take place at Europa Banquet Hall, on Dundas St., not too far from the school, on Thursday, June 10th, 2010, at 5 p.m., right after the first day of the June exams in my school. The retirement party remains one of my most cherished moments.

Lydia served as the Master of Ceremonies for the occasion and she kept the evening rolling at a brisk pace, especially when it came to speeches. No one enjoys listening to long speeches in such occasions. The rule of thumb is simple: "make them short and sweet". Most people did. I was surprised by the amount of work that the organizing committee had put into my retirement party. They had thought of everything. The hall looked beautiful. There were yellow fresh flowers on the tables, yellow napkins in the wine glasses, a yellow streamer on the stage with the words Happy Retirement written underneath it. As guests arrived, they were greeted by the music of a String Quartet consisting of Poanna, Asa, Fei Ran, and Alex, all current students at the school. A nice touch coming from Renata. After mingling for an hour, dinner followed at 6 p.m., followed, in turn, by the presentations at 7 p.m. and dancing for those who were in need of burning a few calories at 8 p.m.

As is the custom in such occasions, after the meal some speeches were made by several of the guests in attendance. What made this particular feature different from most was that the speeches themselves were interspaced with entertainment. At one moment my two Vice-principals, Janice Gladstone and Renée Bouthot, accompanied on the guitar by Julian Lee, a student, sang a variation of *Yesterday*, a song made famous by the Beatles. It went like this:

Yesterday
Leaving teaching seemed so far away
Now it looks as though today's the day
Oh, I believe
In yesterday
Suddenly
I'm about to start my Ph.D.
There is a thesis hanging over me
Oh, yesterday
Came suddenly
Why I
Had to go I don't know
Students wouldn't say
I never
Taught a thing wrong now I long
For yesterday
Yesterday
Teaching was my only game to play
Now I finally get to go away
Oh, I believe
In yesterday
Why I
Had to go I don't know
Students wouldn't say
I never
Taught a thing wrong now I long
For yesterday
Yesterday
Teaching was my only game to play

> Now I finally get to go away
> Oh, I believe
> In yesterday

My very good friend and colleague at the TDSB, Lucien Benacem, said a few words about our long-standing friendship and my devotion to everything French, including being a member of the Conseil d'administration de l'Union des Français de l'Étranger, of which he was Président. Professor Paulette Collet, a mentor and my artistic director, praised me for my commitment to education and for not only promoting the arts, but actively participating in them. She was referring, of course, to my participation in the French plays. In passing, she also said that I was too young to retire at fifty-seven. Madame had been forced to retire at the age of sixty-five, as was the custom in those days, a fact of life that did not agree with her own work ethic at all in that she felt that she still had much to contribute to university life. Renata Todros, the CL of Music, Drama and Visual Arts, spoke of our numerous trips with students overseas and, closer to home, to the lovely music retreats spent at Teen Ranch with the Harbord Collegiate choir that turned out to be great fun for all. Peter Roffman, my ACL responsible for the delivery of the English program, a real *mensch*, a collaborator, someone whom I admired and respected a lot, summarized, in typical succinct form, my entire career. Principal Rodrigo Fuentes followed suit by thanking me for all the work that I had done for the school and its students for twenty-seven years. Natasha, my daughter, spoke of me as a dad and as a consummate teacher. Finally, it was my turn to say a few words myself. It was about time. Halfway through my speech, a former student of mine, Suzane, someone who had participated in so many of my shows called Noite de Teatro at the school, and who had been my student in Portuguese and Spanish for three consecutive years, interrupted it by asking permission to say a few words impromptu. I immediately agreed, of course. She came to the podium and described one of my trademarks as a teacher when writing a sentence or two on the blackboard: my extra-long acute accent marks, one of my "special" ways of conveying to students that accent marks are part and parcel of correct spelling habits and that they should not be overlooked. All in all, it was a most memorable retirement party, especially for me. Woefully, Penny Vincent, one of the organizers and such a dear friend, could not celebrate the happy occasion with the rest of us because she was at Western Hospital undergoing hip replacement surgery. A few days later, as a token of my appreciation, I took the other members of the organizing committee to a Portuguese restaurant for lunch and paid Penny a visit at the hospital. She was recovering well. It was the least that I could have done for them after all the trouble they had gone through to make my Retirement Party so special.

With part of the money that the invitees had contributed to the event, a scholarship was created in my name for the grade 12 student with the highest standing in the Extended/Immersion French Program. At Commencement, every year since 2010, I have been invited to meet and give the lucky recipient his or her prize. It's always a pleasure to return to Harbord Collegiate, especially on such an important occasion for the graduating class, and be part of the platform party. Every time, for a few fleeting moments, I have the impression and the strong feeling that I have never left the school. It's like being home away from home. It's a marvelous feeling.

Looking back at my long career as a high school teacher, my contributions to it can be put into several categories: 1) in a position of added responsibility, b) committee work, c) as a classroom teacher, and d) teaching related. All were equally fulfilling and gratifying.

My first positions of added responsibility occurred in the summers of 1986 and 1987 when I was given the chance to be the lead teacher in French at Harbord's Summer School. It prepared me for all future positions of added responsibility that culminated as Head of Moderns at Malvern Collegiate and Curriculum Leader of Communications and Languages at Harbord Collegiate.

I cannot understate the value of volunteering one's time to participate in so-called committee work at the local school level. It allows one to have significant input in setting school policies and the overall tone of a school. To that end, I volunteered over the years to be a member of the following committees: Restructuring, Evaluation, Staffing, Transitions, School Planning, Review, and Improvement Team, Chair of the Assessment and Evaluation, Chair of the School Wide Activity Day, Chair of the Heads and Assistant Heads Association at Malvern Collegiate and Chair of the monthly Staff Meetings at Harbord Collegiate.

As a regular classroom teacher, I was fortunate to have been given the chance to teach all the language courses in the curriculum for which I was qualified: French (Core/Extended/Immersion), Portuguese and Spanish. In the case of Portuguese and Spanish, I was also given the opportunity to choose the textbooks to be used, an opportunity seldom available to most teachers. Also, I was a teacher of French at the Villefranche Enrichment Program, at Université Canadienne en France, and taught French in Summer School for many consecutive summers.

Finally, in the area of teaching related, my contribution went from attending workshops on Differentiated Instruction, Mentoring, TEL and Markbook, to being part of the Summer Institutes in: Promoting Excellence through Leadership, FSL, International Languages, to being involved in the International Languages Course Profile Writing Team for the TDSB, to Coordinator of Harbord's Education Week Activities, to Oral/Written Examiner for the University of Toronto/York University/Glendon College French Contest, to Judge for the TDSB's Concours d'Art Oratoire, to Staff Advisor for both the Portuguese and Hispanic Clubs, to Coach of the Junior Boys Soccer Team, to Sponsor of Trips Abroad, to Co-chairperson of the Working Group for Portuguese Studies at Glendon College, to Associate Teacher of French and Spanish from 1981 to 2010, and the list goes on. Consequently, by 2010, I felt that I had had a most satisfying and fulfilling career and that I was ready to embark on a new academic adventure. I looked with trepidation and anticipation to the next few years.

Life was excellent!

19

A Ph.D. in Québec Literature, 2010-2017

Any School of Graduate Studies is governed by stringent deadlines that must be adhered to at all times in order for "things" to move along smoothly from beginning to the end of one's studies. For me, the first one that came up was on January 15th, 2010. I had to go to the School of Graduate Studies online application website and submit my dossier which included the following documents:

One copy of the official transcript from each university must be sent by the Registrar directly to the Department in a sealed envelope, two academic letters of recommendation and a sample of written work in French completed as part of the applicant's bachelor's or master's program in French in literature or linguistics as appropriate." It also stated that: "Applicants holding a Master's degree must submit a statement of purpose in French (maximum 500 words) which clearly outlines the area in which the applicant intends to pursue research in French literature or linguistics.

With regards to the two letters of recommendation, I contacted two professors who knew me well: Professor Jean-Claude Susini and Professor Paulette Collet. They were happy to sing my praises. The other requirements were simple to put together and I even included, for good measure, a CV that summarized my entire academic and professional achievements.

On April 29th, 2010, I received the following letter from the University of Toronto:

Dear Mr. Machado,

On behalf of the School of Graduate Studies, I am pleased to offer you admission to the program of study described below, and hope you will be able to accept this offer. [...]

Session:	2010 Fall
Student Number:	731440100
Program Begins:	September, 2010
Status:	Full-time
Department/Centre/Institute:	Department of French
Degree:	Ph.D.-French
Field:	Literature

Yours sincerely,
Heather Kelly
Director, Student Services

Attempting to do a Ph.D. is not an easy task by any stretch of the imagination at any age. Trying to do it at the age of 57, it goes without saying, is even more challenging. Time has taken its toll. The level of energy is not the same as that of a twenty something year old. That said, on the plus side, one is not necessarily doing it anymore in order to start a brand-new career in academia. So, in that regard, the pressure is off which allows for some fun as the process itself unfolds.

I had, by June 10th, submitted my choice of courses of study and, by July 20th, I got my teaching assignment: I would be one of the course instructors (CI), from January 1 to April 30, for FSL421Y1Y (s) L5101 T 6-8 R 6 NF 113, under the immediate supervision of Professor Marie-Anne Visoi. It was a fourth-year undergraduate course that ran on Tuesdays from 6 to 8 o'clock and on Thursdays from 6 to 7, at Northrop Frye (Victoria College), in room 113. I was thrilled.

With regards to the courses of study, the Department of French stipulated that: "A student admitted on the basis of a **master's degree**, must complete 3.5 full-course equivalents during the first year of the program. With the Department's permission, the student may take one full-course equivalent outside of the Department."

Taking this advice into consideration, I chose the following course load: FRE 1201H-F (Méthodes de recherche en études littéraires et linguistiques), with Professor Pascal Michelucci, a mandatory course for all students; FRE 1613H-F (Les récits de voyages dans la littérature française des XVIe et XVIIe siècles), with Professor Grégoire Holtz; FRE 1928H-F (Zola), with Professor Charles Elkabas; FRE 2007H-F (Littérature éthique), with Professor Pascal Riendeau, a future member of my thesis committee; FRE 2103H-S (La nouvelle québécoise contemporaine), with Professor Michel Lord, my future thesis director. Given that I wanted to write my thesis on the body of work of a Québec playwright, Marcel Dubé, and because there were no drama courses offered by the French Department, I was obliged to go to the Drama Department to take a couple of courses: DRA 3901H-F (Topics in Theatre Drama Performance 1 – Dramaturgy of Sound), with Professor Damiano Pietropaolo, and DRA 3903H-S (Topics in Theatre Drama Performance 3 – Performing Commedia dell'Arte), with Professor Domenico Pietropaolo. By the way, the two professors are indeed brothers and, finally, RST 9999Y, which refers to Research/Thesis, an on-going independent course that starts in year one and only finishes when the candidate defends successfully his or her thesis.

As for the statement of purpose in French, I had already a good idea about the title of my thesis; it would be about Marcel Dubé's dramaturgy. What I was not quite certain about just yet was from what literary angle I would be analyzing his body of work or, at least, part of it.

Furthermore, the brochure from the French Department stated in very clear terms: "To remain in good academic standing and to continue in the Ph.D. program, a student must complete 3.5 full-course equivalents, with an average grade of at least A-, by the end of the first year of the program."

The first year of the Ph.D. program was certainly one of the most academically demanding but also the most fun for me. The list of mandatory readings for each course was out of this world and the oral presentations and essays kept on happening one after the other if not simultaneously. Classes were fairly small and the pressure to perform was relentless. One had to prove that one was "brilliant" at all times. On the fun side of things, it was only during classes and at special social events that I saw my fellow Ph.D. students, my cohorts.

The cohort class of 2010 in the French Department consisted of ten students, most of them in the literature stream. By the end of October, however, we had been reduced to seven. Three people had abandoned altogether their dream of pursuing a Ph.D. And the first one to defend successfully his thesis was Frenand Leger in 2016 followed by myself in 2017. As for the others, they slowly vanished from the School of Graduate Studies. The drop-out rate at the Ph.D. level is very high.

Although I met other students who were ahead of me or in their studies, mostly because of the assistantships where sometimes up to five of us worked together in the delivery of an undergraduate course under the supervision of a professor, I can honestly say that I only became friends with two or three among whom the aforementioned Frenand who actually helped me quite a bit by offering valuable information and suggestions about writing proposals for grants and the like. He was in his thirties and much more familiar with the academic expectations than I was. The last time that I had graduated from the School of Graduate Studies was in 1989, twenty-one years earlier.

On Thursday, September 2nd, 2010, I attended the TATP TA Day, the Teaching Assistants' Training Program, at the Centre for Teaching Support & Innovation. It entailed a full day of workshops. There were hundreds of us. In the morning, the workshops were for everybody. After a Keynote Address and a presentation by CUPE (Canadian Union of Public Employees), another one on Supporting Students at the University of Toronto and a final one on Teaching Tips from the 2010 TATP Excellence Award Winners, there was a light lunch provided. In the afternoon, there were concurrent sessions and choices to be made by all of us. I opted for a first one called Preparing for Your First Class in the Humanities & Social Sciences and a second one entitled Great Expectations: A Workshop on Marking Papers in Humanities & Social Sciences. Except for the CUPE presentation, the assumption by all presenters was that none of us had any teaching experience whatsoever before registering at the School of Graduate Studies. And, looking around me, I could see why. Most graduate students were in their twenties. They had enrolled in a doctorate program right after finishing an undergraduate and a masters and, therefore, they could not have had much experience teaching at any level. I, on the other hand, was coming into a Ph.D. program after having taught for 30 years at the high school level. I had also been an associate teacher for over 25 years. It meant that I had shown the ropes to adults who were attending FEUT/OISE and assessing their potential as future teachers. I quickly realized that I had a tremendous advantage over my fellow Ph.D. students.

A few days later, the French Department, staged its Semaine d'Orientation for incoming and returning Ph.D. students and candidates. It went on for three consecutive days, from Wednesday to Friday. Returning students were required to attend the mandatory sessions on Wednesday morning, the lunch offered by the Department, and the Réunion de coordination for the specific course that they were teaching starting on Thursday afternoon and continuing on Friday morning if necessary. The new cohort of 2010 had to attend the entire three days of activities.

The information given out by all presenters was most useful. It was also the first opportunity that I had to meet personally some of the professors with whom I was going to be in close contact for the foreseeable future such as Professor Danièle Issa-Sayegh, Professor Jeffrey Steele, Professor Marie-Anne Visoi and Mr. Damion Renner, the Multimedia Lab Technician whose laboratory was located at Carr Hall. Professor

Issa-Sayegh provided information about our contract and working conditions, Professor Steele focused on the teaching of oral skills, Professor Visoi addressed the goals of the particular course that I would be teaching as of January, FSL421Y and, finally, Mr. Renner, explained the mysteries associated with the Language Lab itself and Blackboard, the platform used to input such important things as students' marks. Also, there were presentations made by SESDEF (Société des Études Supérieures du Département d'Études Françaises), TATP, CUPE, the Accessibility Office, etc. There was a lot of information to digest before the first day of classes the following week.

It was with a lot of anticipation that I started looking forward to the beginning of my fall courses and meeting the individual professors and, in January of 2011, meeting my FSL 421 class. In the meantime, I tried to get involved in the activities of SESDEF. I felt that the younger generation should be the one assuming the major roles such as President, Vice-president, Treasurer, etc. I put down my name, together with Frenand, for those members who would be « responsables des activités socio-culturelles ». Every once in a while, there was a *causerie*, a friendly talk, given by a candidate on his on-going research followed by a *coup*, a glass of wine or beer, at a local pub or restaurant. Also, the plans for some sort of a Christmas party began to be discussed in the fall of 2010. I soon found out that most students or candidates in the Ph.D. program just did not have the time for such distractions. In other words, there was not much of an *esprit de corps*, solidarity, uniting all of us. I made a mental note about this unfortunate state of affairs.

During the fall of 2010, my colleague from the secondary school panel, Gord Berg, the former Head of Moderns in a school in Scarborough, Albert Campbell Collegiate Institute, and now retired, upon finding out that I, in turn, had retired from Harbord Collegiate asked me if I would be interested in joining a volunteer not-for-profit organization called CEEF (Canadian Education Exchange Foundation) specializing in international reciprocal exchanges for high schoolers. There were four European countries that participated in the exchanges with

Canada: France, Spain, Italy and Germany. Canadian students could opt for a two-month or a three-month exchange during the school year. They would live with a family overseas and attend a local school for the duration of the exchange. The "job" entailed visiting some high schools in Toronto and the Peel Region, that is to say Mississauga, Brampton and Caledon, to do presentations in order to make students aware of these wonderful academic and cultural opportunities that would be an adventure of a lifetime for them. My reward for promoting the program would be a chance to either take a Canadian group overseas at the beginning of the exchange or to bring one back at the end of it. For the first two years of the Ph.D., it was out of the question to take a group overseas in early February because my own courses and undergraduate teaching would be in full swing. That said, I could certainly bring a group back in late April. Although I was terribly busy already, I accepted his offer. It was the beginning of a friendship with Gord and the other very fine volunteers who put in so much time and effort of their own for the next ten years, until 2020. Sadly, it took a global pandemic, COVID-19, to put an end to such a worthwhile program. More about CEEF later.

Inevitably, because class sizes are so small at the Ph.D. level, one develops close relationships with the professors delivering the courses. Classes tend to be more like a constant dialogue if not a friendly chat between the professors and the graduate students about the content of the course. I was very fortunate to have picked courses taught by extremely competent, experienced and approachable professors who, although experts in their respective fields, and highly respected as a consequence, did not look down upon us students, but rather considered us future colleagues worthy of attention and respect. Also, because of the intimate nature of the classes, I quickly found out not only the academic interests of the professors, but also their availability as potential members of my Thesis Committee, not to mention what they were like as fellow human beings. This last piece of information is rather important because one is looking for a long-term relationship between oneself and the trio that makes up that committee, a relationship that will last for at least four years if not more. So, one wants to avoid at all costs the remote possibility of a personality clash that would interfere with the completion of the task at hand. The bottom line is that, before the end of the first year of the Ph.D. program, a student has to find three willing professors to form his or her Supervisory Committee. Consequently, the pressure is on the student, from almost day one, to put together this team who will guide and advise him or her for the most important component of the Ph.D. program, the writing and defense of the thesis.

To that end, I asked Professor Lord, in the spring of 2011, a Québécois, who taught La nouvelle québécoise contemporaine, but who knew quite a bit about Québec drama, whether he would be willing to be my thesis director. I intended to focus my thesis research on the great Québécois playwright Marcel Dubé. Luckily for me, he quickly acquiesced to my request. Next, I contacted Professor Riendeau, also a Québécois, who taught Littérature éthique, and who had started his academic career by writing a lot about Québec theatre himself, if he would accept being part of the Supervisory Committee. He also said "yes". Finally, thanks to Professor Lord, he recommended that I contact Professor Salvatore Bancheri, from the Italian Department, someone who was very much interested in theatre and its staging, to find out whether he would be willing to join the team. He quickly agreed to it, too. What a relief! Now, with this challenge out of the way, I could focus exclusively on the mountains of work at hand before the Field Examinations that would occur at the end of April of the second year. That said, by October of the second year, I had to come up with a title for my *sujet de thèse* as well as determine its *objectifs*, *problématique*, *méthodologie* and *corpus*. There was no shortage of items to think about. This is why people say that working on a Ph.D. is an all-consuming affair, and rightly so.

January promptly arrived and I met my FSL421Y class. They turned out to be a lovely group of students who were in the process of finishing their undergraduate studies, including their particular study of the French language. Like any group of students, at any level, from elementary school to university, some of them were more committed than others to get the most out of the course. Overall, though, I was surprised to find out that some of them, even after having finished a few undergraduate French courses, were still struggling with the acquisition of the language. In fact, compared to my grade 12 French Immersion class at Harbord Collegiate, they were not as fluent in their command of the language. That was a bit of a disappointment for me. Another one came one evening when I asked the group, approximately thirty of them, if anyone was contemplating teaching French at the elementary or secondary panels as a career option; only three raised their hands. The most noticeable difference between my grade 12 French Immersion class at the secondary and my fourth-year undergraduate group was in terms of overall maturity, of course. All of my students now were young adults who had gone through many more life experiences than my previous teenagers. But, all in all, it was a pleasure and a privilege to teach them French. I was looking forward to more of the same in future years.

On January 22nd, 2011, Professor Domenico Pietropaolo organized a conference entitled Staging the Outlandish and Clowning the Lyrical – Legacy and Transformation of the Commedia dell'Arte, at the Robert Gill Theatre. The Conference was sponsored by The Emilio Goggio Chair in Italian Studies and The Graduate Student Centre for Study of Drama at the University of Toronto. He asked a few of us in his class to serve as Chairs for the different sessions. I was one of the lucky ones to be chosen. I was honored to participate in the Conference. I had found Professor Domenico Pietropaolo's course extremely useful in that it had opened my eyes to just how much Molière himself had been influenced by the Commedia and how much he had exploited it in so many of his plays.

Aside from these activities that consumed most of my time, I was still very much involved in the production of the yearly French play by La Troupe des Anciens at the University of Toronto. My role now was mostly in the areas of the *régie*, stage directions, liaison with high schools, publicity, and ticket reservations and sales. It was a commitment that required quite a bit of my spare time but one that brought many rewards on account of the fact that I kept on learning quite a bit about staging a play from Madame as well as about all aspects concerning French, ranging from pronunciation and phonetics to theatre history. Rehearsals were, in many ways, like taking a course on Theatrical Production under the stewardship of a consummate perfectionist becoming, thus, an ideal learning opportunity. Also, they enabled me to socialize with cast members whom I had known for decades and meet new ones as they joined the troupe. In April of 2011, La Troupe des Anciens staged *L'Avare*.

Shortly after the shows, Filomena and I flew to Rome via Paris to pick up the CEEF students who were on exchange in Italy. We spent a lovely week in the capital and another one in Florence. It was the first time that Filomena found herself in Italy and, because I had been there with my own Harbord Collegiate students on two occasions, I was more than glad to serve as her guide. We had a great time.

In June of 2011, Natasha graduated from Saint Michael's College with High Honours. It was a fantastic personal accomplishment. She had been accepted into the Faculty of Forestry to do a Master of Forest Conservation, a program that interested her a lot. In the meantime, for the summer, she was going to work at Ontario Travel. Life was unfolding for her as it should, so to speak.

As for me, during the summer, I started researching seriously my thesis topic in view of the Field Examinations that would take place at the latest at the end of April, 2012. According to the French Department's brochure:

> The Field Examination is designed to demonstrate that the student is sufficiently familiar with the primary and secondary works in his/her field to be able to proceed to original research and preparation of the doctoral thesis.
>
> No later than the second session of the second year of registration in the Ph.D. program, in the case of a student admitted on the basis of a master's degree, [...], a student must pass the two parts of the Field

Examination: a written part to be taken my March 15 and an oral part taken by April 30.

Furthermore, according to the Department's instructions:

A student must submit by September 15 of the second year of the doctoral program, his/her thesis subject indicating the aims, the general framework and issues, the methodology and the corpus of the doctoral thesis. This form must also contain the names and signatures of the thesis supervisor(s) and members of the supervisory committee.

The student's thesis subject must be approved by the Curriculum Committee and by the General Assembly of the Graduate section of the French Department. Once the thesis subject is approved, the student will then meet at least once with the supervisory committee to clarify and specify the thesis topic.

By November 15 of the second year of the doctoral program, the student will produce a written document of at least 10 pages (double-spaced) outlining the major area – the literary or linguistic corpus, the methodological and theoretical perspectives and approaches – from which the thesis will be derived, together with a thematically organized bibliography indicating the primary and secondary works relevant to this area that the student is expected to know in detail. This document will form the basis for the written part of the Field Examination. The thesis supervisor will certify to the Department that the document is satisfactory by signing a copy which is to be kept in the Department. The student will then distribute a copy to each member of the supervisory committee.

As you can see from the previous quotes, there was no shortage of items to think about during that summer of 2011. That said, every once in a while, all three of us in our family still managed to travel by car within Ontario's borders whenever our daughter was free from her summer job at Ontario Travel. We made it to Point Pelee National Park, Windsor, Sauble Beach, Bruce Peninsula National Park, Tobermory, Fathom Five Marine National Park, etc. Natasha was getting a lot of practical information about Ontario, information that she could share afterwards with the tourists that dropped by Ontario Travel. Other side benefits from these trips were that they allowed us to spend quality time together and, in the process, discover parts of Ontario that we hardly knew.

On June 28th, 2011, I got my second teaching appointment; it would be again FSL 421Y(s) L0301 T 10-12, R 10 CR 103, from January 1st to April 30th, 2012, under the supervision of Professor Visoi who had already given me a fine « Grille d'évaluation – Visite pédagogique » when she had visited my class on February 10th, 2011. The good news was that I would be teaching the same course once again, one that I was already familiar with; the bad news was that the end of the course would coincide with the Field Examinations. Nothing is ever perfect in life. So, one adapts to new circumstances and moves forward making the necessary adjustments to one's priorities to accommodate what is coming down the pipeline. Knowing what was coming, I took full advantage of the time between September and December to do as much research as possible in order to prepare for the Field Examinations.

On Thursday, October 27th, 2011, I received an email from the Department entitled « Sujet de thèse approuvé et prochaine étape » in which Professor Barbara Havercroft, the Associate Chair, Graduate Studies, related the good news:

> Cher Roberto,
>
> J'ai le plaisir de vous confirmer que, lors de l'Assemblée générale du Département d'études françaises du mercredi 26 octobre 2011, la section des Études supérieures du Département a approuvé votre sujet de thèse.
>
> Veuillez accepter toutes mes félicitations d'avoir franchi cette étape importante dans vos études doctorales.

I decided, right afterwards, that the title of my thesis would be « Le théâtre de Marcel Dubé: une transformation dramaturgique ». In it, I analyzed from a socio-semiotic point of view five major plays written by the playwright between 1953 and 1977. They were: *Bilan*, *Florence*,

Un simple soldat, *Un matin comme les autres*, and *Le réformiste ou L'honneur des hommes*.

That fall, I also did my fair share of classroom presentations for CEEF. Given the fact that I was going to be teaching from January to April and that the Field Examinations were also in March and April, I asked Gord not to assign me any escort duties for 2012. It was the reasonable thing to do. I needed to prepare adequately for those exams and wrap things up at the conclusion of the course that I was teaching, always an extra busy time.

In April, La Troupe des Anciens put on *La Cantatrice chauve* and *Les Précieuses ridicules*. The former meant a lot to me because I had acted in it a couple of times. The latter is one of Molière's funniest comedies. The matinées for the students and the evening performances for the public at large were a huge success.

My involvement in the activities of SESDEF, as the years passed, became more and more selective. In 2011-2012, I participated with Elena Stoica, a fellow Ph.D. candidate, in the selection of the proposals submitted by all sorts of Ph.D. candidates for the Department's graduate student conference entitled « Sens dessus dessous » taking place in the spring. It meant reading them carefully and deciding, as a team of two, which ones would be the most informative and interesting. It took several meetings between the two of us to arrive at a final decision. Also, every once in a while, I would attend a *causerie* given by a fellow Ph.D. candidate. With regards to social activities, although I was still somewhat involved in them, I made the irrevocable decision that I would participate less and less in them. The *esprit de corps* between SESDEF members was just not there.

I would like to return momentarily to December of 2011 because it marked a major milestone for Filomena. After more than three decades in banking, starting with the East Cambridge Saving, a bank in Somerville, Massachusetts, and then the Royal Bank in Toronto, she was more than ready to retire. She was tired of the daily commute from Mississauga to Toronto at the beginning of the day and from Toronto back to Mississauga at the end of the day. In addition, dealing with the public on a daily basis had taken its toll. Although most of the clients were polite, every once in a while, she had to face a real jerk, an experience that would sour the rest of her day. And, as anyone who has worked with the public knows, "the customer is always right no matter what". There is so much that anyone can take before deciding that enough is enough. It was the right time to let go. Looking forward, she wanted to relax and unwind and enjoy her new found freedom for a while. Afterwards, she planned to volunteer at the local church and take a vacation whenever the opportunity came up to travel, something that she had already started doing in 2008 when she had participated in a fascinating excursion to Israel, Jordan and Egypt organized by our local parish. Within the next few years, while I was tied up with my studies, she would travel several times to Florida, the Azores and mainland Portugal, always in the company of friends or family.

To celebrate Filomena's retirement, *comme il se doit*, that is to say properly, we rewarded ourselves by going on a one-week Caribbean cruise during Reading Week at the University of Toronto. We invited Filomena's sister and brother-in-law, who live in the Boston area, to join us in San Juan, Puerto Rico. As two people who loved cruises and who had participated in over twenty of them, they readily accepted our invitation. For the two of us, it would be a first. The ship, the Celebrity Summit, was beautiful and it offered all the amenities that cruisers have come to expect. Unfortunately, many of the passengers were obnoxious Americans who never failed to make idiots out of themselves wherever they went. The starting and final point was the city of San Juan with the following ports of call along the way: Bridgetown, Barbados, Castries, St. Lucia, St. Johns, Antigua, Philipsburgh, St. Maarten, Charlotte Amalie, St. Thomas, and back to San Juan. The entire first day was spent at sea and it was by far the most relaxing and pleasant of the seven-day cruise. That said, at every port of call we participated in what is referred to as Shore Excursions which were mostly disappointing endeavors by the local Sightseeing Tour companies at highlighting the individuality of each one of the islands. We were constantly on the go to fully appreciate the natural beauty of each island and much less to have a sense of what daily life was like for its inhabitants. Rushing from one spot to the next in an attempt to cover as much of the island as possible was not ideal. Even going to local beaches was a hurried affair and, once there, they tended to be overcrowded with rude tourists, polluted, and too noisy. By the end of the week, Filomena and I had concluded that cruises were definitely not our cup of tea.

For me, however, the highlight of 2012 was certainly the Field Examinations. The written part consisted of a take-home examination. There were four questions, two about theory and methodology and two on the corpus itself. I was to answer one in each category. Each answer had to be between 3,000 and 4,500 words. I was given one week to answer the two questions. The answers were due on April 18th. Once again, according to the French Department's brochure: "The written part is evaluated by three voting members of the thesis supervisory committee solely on the basis of content (Pass/Fail). A simple majority (two positive votes out of three) is required for successful completion." Furthermore, the Department stated that: "A student may not proceed to the oral part of the examination until he/she has successfully completed the written part."

A few days later, I received an email from Professor Barbara Havercroft in which she announced: « J'ai le grand plaisir de vous annoncer que le jury de votre examen écrit vous a décerné la mention « Pass » à l'unanimité. Comme Associate Chair, Graduate, je vous exprime mes félicitations pour ce travail bien fait. » Some comments and suggestions made by the three members of my Supervisory Committee followed. Fortunately for me, everything had gone well. It was time to focus on the oral part now. Its instructions were as follows:

> The oral part of the Field Examination is to be taken by April 30 of the second year of the doctoral program. It is based on a document consisting of 15-20 pages (double-spaced) thesis proposal accompanied by an appropriate bibliography. The preparation of the document is

entirely the responsibility of the student. This part of the examination will be conducted in French. Exceptions may be made only for extra-departmental members of the supervisory committee. Students must submit their written document to each member of the supervisory committee and to the Department one week before the date of the oral part of the examination which will be chaired by an officer of the Graduate section of the French Department, or delegate, who does not vote on the student's performance.

The student will make a 20-minute oral presentation, followed by questions from the committee. Evaluation of the oral part of the examination is on a Pass/Fail basis and takes into account both the written document and the oral presentation. A simple majority (two positive votes out of three) is required for successful completion.

The written document and accompanying bibliography must be filed with the French Department by the student once he/she has passed the examination.

Everything went well during the exam. Now I was called a Ph.D. candidate. I was on my way and more or less on my own for the next three years or so to complete the "real" thing, the doctoral thesis with much encouragement and sound advice from all members of my Supervisory Committee, especially Professor Lord, the kindest and most patient person in town.

The summer of 2012 was a relaxing one. There were no major trips abroad for my wife and me. Natasha, however, was lucky enough to go to Malaysia on a field trip organized by the Faculty of Forestry. It was an eye opener for her and once back, she did an Internship at the St. Lawrence National Park as mentioned previously. So, every once in a while, my wife and I used to visit her in Brockville. That said, at some point that summer I was scheduled to do research at the Société d'État Radio-Canada, in amazing Montréal. To that end, my wife and I booked ourselves into one of the student residences belonging to Université du Québec à Montréal (UQÀM), on boulevard René-Lévesque Est and within walking distance to the Radio-Canada tower, next to the bridge Jacques-Cartier. While I was in Montréal to consult the archives and to research Marcel Dubé's contribution to TV programing over many years, Filomena was there to do some shopping and to enjoy the sights. So, every day, after breakfast, I used to depart to Radio-Canada and stay there until about four o'clock at which time I would return to the residence and the two of us would go for a walk in Old Montréal or around Place des Arts, followed by a delicious dinner in one of the many downtown restaurants and, afterwards, we would attend a show.

I also wanted to visit the theatres where Dubé had staged some of his plays such as: Théâtre du Nouveau Monde (TNM), a theatre that was celebrating its 60th anniversary in 2012, Théâtre d'Aujourd'hui, Théâtre Quatre Sous, Théâtre du Rideau Vert and, finally, Théâtre Duceppe, named after one of Dubé's favorite actors, Jean Duceppe. We had a terrific time in lovely Montréal.

After the research was done at Radio-Canada and before heading home, we drove back by way of Ottawa, a city that we had not visited in such a long time. It is such a pleasure to see personally important landmarks in one's own capital city, especially the frequent ones that one sees on the news on a daily basis. We stayed in Ottawa for a couple of nights, enough time to revisit old familiar places and find out what was new. Our capital city had grown quite a bit ever since 1979, the last time that we had been there. It had become more cosmopolitan and more physically attractive too.

On the way from Ottawa to Mississauga, it goes without saying, we made a pit stop in Brockville to spend a few hours with Natasha. Everything was going well and within a few more weeks the internship would be over which meant for her a return to Mississauga and, shortly afterwards, to the flat on Robert St. that she shared with her friends and which, in the meantime, they had sub-let for the summer, to complete her master's degree before Christmas.

As usual, my teaching assignment arrived without fail on June 22nd, 2012. I would be one of the CIs for FSL 221Y (f) L0301 T 9-11, R 9 UC 328, under the supervision of Professor Sébastien Sacré, one of the youngest rising stars in the French Department. In October, after attending one of my classes, he wrote on my « Grille d'évaluation » the following comments:

> Avant que le cours ne commence, Roberto est dans la salle de classe et une chanson française passe discrètement sur un lecteur CD.
> Plusieurs informations liées à l'activité du jour et à l'actualité sont inscrites sur le tableau (date, concordance des temps et une phrase sur l'ouragan Sandy). Dès le départ, l'atmosphère est détendue et professionnelle.
> Le cours lui-même est dynamique, intéressant, très bien présenté par Roberto, qui a une parfaite maîtrise de son cours et de son matériel, si bien que tout se déroule sans difficultés.
> [...]
> Bref, il est clair que Roberto est un instructeur expérimenté qui a l'habitude d'enseigner : il fait preuve d'une aisance naturelle, maîtrise le matériel qu'il présente et sait créer une atmosphère propice à l'apprentissage.

All those years of teaching at the secondary level and, afterwards, in years one and two in the Ph.D. program, had served me well.

A couple of months later, back at the University of Toronto main campus, on August 16th, I got Professor Michelucci, now the Chair of the French Department, to write a note on my behalf to the Kelly Library asking for a 3rd floor private study carrel and the request was granted. That carrel would become a home away from home for the next four years. I spent an enormous amount of time at that library, the closest to the French Department. Speaking of the French Department, that September I had the distinct pleasure of meeting André Tremblay, a great guy and the new Graduate Counsellor and Administrative Assistant who was replacing Mme Monique Lecerf who had retired and whom I had known ever since my M.A. days in the mid-1980s. André quickly became a trusted friend. I used to confide in him my troubles and tribulations when it came to my on-going thesis and the personal challenges that it was imposing on my personal life and he used to provide good advice. He had incredible interpersonal skills and he was an attentive listener. We were sort of kindred spirits and, when it came to having a good time, we were always ready for it. Also, because of the publicity that he provided throughout the Department for the annual French play, La Troupe des Anciens used to reward him with a couple of free tickets for one of the evening performances. As for me, I used to invite him for a beer and he, in turn, used to invite me for his Union Christmas Party and the Spring Party where beer flowed freely. In between these two occasions, every once in a while, we used to go for dinner at a little Mexican restaurant on Yonge St. called Como en casa where we had befriended the two owners, Fernando and Carlos, two wonderful men. My friendship with André is one that has lasted well beyond my days at the Department that came to an end in 2017. And, when he retired in September of 2019, he, naturally, invited me to his retirement party held at the pub on Bay St. that the two of us used to frequent often, Mullin's Irish Pub.

Aside from my teaching assignment, the bulk of my time in 2012-2013 was devoted to research in preparation for my yearly meeting with the members of my thesis committee in the spring. So, I spent a lot of time at the University of Toronto main library, the Robarts Library, or at the Kelly Library where my carrel was located, with less frequent incursions into the Pratt Library, part of Victoria College, in search of a book or a document that could not be found in the previous two libraries.

I found that doing research was both exciting and a pleasant way to spend time. One writes a lot of succinct notes, makes sure to record carefully where the bibliographical information came from in order to avoid future headaches and a waste of one's time trying to find it again and, then, comes the hard part, that is to say putting it all together in a chapter. Writing a thesis chapter is tedious work. Several drafts are called for until the material is presented in a straightforward, logical and scientific manner in order to be forwarded to the committee for input at least two weeks in advance of the date of the annual meeting, Invariably, there are corrections, suggestions and improvements to be made to the chapter thanks to the keen and critical eyes of the committee members. Once those are taken into account, the chapter is rewritten and resubmitted to the thesis director for final approval, and if one gets his or her OK, one moves on to the next chapter which, once written, will call for the same type of oversight and review by the committee. This is why writing a thesis takes years and tests the patience and resiliency not only of the candidate, but also of the professors who agreed to guide the candidate. One needs to keep focused on the ultimate goal, namely that of earning the Ph.D. degree. If one cannot remain focused for whatever reason, it will be next to impossible to achieve it which explains why the drop-out rate is so high at the doctoral level. In this regard, I was very fortunate to have chosen Professor Lord as my thesis director. I met with him informally numerous times at his office at UTM (University of Toronto at Mississauga). He was always cordial, generous with his time, and encouraging. His sound advice helped me a lot, especially when it came to writing succinctly, clearly, logically and scientifically.

On another front, my fifteen CEEF presentations in high schools in Toronto, Mississauga, Brampton and Bolton were mostly completed by early December. In January, the Pre-Departure evening meeting with the students and their parents went on as usual. I would be picking up students in France on May 2nd in order to bring them back to Canada. Therefore, Filomena and I decided that we would travel to Paris on April 22nd and, after a few days in the city, take the TGV to Nice and revisit the Côte d'Azur and Monaco. Although the weather was rainy in the South of France, it was pleasant in Paris. One of the highlights of the trip came when we attended a performance of *Les Trois Sœurs* by Anton Tchekhov, in the famous Salle Richelieu of the Comédie-Française. It was an evening to remember. On May 2nd, we met the students at Charles de Gaulle without a single one missing in action which is always a blessing because, as we say when working with young people abroad, or even at home, expect the unexpected.

In January of 2013, an acquaintance of mine, a teacher of French at Blessed Cardinal Newman C.H.S., Ginny O'Sullivan, asked me, upon finding out that I was doing a Ph.D. on Marcel Dubé, if I would be interested in doing a presentation on *Zone*, one of Dubé's most staged plays, at her school. Needless to say, I told her that I would be delighted to do so. Afterwards, as the word got around throughout the secondary school panel that I was willing to do presentations on Dubé's plays, I got invited to other schools such as Cardinal Carter Academy, this time to chat with students about the significance of *Florence* as an early example of the women's emancipation movement in Québec society, Upper Canada College, to explain why a playwright such as Michel Tremblay considered *Un simple soldat* one of the most influential Québec plays of all time, and to Professor Rosa Saverino's French class, at the University of Toronto, to give presentations on *Au retour des oies blanches*, considered by many critics as perhaps the first modern Québec tragedy.

That April of 2013, La Troupe des Anciens staged *Le Malade imaginaire* and, as usual, I was very much involved in its production. It took my mind away from the thesis work that was ongoing and, in that sense, it was very much a therapeutic measure.

In March, Professor Paul Bessler, who was in charge of the University of Toronto's French Contest, asked me to lend a hand in its planning since I had been involved in it for so many years. I gladly obliged. That said, in terms of its former self, the French Contest had been scaled down substantially and was nowhere close to its former glory days. Times were changing and budgetary constraints were everywhere.

Also, in March, I made myself available to be part of the Department's Open House. It entailed providing undergraduate students with information about the wide-range courses offered by the Department and what the course load would be like, and explain the third-year abroad program, and some of the opportunities in Canada such as the MyExplore Program.

As the third year unfolded, Professor Pascal Riendeau, one of the professors in my thesis committee who taught at UTSC (University of

AN AZOREAN IN CANADA

Toronto at Scarborough), asked me if I would be interested in helping him out with the marking of his students' final essay in FREB37, Contemporary French Drama, a course where students analyzed four plays by four different Québec playwrights: *Tit-Coq* by Gélinas, *Les Belles-Soeurs* by Tremblay, *Les feluettes* by Bouchard, and *Les sept jours de Simon Labrosse* by Fréchette. The essays would be between 4-5 pages long and contain between 1,500 and 2,000 words. Of course, I said "yes". Although marking students' work is time consuming, the experience would be interesting because I would be able to assess the quality of the undergraduates' written work in a strictly literary course. While correcting them, I quickly found out that, although the ideas put forward by some of the students were many times interesting and original, their grammar mistakes still left a lot to be desired, so much so that sometimes they impeded immediate comprehension of what they were trying to convey to the reader. My conclusion was that a good many of the students enrolled in the course still needed more grammar acquisition to attain a higher degree of accuracy in the use of the French language.

Before my yearly meeting with the thesis committee, I met informally twice with Professor Lord to make sure that my chapter was going to meet the committee's expectations for the upcoming meeting in May. With the exception of a few points here and there, according to him, everything was coming along relatively well. Going forward, these informal meetings with him became a useful tradition. The June committee meeting came and went and more suggestions for improvements were made by all three professors and these were acted upon immediately by yours truly to the satisfaction of all concerned. My dissertation was taking shape slowly but surely.

In late May of 2013, Filomena and I flew to Lisbon where we met her sister Eduarda and brother-in-law, Constantino, who live in the Boston area, for a two-week tour of Lisbon and the Algarve. They had never been to Portugal's capital city before and, much less, to the Algarve. On the way to Lisbon, the SATA International airplane landed in Ponta

Delgada for a couple of hours before proceeding to Lisbon. It always gives us renewed pleasure to see the city from the air where both of us were born, even just for a few brief seconds. That time, as an added bonus, the pilots flew just south of the twin lakes of Sete Cidades, in my opinion, the most emblematic sight of São Miguel. We were lucky to be seated on the left side of the airplane with an unobstructed window view. It was a glorious morning and the sight was simply incredible. While at the airport, Filomena took advantage of the stopover to phone her father who was living in Ponta Delgada at the time.

The last time that we had been to Lisbon had been in 1981 when we landed there briefly before proceeding to Ponta Delgada to attend my mother's funeral and we had not seen much of the city. The very first time that we had visited Lisbon and had been to the Algarve was in 1978, when we had gone to São Miguel, continental Portugal and Madeira on our honeymoon. Lisbon and the Algarve looked better than ever before. In the Algarve, we stayed in Montegordo, a town on the eastern part of the province, relatively close to Vila Real de Santo António, the last Portuguese city in the Algarve before reaching the border with Spain. We stayed at our compadres' (Eduardo and Ana) lovely condominium facing one of the longest beaches in the entire Algarve. It was a great place to unwind after all the sightseeing in the Lisbon area. That said, we did not stay put in Montegordo, we visited several other places such as Faro, the Algarve's capital city, where we enjoyed a great dinner in a restaurant named Dois Irmãos, Tavira, from where we took a pleasant boat ride in the company of other tourists and a trio of jazz musicians to the island offshore to enjoy its beach, Albufeira, where Filomena and I had stayed in 1978, Portimão, Sagres, and even Seville for a day. After a most pleasant stay in the Algarve, we drove back to Lisbon for a couple more nights during which we still managed to fit in a Fado Night at a great spot named O Faia, where a delicious meal was also served, before returning to North America. All in all, it was a most pleasant vacation, spent with family members, in our home country.

On July 3rd, I received my teaching assignment for September; I would be a TA in FRE280Y5Y, a full-year course that finished in April. It was also the first time that I would be teaching at the University of Toronto at Mississauga (UTM), under the supervision of Professor Mihaela Pirvulescu. In reality, it was Dr. Mamadou Soro, from the Alliance Française de Toronto, who would be the course instructor and, therefore, the person with whom I would be working with closely. Teaching at UTM proved to be a blessing in disguise for me as the campus is relatively close to my home in Mississauga. It also afforded me the opportunity to meet very fine people in the Department of Language Studies under the leadership of Professor Emmanuel Nikiema, an accomplished leader and one of the finest individuals for whom one could possibly work.

The Department of Language Studies at UTM is much smaller than the main one on the St. George campus. Everybody knows everybody and the campus itself is beautiful, almost integrated into Erindale Park. So, it's not unusual to see deer grazing on campus as one moves from building to building. Aside from being in close contact with nature, many of the buildings are fairly new and comfortable; furthermore, the audio-visual equipment available in the classrooms is the latest and most reliable. All these features make the campus a pleasant place to engage with the students formally and informally.

In September, I volunteered to represent the Department in the so-called Ontario University Fair at the Metro Toronto Convention Center, an event that attracts students from many high schools in the province in search of a university to further their education. I was to speak with students and parents about the Mississauga campus as well as the courses available in the Department of Language Studies.

In December, I gave my first presentation at York University, in the Département d'études françaises. The title of my address was: « Une analyse socio-sémiotique de trois pièces de Marcel Dubé. » The presentation was pretty much aligned with the type of research that I was doing for my thesis. Professor Ross Bilous had put together a roaster of eleven presenters, some were professors, others were Ph.D. candidates like myself, and the whole enterprise was presented under the banner of Conférences au Département d'études françaises de l'Université de York. My colleague and friend Frenand, who was teaching now at UTM too, was kind enough to attend my presentation and provided some very useful feedback that I put to good use almost immediately, in February, at the University of Toronto's Faculty Club. My good friend and former colleague at Harbord and Malvern Collegiates, Penny Vincent, asked me to do a presentation for the members of Club 48, The Superannuated Secondary Teachers of Ontario, of which she was an active member. I agreed, of course, to do it. One is always curious as to what kind of reaction one is going to get from people who normally are not that familiar with a particular author's body of work. So, in order not to bore my audience and lose their interest in my topic, I did not go into technicalities and terminology that most people would not be familiar with unless they were into socio-semiotics. Keeping my audience in mind, I entertained them with pertinent information about the playwright himself, his life and times, and mentioned the features that made some of his plays so successful for three decades in Québec. All this was done in English because most of the attendees did not speak French. Judging from the questions that followed the presentation, they rather enjoyed it. Among them was an old friend and colleague from Harbord Collegiate, Larry King. After most people had left the room, Penny, myself, and Larry went to the pub downstairs to have a pint of beer and to further engage in conversation about Dubé.

I also had a chance to participate in the activities of the Journée FrancoFun 2014 at UTM. It was a day devoted to showcase the courses, cultural and social activities of the Department of Language Studies. I was in charge of the literature component and took full advantage of the opportunity to promote Marcel Dubé and his plays.

In April, La Troupe des Anciens put on *Les Femmes savantes*. I was in charge of ticket sales for both the student matinées and the evening ones for the public at large, not to mention publicity. Also, I was very much involved in the rehearsals, as in the past, a commitment that required my presence for a good fifteen of them.

After the Troupe's production in April, my wife and I travelled to Nantes via Paris to pick up the students who were on exchange there with CEEF. They had been dispersed along the Atlantic coast and the pick-up city was Nantes. We took advantage of being there for a week to explore the city itself, which we did not know at all, as well as a bit of the countryside going as far as St. Malo and Mont St. Michel towards the north-west, a first for us, and as far south as La Rochelle. For the purpose of discovering the region, we had rented a car which facilitated substantially our daily escapades into the countryside. In one of those escapades, we visited La Baule, a resort town with a lovely beach that really enchanted us.

As I look back at this particular trip, one event that stands out in my memory actually occurred in Paris before we moved on to Nantes. We had made reservations for a show playing at the Théâtre des Nouveautés, on Boulevard Poissonnière, not too far from our hotel, entitled How to become a Parisian in one hour? The show was animated by a talented stand-up comedian named Olivier Giraud. It was a barrel of laughs from beginning to end, as the title indirectly suggested. My wife was laughing quite a bit at his jokes and we were seated on row B, center orchestra. Olivier took notice of her reactions and, I am sure, her good looks, and towards the end of his performance asked her, and another fellow who was seating nearby, to join him on stage. Filomena accepted right away; the fellow, however, had to be encouraged by his wife to step on stage, a situation that produced some laughs from the public. Olivier's idea was, of course, to exploit to maximum advantage the comedic elements in his show. His ultimate goal was to make the audience laugh at the ability, or inability, of his two guests to carry out what he was directing them to do. All in good taste, of course. All I can say is that Filomena did herself proud on that Parisian stage. After the show, Olivier joined the public at the lobby and made it a point of thanking personally my wife for being a good sport and contributing directly to the success of his performance. We asked someone nearby to take a picture of the three of us. A wonderful souvenir of the evening. The irony of the situation is that although I was the one who had been involved in plays and performances for years and years, I cannot say that I ever stepped on any stage in Paris.

After the performance, while enjoying a pizza in a nearby restaurant, we were seated next to a couple from, of all places, Mississauga, who had attended the same performance. We started talking about the performance and the woman said to my wife that she would not have been able to do what Filomena had done simply because she did not have the courage to do it. A wonderful acknowledgement of my wife's many talents. We flew, a couple of days later, to Nantes where, on May 6th, we would meet the students to bring them back to Canada via Paris.

In May, I participated, as an oral interviewer, in the Concours de Français which was held at Glendon College. I found it to be the most disorganized of all the Concours in which I had participated up to that moment. I decided that, in the future, I would not be part and parcel of it anymore.

Because of my light teaching assignment in 2013-2014, I found that I could devote a lot of my time to do further research on Dubé and to set aside chunks of time to do the actual writing of the thesis. Consequently, the number of written pages accumulated at a brisk pace. I found the writing process itself rather enjoyable. I had more time to write, edit, revise and rewrite. Also, I had more spare time to dedicate to other activities that brought me satisfaction such as the CEEF presentations in high schools, the regular meetings and activities of UFE, the rehearsals for the French play, etc.

In the summer of 2014, Professor Corinne Denoyelle picked a few of us Ph.D. candidates to update the « Visibilité de la recherche au Département ». Each one of us was given a certain number of professors and our job was to see to it that their research activities as well as their refereed and non-refereed publications were all up-to-date, with their permission, it goes without saying. The idea was to put up their

Research Endeavours and their Scholarly and Professional Work on Academia.edu in view of increasing the Department's visibility as much as possible. I quickly found out that some professors can be very touchy when it comes to what they have been up to. Moral of the story? Always consult with them before forwarding their information elsewhere.

Also, that summer, my wife and I returned to São Miguel. My father-in-law had remarried for the third time and we wanted to meet personally his new wife who was as young as his two oldest daughters. Filomena's sister, her husband and their son Jason, his wife and their two young daughters also joined us there. The fool, who had turned 86 years old in the summer of 2013, had married that fall someone who was only 63 years old. Needless to say, she had agreed to marry the old geezer because he had accumulated some financial means and she had none. Furthermore, educationally-speaking, she was much more advanced than he was. I only discovered after his death what I had suspected for many years, that he was almost illiterate in Portuguese and certainly so in English. She, on the other hand, bragged to anyone who was willing to listen to her, that she had "written" a book entitled *Os Meus Passos*. One would think that she would want someone, me, who was working on a Ph.D. in literature, to read her "masterpiece" for an opinion, but she never did. I do wonder why not. Meeting her personally proved my wife's suspicions and worst fears: she had married the old man to rob him of his money, an objective that she proceeded to execute methodically during the next four years, until his death in 2018. Her plan of action was quite simple: isolate the bugger from the rest of his family to manipulate him and exploit his weakness and his ensuing vulnerability to her advantage. My father-in-law, the *ignoramus*, was taken for a ride at the end of his life on account of his own stupidity and egotistical ways leaving a legal mess to be sorted out, with the professional help of a lawyer, by his surviving children.

That July, I received my next teaching assignment, it would be the same as the previous year, which meant that I would be a TA in FRE280Y5, from September to April, at UTM, under the supervision of Dr. Caroline Lebrec with whom I would develop, during the next few years, a wonderful professional relationship based on mutual respect and close collaboration. One of the most interesting activities that the French unit of the Department of Language Studies offered its undergrad students was the possibility of participating in a Soirée des Talents in March. Caroline took charge of this initiative. It was an opportunity for students, and willing staff members too, to display their talents in French. So, some of the participants recited poems, others sang songs, still others did a skit, etc. In March of 2016, I was honored to MC the show and participated in it in another capacity, that is to say that at one moment I told a series of jokes with the intent of making people laugh. I also recited a poem: *Le chat et l'oiseau*, a famous poem by Jacques Prévert. The evening, staged at Erindale Theatre, was a success by all accounts and it would be repeated over the next few years. The following year, in 2017, I recited another poem by Prévert: *Page d'écriture*. Caroline and I kept in touch after I finished my Ph.D. in 2017 and left the University and, in 2019, she asked me to come back and assist in the Soirée des Talents' proceedings by being a judge because there were prizes to be given out to the best student performances in each category. It was a lot of fun.

Another very worthwhile initiative of the Department of Language Studies was the Awards Evening and Music Gala. It was an opportunity for the various units within the Department to honour its most outstanding students. There were Language Awards in Arabic, Chinese, German, Hindi, Latin, Persian and Spanish; French Awards, Italian Awards, Linguistic Awards, Concurrent Teacher Education Awards, Language Studies Academic Society Award and even Course Instructor Awards. It was a wonderful chance to put the spot light on the tremendous accomplishments of both students and staff associated with the Department.

Since FRE280Y5 was a repeat course, I also applied for a second teaching assignment and, in August, I was given the position of CI in FSL321Y1 (s) L0101 M 10-12, W 10 TF202, from January to April, at the St. George campus, under the supervision of Professor Paul Bessler, a very nice fellow whom I had met on several occasions in connection with the French Contest. I was looking forward to the teaching of FSL321Y1 because it would be one more course in the sequence of the mandatory course progression for undergrads who wanted to specialize in French; I had already taught FSL421Y1 (twice) and FSL221Y1. This wish, however, was seriously impacted by the labour dispute between CUPE and the University of Toronto that took place across the three campuses in the winter of 2015. Throughout my entire professional life, I have always been a strong union supporter and, consequently, when CUPE asked course instructors (CIs) and teaching assistants (TAs) to boycott classes and to picket, I did not hesitate to answer the call of duty. The strike went on for weeks during a bitterly cold winter. There were planned demonstrations across the university and rallies to promote unity amongst the ranks of picketers and to update the members on the latest developments. After much wrangling, the University of Toronto came to its senses as the most important and the largest university in the country and agreed to a reasonable contract. That said, the whole ordeal left a sour taste in all concerned. In my case, the teaching of FSL321Y1 was just collateral damage. When classes resumed and I returned to the classroom, the school year was almost over. Such is life.

The school year 2014-2015 was a very busy one for me. I participated, starting in October and finishing in February, in the Second Language Teaching and Learning Workshops Series organized by the French Department under the leadership of Professor Jeff Steele. These workshops were most useful and provided a lot of insight into all aspects of language acquisition and eventual fluency.

I also lent a hand in October to Professor Paul Bessler in the Fall Campus Day at Hart House by promoting the Department and the University of Toronto to visiting high schoolers in search of the ideal university in order to pursue their post-secondary education. The students were curious, their parents inquisitive, and the people from the Department of French who had volunteered for the occasion were courteous and eager to answer all sorts of pertinent questions. All these factors made it a most enjoyable experience.

In January of 2015, I submitted ninety pages of my thesis for Professor Lord's consideration. It contained three chapters. The first one dealt with *Zone*, the second one with *Florence* and the third one with *Un simple soldat*. Each chapter was approximately thirty pages long. Previously, in 2014, I had submitted a chapter on the theory and methodology that I would be using to analyze the corpus and in 2013 a chapter dealing with the overall state of affairs in Québec's theatre world before, during and after Dubé wrote the bulk of his production which happened to be before, during and after the Quiet Revolution, a pivotal period in Québec's history, as well as a justification for my choice of plays. I was hoping that after having analyzed Dubé's plays that dealt with the working class, the three plays mentioned above, I would be able to move on to analyze the four plays in which he dealt with the middle class, the bourgeois: *Bilan*, *Un matin comme les autres*, *Au retour des oies blanches* and *Le Réformiste*. The ninety pages were in preparation for the annual meeting with the thesis committee coming up in June. As usual, a couple of weeks later, Professor Lord provided useful feedback that helped me refine the content of the submission. Therefore, I worked on it some more and two weeks before the June get together with all committee members, I forwarded a copy to each one of them so that they could read it and make comments about it during our meeting. At the meeting, I was given the green light to proceed to the second part of the thesis which dealt with the middle class.

In February, I had the pleasure of doing a presentation at St. Joseph Catholic High School on Molière and Courteline, two playwrights who would be featured in the Troupe des Anciens' production in April. The Troupe would be presenting *George Dandin*, and *Le Commissaire est bon enfant* and the students in question would be attending a matinée performance.

That same February, Filomena and I also had the chance to spend a lovely week in Naples, Florida, at our *compadres*' condominium. It was great to enjoy the mild weather down south, go to the beach, and relax as much as possible. Nevertheless, when one is in the middle of a project such as a thesis, one cannot forget about it altogether. It becomes a sort of obsession that follows you everywhere. So, I took my laptop along and, after lunch, I put in a few hours to add to what I had already written and to edit its content, the latter an aspect that, I must confess, I did not enjoy much. After investing considerable time researching, writing notes, writing a first draft and, afterwards, a second and a third one with the intent of making a chapter as readable, logical and scientific as possible, having to cut something out was the most painful part of writing a thesis. In my mind, all of it was so very important. Eventually, however, common sense prevails and entire paragraphs, pages and, sometimes, even a whole chapter, are eliminated.

In April, the two plays mentioned above were staged by La Troupe des Anciens to the delight of both high schoolers and the public at large. Under the artistic direction of Professor Collet, La Troupe des Anciens kept on producing one smashing success after another.

By the end of April of 2015, all course work was finished and I was on my way to Berlin, Germany, with my wife, to pick up the students who had been there on exchange for three months under the banner of CEEF. It was our first time in that fantastic city, one of the great cities of the world, and it turned out to be a wonderful way to unwind after an extremely busy year in the French Department and also in terms of visits to schools in order to promote the international student exchanges. We flew with KLM from Toronto to Amsterdam. At Schiphol's International Airport, we boarded a Lufthansa flight to Berlin arriving at Tegel Airport towards noon.

Berlin. It's a city with such a long and controversial history. Nowadays, though, it has become a city in the avant-garde of the arts scene. One cannot visit Berlin without noticing right away the 368 meters tall Television Tower; it is Berlin's tallest structure. For those who enjoy a bird's eye view of cities, it is a must stop. Our list of places to see included: the Brandenburg Gate, a symbol of German unity today, and a stroll down Unter den Linden, Berlin's version of the Champs-Élysées, the Reichstag/Bundestag Building, the seat of the German government, with its ultra-modern dome, Platz der Republik, right in front of it, where the German reunification celebrations occurred on October 3rd, 1990, "Red Town Hall", the seat of the governing Mayor of Berlin, the somber Memorial to the Murdered Jews of Europe, Potsdamer Platz, with the Sony complex, the Berlin Cathedral, Berliner Dom, Philharmonic Hall with its unique architecture and acoustics, Victory Column topped by the Goddess Victoria, the amazing Tiergarten, the largest green space in the city with an area of 207 hectares, Soviet War Memorial, the first Soviet cenotaph of the city, Schloss Bellevue, seat of the Federal President, Museum Island, a paradise for visual arts lovers, the very touching Jewish Museum, Checkpoint Charlie, Topography of Terror, Olympia Stadium and, finally, a trip to the amazing KaDeWe department store where clothes, food and drink combine under the same roof to the delight of most locals and tourists. One week was definitely not enough to explore a city that has so much to offer and the two of us promised to return soon.

I attended, in May, the Department of Language Studies Retreat at the Columbus Center, a very interesting event put together by Professor Emmanuel Nikiema and staff with the ultimate goal of refocusing the Department's objectives going forward and promoting further its many strengths.

For the summer of 2015, Professor Rosa Hong was in charge of a French Summer Camp for young children at UTM. The idea was to encourage in them the use of the French language in all sorts of every day fun activities. She asked me if I would be interested in being Assistant coordinator. It meant essentially that I would be working with and supervising the undergraduate students who would be delivering the program on a daily basis. The camp would run from July 27th to August 21st. I accepted her offer because I thought that the program would be an effective way to develop in children a certain degree of fluency in French. I had seen first hand how quickly my own daughter had acquired fluency in French once enrolled in senior kindergarten at St. Jean-Baptiste.

That May, we also flew to Punta Cana, in the Dominican Republic, for a so-called destination wedding that almost turned into tragedy for one of the attendees. I explain. Wendy, one of Eduarda's two daughters was remarrying a very nice fellow, Sam, and they had invited a select number of family members and friends to attend the ceremony in a gated resort in Punta Cana named Dreams Resort & Spa. We accepted their kind invitation and combined it with a one-week vacation there. The last time that we had been in the Dominican Republic had been in 1988 and we had loved it. We arrived at the resort the evening before the ceremony to find all family members and friends up in arms: Eduarda, while having dinner in one of the several restaurants, choked on a piece of steak and collapsed on the spot. She had to be rushed to a local hospital in serious trouble with a collapsed lung. Unhappily for her, the local hospital had limited resources and could not deal with the aftermath of the situation. For the next few days, she was in limbo until she, accompanied by her husband, were transported by air ambulance to a Miami hospital for a proper diagnosis and treatment that lasted over a month. Although everybody was saddened by the turn of events, the wedding still proceeded without, of course, the bride's parents in attendance who were in the hospital. That said, Gabriela, Filomena's younger sister, the Down syndrome sister, had flown with Eduarda and her husband from Boston to Punta Cana to attend the wedding. Now, there was a problem in that she could not return to Boston because Eduarda was recovering in a Miami hospital and nobody knew when she would be released from it. Eventually, a solution was found: Gabriela would fly with us to Toronto and, whenever Eduarda and Constantino returned to their home, Filomena would take her back to Boston. That said, finding an empty seat last minute in an airplane returning from a destination spot such as Punta Cana is not an easy matter. So, the Sá Ponte family had to pay for the only place available in our scheduled return flight, a business-class seat for Gabriela. Thankfully, the wedding itself at Dreams was just lovely and the rest of the vacation was uneventful. All in all, the turn of events could have been much worse for all concerned, especially for Eduarda who could have passed away the evening before her daughter's wedding at Dreams, in tropical Punta Cana.

In June, it was time to meet with my thesis committee for the annual conference. The meeting was as cordial as ever. More suggestions and positive criticism were expressed by my trio of professors in view of improving the overall quality of the chapters submitted after which we wished each other a wonderful summer and went our separate ways. By now, I had already written a good 190 pages having to do with the introduction and the first part dealing with protagonists that belonged to the working class. That said, it was becoming obvious that at the pace that I was writing, I would not be able to finish the thesis within the prescribed time, that is to say within five years. In practical terms, it meant that I was falling outside of the funding package offered by the School of Graduate Studies. The remedy was to apply for a Doctoral Completion Award (DCA), a very common "cure" because very few candidates are capable of defending their thesis within the time frame allowed. Therefore, I applied for it and by June 5th, 2015, I got a reply from Professor Barbara Havercroft, the Associate Chair, Graduate Studies: "I have the pleasure of writing to inform you that the Doctoral Completion Award applications have been evaluated by our Graduate Scholarships and Awards Committee and that you have been awarded a DCA for the 2015-16 university year."

It's interesting how, as time moves on, the overall internal structure of a thesis comes together almost by its own internal logic. Mine, by the end of the summer of 2015, was pretty much set and did not change drastically afterwards. It contained an introduction divided into two parts, followed by a first part which included three chapters, each one dealing with a specific play concerning the working class, and this concluded with a partial conclusion based on the analysis; this first part was followed by a second one which included four chapters each one dealing with a specific play analyzing the trials and tribulations of the middle class; this second part also ended with a partial conclusion based on the analysis discussed. Finally, a general conclusion was put forth and a detailed bibliography ended the thesis.

In July, Filomena and I flew to Portugal. We had planned carefully another vacation with Eduarda and Constantino. This time we were going to meet them in Porto and "discover" northern Portugal during a two-week vacation. For that purpose, we had rented a couple of comfortable condominiums in Porto for the first week and then booked a series of hotels going all the way north to Viana do Castelo and as far south as Coimbra and Figueira da Foz for the second week before returning to Porto and boarding our respective planes back to North America. Needless to say, given what had happened to Eduarda in Punta Cana, they could not join us. After six weeks at the hospital, she had to wait another month in Miami before she could fly back to Boston. In spite of this setback, Filomena and I enjoyed very much our trip. The last time that we had visited some of the places in our itinerary had been during our honeymoon back in the summer of 1978. We arrived back in Canada on July 26th, one day before the Summer Camp was going to start at UTM.

The experience reminded me of the Summer Camps run by the West End YMCA in which I had been involved as an undergrad myself. A big difference, though, was the undeniable fact that now I was in my sixties and did not have any more the same level of energy as when I was in my early twenties. But, thanks to the undergrads that I was supervising, they kept the children entertained. They were kept busy with all sorts of fun activities in a beautiful setting, the UTM campus. They were encouraged by all of us to express themselves as much as possible in French and I am convinced that the experience was a positive one for the vast majority of them.

On June 26th, I had received my teaching assignment for 2015-2016; it would be once again FRE280Y5, under the supervision of Dr.

Caroline Lebrec, someone I had gotten to know really well and with whom I enjoyed teaching.

In September, October and November, I was busy with CEEF presentations, attending the RGASC Writing TA Training Program at UTM and the SLTL and TATP Workshops at St. George Campus. In late September, La Troupe des Anciens Board of Directors' meeting took place and it was decided that, in April, the troupe would stage *La Cantatrice chauve* followed by *Le Médecin malgré lui*.

In the meantime, the writing of my thesis was moving along at a brisk pace because in early December I had to submit another chapter of the thesis to Professor Lord in order to prove to the Awards Committee that I was not lazing around. It was one of the stipulations to be able to receive the second financial instalment of the DCA. Everybody was satisfied that good progress was being made as far as that was concerned.

In January of 2016, Caroline went on sick leave and for the duration of her absence Professor Nikiema asked me to replace her as the CI in FRE280 which I did with pleasure. It made me happy to know that the Department trusted me to carry on in a capable and efficient manner.

Also, at the end of January, I had completed the last chapter of the second part which I submitted to Professor Lord for his feedback. That chunk of work and the chapter that I had submitted to him in December would be the basis of the committee's annual meeting in June, so I thought. A couple of weeks later, I received Professor Lord's suggestions for the improvement of its content. He wanted to see me in person to discuss the overall length of the project and the use of the SGS mandatory template for the next submission to all committee members. We found a common time in February and, during the meeting, it was decided that one of the plays in the second part of the thesis would have to be sacrificed. There were four. I needed some time to figure out which one to eliminate and resubmit a fresh version to him. He gave me a couple of weeks to accomplish the task. I eliminated *Au retour des oies blanches*. The elimination of one of the chapters, although painful to me, actually made sense because it would balance things out in that there would be three plays concerning the working class and an equal number concerning the middle class. This proved to be relatively easy to fix. What was not so easy to fix was the application of the SGS template to everything that I had written. I wished that someone in the Department had told me right from the start to have used it. Consequently, I spent countless hours formatting the thesis properly, a very frustrating exercise but an indispensable one.

Inevitably, as this flurry of activity was going on with respect to my thesis, other events were happening as well. I supervised one of the Soirée Ciné's showings at UTM, another excellent initiative of the French unit of the Department, coordinated with Caroline the content of Soirée des Talents, and did my fair share of work in rehearsals for *La Cantatrice chauve* and *Le Médecin malgré lui*.

In March and April, I met again with Professor Lord and it was decided that the entire thesis would be presented in June to all committee members for a general discussion. I added the Final Conclusion and resubmitted the very latest version for his opinion. A couple of weeks later, by now we were into April already, I received some more pertinent comments, pointers, suggestions and corrections and the go-ahead to send a final corrected version to all three members of the committee in preparation for the discussions that would form the basis of our annual meeting. Adapting my thesis to the SGS template proved to be more challenging than I had anticipated. All sorts of unexpected formatting problems kept on occurring. I sent a version to the committee on April 17th, the day that I was leaving for Europe on CEEF business, only to realize once in Italy that there were technical issues with it. Fortunately, I had taken my laptop with me and late at night tried to fix them to the best of my ability. Finally, to my great relief, already back in Canada, on May 9th, the very latest version was forwarded to all three members of the committee. But since none of them were going to be available in June for the annual meeting, the date of May 31st was chosen.

On March 31st, I attended a workshop given by Professor Barbara Havercroft entitled « Comment se préparer pour la soutenance de la thèse ». It was very *à propos*. Professor Havercroft invited for the occasion a candidate who had just successfully defended her thesis, an aspect that made the workshop even more relevant for all in attendance.

In April, the performances of *La Cantatrice chauve* and *Le Médecin malgré lui* went on as planned. The former, as always, was a tremendous hit with the high schoolers in attendance at the matinées because it's a play emblematic of the theatre of the absurd, something that we found had a special appeal to our teenage clientele. The latter, although not as popular or as known as the former, is a farce with scenes typical of the Commedia dell'Arte and, consequently, pleased all in attendance too.

And, as if all these activities were not enough, on April 29th, after the French Play, my wife and I were scheduled to pick up a group of students on a CEEF exchange in France. Since our daughter was getting married in the fall of 2016, we decided to invite her to come along with us. It was sort of a wedding gift in advance of the wedding itself. Of course, she gladly accepted the generous offer. We would fly to Paris on April 17th and, from there, onwards to Venice. My daughter had never been to Paris or Venice and my wife had never visited Venice. We booked a condominium in Padova for four days and a hotel in Verona for the same length of time too, and from there we would go on day trips to explore this gorgeous region of Italy. Afterwards, we would fly back to Paris for the final four days and pick up the exchange students at Charles de Gaulle Airport on April 29th. It was a memorable trip, not only because our daughter was with us, but also on account of the spring-like weather that we enjoyed in Italy. In Paris, however, it was a different story because of cold temperatures and rainy days but, in spite of this minor *contretemps*, all three of us had a great time.

As it turned out, 2016 was a memorable year in many ways for ourselves and for our little girl who was not so little any more. With regards to trips, aside from the one to Paris and northern Italy, she had already been in the winter to St. Maarten, in the Caribbean and, after the European trip, she went in the fall to Iceland. In between trips, she managed to plan successfully, albeit with a bit of help from mom, her wedding on October 22nd demonstrating, in the process, very capable organizational skills.

In any case, upon returning from our glorious trip to Italy and France, from May 3 - 6, I drove up to Barrie on CEEF business. Every May, a few of us, under the leadership of Gord Berg, got together in that city in order to go through the "matching process". It entailed matching Canadian students with their French counterparts. A meticulous process that took into account many factors about the candidate such as age, gender, academic background, hobbies, specials talents, parents' occupations, etc. so that a "perfect" match would become a reality. It was also an opportunity for us to socialize at the end of the day over dinner and, perhaps, view a movie at a local cinema before retiring for the night at the hotel.

After that, it was time to start preparing for the annual thesis committee meeting. By this time, the entire project had been consuming me for six long years and I was getting desperate to just move on to other passions. As it turned out, although I thought that the latest version was quite polished, my three professors still found typos, minor contradictions and redundancies here and there that had to be addressed in order for the final approval of the thesis to take place. Of course, I was disappointed but I put my mind to it and literally spend the summer of 2016 at the Kelly Library perfecting as much as possible the "bloody" thesis.

The very same day I applied for a so-called "first extension of time to complete the requirements for the Ph.D. degree" which was granted by the Department on June 2nd. In June, July and August, I went methodically through the entire thesis: Introduction, First Part, Second Part and Final Conclusion. In late August, it was ready to be sent to my trio of Professors again but I did not do it. Instead, I put it in the back burner for a while and, every once in a while, I would reread it and "perfect it". And, every time that I did that, I still found a typo here and there. By early December I had had enough of it. On December 6th, I sent the entire thesis to my committee. It was approved just in time for Christmas. On January 31st, 2017, I submitted it to the French Department and the SGS. Its defense would take place on May 11th, 2017, at 11 o'clock in morning, at Odette Hall.

Back on July 28th, 2016, I had received one of my teaching assignments for 2016-2017. I would be one of the CIs in FSL 121Y1Y L0201 TR 1-3, from September to April, under the supervision of Dr. Marina Marukhnyak. The assignment for the other course arrived a few days later, on September 2nd; I would be a TA once again in FRE280Y5, under the supervision of Caroline Lebrec, from September to April too. I was very happy to be involved in the teaching of FSL121Y1 because it would complete the series from beginning to end and because it would give me a hands-on understanding of the entire program. Also, I would be working side by side with Dr. Elena Stoica, the other instructor aside from Dr. Marukhnyak and me, someone I knew well and respected a lot.

In September, I attended the Orientation Meetings for CIs and TAs at both the French Department at St. George, organized by Professor Jeff Steele, and the one at UTM, organized by Professor Claude Evans. Also, in September, the regular CEEF visits to high schools to promote exchanges started in earnest and they would last until early December.

In October, at La Troupe des Anciens Board of Directors' meeting, it was decided to stage *Le Bourgeois gentilhomme* in April of 2017. As in previous years, I would be sharing the bulk of the rehearsals with a couple of colleagues as well as be in charge of ticket sales for the student matinées and the evening ones.

October also marked another milestone in the life of the Machado family. Our "little girl", Natasha, got married on Saturday, October 22nd, at the Ivy Lea Club, a beautiful setting, in Lansdowne, between Kingston and Gananoque, Ontario. It was an emotional moment for my wife and me. In typical Portuguese tradition, it's the parents of the bride who pay for the reception and we were happy to oblige. Unfortunately, the venue itself could not accommodate as many people as we wanted to invite, family and friends, who had accompanied us all along our lives and whose sons and daughters had already gotten married and who had invited us to their weddings. Life is full of compromises and the choice of the Ivy Lea Club and the number of guests that it could accommodate was a big one. But it was a venue that appealed to our daughter, ourselves, and Joel, the groom, who was delighted when he found out that he did not have to incur a big expense.

The month of October can bring both beautiful cool sunny days and chilly rainy ones. Except for the Sunday, a glorious fall day, the weekend of October 22nd was a rainy one. Therefore, none of the activities associated with the wedding itself and the reception that followed, some of which were planned to occur outdoors, could be held in the patio and surrounding gardens whose trees were in the process of changing colours. But, alas, one does not have control over such matters.

We arrived in Gananoque on Friday afternoon for the wedding rehearsal at the Ivy Lea Club. Afterwards, the wedding party went to a mini reception organized and paid for by both the bride and groom at a wonderful Italian restaurant in Gananoque called Riva. Later, we went to a local micro-brewery around the corner from the restaurant where we sampled different types of beers accompanied by someone playing the guitar and singing in the background. After that, Filomena and I retired to our hotel while the couple and their friends continued the festivities late into the night at the pub. In the meantime, our family members form the US had already checked in at our hotel and we invited some of them to come to our room to chat and to sip some Port wine that I had purposely brought for the occasion. The least that can be said is that the two bottles of Port wine certainly added to the general happiness and merriment of all those who partook in the drinking.

The day of the wedding the skies were covered up and every now and then there were showers. We returned to the Ivy Lea Club in the morning to help set up for the evening reception and then all of us returned to the hotel to relax a bit and get dressed for the special occasion. Later in the afternoon, before the arrival of the guests at the venue, the wedding party made it back to the Club in order to take some pictures and enjoy each other's company. When the two of us saw Natasha dressed in her wedding gown, we were blown away by how beautiful she looked. It was hard to believe that she was all grown up and ready to start an independent life of her own. Her bridesmaids: Marina, who had been her best friend ever since elementary school, was the maid of honour, Rebecca, whom she had met at the Faculty of Forestry, was a bridesmaid as was Jena, Joel's sister. They all looked lovely. As for the groom, his best man and friends, all of them looked sharp in their dark grey suits. Soon afterwards, the guests started arriving and before we knew it the Ivy Lea Club was packed.

For the wedding ceremony, my wife and I had decided that both of us would walk with Natasha to the front of the room, a room that had been prepared especially for the wedding ceremony with rows of chairs fanning out from a huge floor to ceiling window overlooking the St. Lawrence River, where the Justice of the Peace stood and a small table was set up for the signing of the marriage contract. In most weddings, traditionally, it's the father of the bride who walks her to the altar and hands her over to the groom. However, since both of us had spent so much time with Natasha over the years and since both of us loved her equally, we felt that it was only right that the two of us participate in the ritual. The ceremony itself was simple but beautiful. At one moment Sue, Joel's aunt, sang a song accompanied by the banjo, a nice touch, and before we knew it the ceremony itself was over and all of us made it to the main restaurant. There was an open bar, thanks to Joel, and tasty appetizers started being served by the staff for the delight of the guests. This *avant-goût* was followed by a complete dinner and, at some point, the MC for the evening, one of Joel's friends, went to the podium and speeches by different people were made, including by myself and my wife. They culminated when the bride and the groom went to the microphone and spoke about themselves, how they had met at the Faculty of Forestry, how they had shared a flat with friends on Robert St., how they had driven to Prince George and back for jobs after graduating, how they had landed jobs with South Nation Conservation, in Finch, etc. Finally, they thanked their families and friends for sharing such an important milestone in their life with them. Dessert, coffee and tea were served, accompanied by *queijadas de nata*, a Portuguese delicacy, and the dancing started. At about midnight, we all returned to the hotel to rest. We were exhausted but happy that everything had turned out just right in spite of the rainy weather. It was a most memorable event.

On Sunday morning the skies were blue and the sun was shining. My wife and I, accompanied by Natasha and Joel, returned to the Ivy Lea Club to settle the wedding bill with the reception manager, a very capable, experienced and pleasant woman who had taken full charge of all aspects of the event to our great relief. After the meeting, we drove back to Mississauga and, the two of them, to Bancroft, where they now lived in a rented chalet on the shores of Baptiste Lake. Both had quitted their jobs with South Nation Conservation. Natasha now worked for the Canadian Institute of Forestry, in Mattawa, and Joel for the Ministry of Natural Resources, in Bancroft. They would take some time yet before buying a house in Bancroft and putting down roots in this lovely area of Ontario.

In November, the CEEF Information Evening for students, accompanied by their parents, who were interested in International Student Exchanges, took place at the TCDSB (Toronto Catholic District School Board). Lots of curious parents and keen students showed up for the presentation.

In January of 2017, I became the *animateur* des *Cafés-rencontre* at UTM, another one of Caroline's initiatives. As such, my goal was to engage with undergrads who were studying French to promote their use of the language and to prepare some of them, if not all, to be participants in the Soirée des Talents. These get togethers took place at noon and coffee and sweets were provided by the Department for the occasion. It was an enjoyable experience for all, including myself, but especially for the students who took the time to participate in them. Also, in January, I wrote an article on Marcel Dubé's contribution to Québec drama for an upcoming publication whose editors were Professors Bernard Andrès and Pierre Hébert entitled *Atlas littéraire du Québec* which saw the light of day in 2020.

In February, I had CEEF airport duty for the Canadian students who were departing on their two or three-month exchanges. Also, in February, the CEEF Home Interviews for the students who had enrolled for a 2018 exchange started in earnest and those would continue into March. Speaking of March, there was the Soirée des Talents during which I recited a poem by Prévert. In April, I participated in the Exam Jam and, of course, there were the four matinées and the two evening performances of *Le Bourgeois gentilhomme*, one of Molière's plays most enjoyed by the public.

In May, there was the CEEF matching of Canadian and European students in Barrie. And then there was the big day, the day of my much-anticipated *soutenance*, May 11th. Believe it or not, seven long years had elapsed since the start of my Ph.D. It was high time to conclude it.

Two weeks prior to the oral defense itself, I received the evaluation of my doctoral thesis from the Exterior Examiner, Professor Jane Moss, from Duke University. In it, she said:

> This is a very well written thesis that makes clear arguments about the contributions of Marcel Dubé to French-Canadian drama and television during three decades important to the development of Modern Quebec society. While it does not argue for an original reinterpretation of Dubé's work from the 1953-1977-period, it does make use of theoretical tools unavailable to earlier scholars. Machado's analyses of the distinct sociolects of the six plays in his corpus and his use of theatre semiotics to map the motivations of the main protagonists enable him to illustrate how Dubé's theatre reflects the sociopolitical and cultural changes of the period. This exercise in sociocriticism leads him to solid conclusions about Dubé's critique of Quebec society and his humanistic vision of the existential dilemmas of modern life.

While not disagreeing with my analysis or conclusions in her written report, Professor Moss had a series of questions some of which she intended to ask during the upcoming oral examination. I considered each one of them carefully and addressed them one by one during the twenty-five minutes that I was allowed for the presentation. Her questions were most helpful in focusing my attention on key aspects of my dissertation that I needed to highlight during the examination.

The day of the examination itself, aside from Professors Lord, Riendeau and Bancheri, the trio who had put up with me for six years, in attendance were the External Examiner, Professor Jane Moss, who turned out to be not only a very pleasant person, but also someone who was keenly interested in what I had written, representing the French Department, Professor Barbara Havercroft and, finally, the Chair, Professor Stanka Radovic, from the English Department, whose role was to make sure that the proceedings moved along at a good pace and that each professor had a chance to ask some questions about different aspects of my thesis. This "rite of passage" turned out to be a very cordial meeting between myself and all the professors present. It took two hours after which I was invited to step outside of the room while the Examination Committee voted on my performance, my preparedness and the quality of my answers. All, except the Chair, had to cast a vote. There were three possible outcomes to the examination: As it Stands (AS), Subject to Minor Corrections (MC) or Subject to Minor Modifications (MM). Luckily, my thesis was approved AS. Naturally, I was delighted with the result. I thanked them all and we shook hands. In advance of the examination, I had chosen a clip from one of my favorite Dubé plays, *Un simple soldat*, as a way of thanking them for being part and parcel of my Ph.D. "adventure". I asked them if they would be interested in viewing it. They said they would. We watched in silence as Joseph, the main character, interpreted by the actor Jean Perraud, raged against his family and himself, in the role of the "ordinary" soldier, giving life to the words written by Dubé in a pivotal play, one that another influential Québec playwright, Michel Tremblay, viewed on TV as a young man, in the company of his deaf father, a play that had a tremendous influence on his concept of what modern Québec theatre should be like. Afterwards, André Tremblay, the Graduate Counsellor, asked all of us to follow him to the staff lounge so that a picture of the group could be taken for posterity. Right after it, I invited the group for lunch but, in typical fashion when it comes to professors, all had previous commitments except my thesis director. The two of us went to a little French restaurant on Yorkville, not far from the French Department, where we shared a delicious meal over a bottle of French red wine while we talked about our respective life adventures. It was a memorable occasion. Before going to the restaurant though, I phoned my wife to tell her the excellent news. She was relieved that everything had turned out OK not only for my sake, but also for hers, too!

Now, according to the instructions provided by the SGS, it was a question of having the thesis printed. I went to the University of Toronto Bookstore, located at the Koffler Center, and within a couple of weeks I had three copies in my hands of my "masterpiece", one for the Department, one for Professor Lord, and one for myself. Also, I had to submit by May 23rd an Electronic Thesis & Dissertation (ETD) to the School of Graduate Studies. My Convocation would be in November of 2017.

In June, Professor Michelucci finished his tour of duty as Chair of the Department of French at St. George. He had assumed that position in 2012 and, five years later, it was time for him to pass the torch to somebody else. He was not the only leader who had served with distinction across many departments at the University of Toronto. Consequently, the University was having a reception to honour all its Academic Leaders on June 14th, at 4:00 p.m. Professor Michelucci had been not only a very efficient Chair of the French Department, but also a tremendous supporter of La Troupe des Anciens during his tenure. Madame and I decided to attend the reception to congratulate him personally for his services to the Department as well as for his unwavering support for our troupe. He appreciated our presence at the party.

For the first time in a long, long time, I enjoyed a summer free from academic endeavors of any kind; instead, I turned my attention to my own backyard and to some serious gardening; it was a refreshing change of pace and scenery. We also visited our daughter a couple of times that summer: first in Bancroft, in June, and in Mattawa, in August. In June, after living in two different chalets throughout the fall and winter, they had rented in Bancroft proper a basement apartment that was, in my humble opinion, a fire trap. It was a depressing place. Fortunately, they did not stay there long. The reason for the trip to Mattawa was mainly to keep Natasha company after work for a couple of days. Although most of the time she could work from home, now and then she was required to travel to Mattawa because that is where the Canadian Institute of Forestry has its main office. We stayed at Le Voyageur Inn, not too far from the Canadian Institute of Forestry. It was an enjoyable time in Mattawa even though there wasn't much to do in the town. Luckily, Le Voyageur Inn, to our great surprise, had a decent Thai restaurant.

In the fall of 2017, I was still entitled to teach from September to December because my graduation was going to take place in November. To that end, I applied for a double TA position: FSL 102H1F TUT 0201 T 4-5 AH 204; TUT 5101 T 6-7 AH 103, under the supervision of Dr. Phoebe Boivy, at St. George, and FRE180H5F, under the supervision of an old colleague, Dr. Caroline Lebrec, at UTM. FSL 102 was going to be exclusively taught online with the exception of the first class. FRE180, was a prerequisite for FRE280, a course that I had taught a few times before. Both courses were for students who had graduated from grade 12 French and intended, perhaps, to go on to do a minor or even a major in French Studies. I was especially curious as to how the online course would play out because I had never taught an online course before. I was intrigued by how the interaction between myself and the students would be like in a remote teaching situation and if it was an effective way to actually teach a language. By December, surely, I would have the answers to my queries, and I did.

On August 29th, the CEEF General Meeting took place in Barrie. On August 31st, it was the Orientation Meeting for TAs at St. George and, on September 5th, at UTM. These would be the last ones that I would be attending; it was a bittersweet moment. In one of them, one of the professors pointed out to those in attendance that I had just defended successfully my thesis. A round of applause followed the announcement. It's always encouraging, especially for those who just started their Ph.D. studies, to learn that someone actually did complete them and was moving on to greater and better things. On September 19th, I attended a workshop at Robarts on Blackboard Collaborate, the platform used for course delivery which proved to be quite useful. On September 27th, Professor Rosa Saverino invited me to do a presentation on *Au retour des oies blanches* in her FRE 314 class, a very enjoyable experience too. The next day, Madame and I met with Professor Alexie Tcheuyap, the new Chair of the French Department, to discuss the publication of a "coffee table" type book celebrating the Troupe des Anciens' 50th Anniversary which would take place in the spring of 2019. We were looking for financial support from the Department for this worthwhile project. He was most receptive to the idea and promised that he would look into it and get back to us soon. In October, I started visiting high schools to promote CEEF exchanges, an activity that would go all the way to the beginning of December. Also, in October, the Troupe des Anciens Board of Directors' Meeting occurred and it was decided that we would stage *Les Fourberies de Scapin* and *Huit jours à la campagne* by Jules Renard in April of 2018. Finally, in October, we returned to Bancroft to celebrate my wife's birthday with our daughter and son-in-law. In November, the rehearsals for the two plays started in earnest and, as in previous years, I did my fair share of them. November 9th, 2017, all of sudden was upon us and it would be a big day for me – it was my Convocation. My wife, my daughter and my aunt, my mother's sister, the only living member of my parents' generation, attended the special event. Afterwards, we went to an Italian restaurant to celebrate the occasion. On November 22nd, it was the annual CEEF Information

Meeting for students and parents who were considering an exchange in 2019. The following day, I did a presentation at Upper Canada College on *Un simple soldat*. A former colleague of mine, Sophie Berezoski, whom I had attracted to Harbord Collegiate many years before, was teaching there now and her students were studying the play. On December 4th, I did another one at Cardinal Carter Academy, this time on *Florence*. It was Anna Faraone, whom I had met through CEEF, and who was a Curriculum Advisor for the TCDSB, who had invited me this time to address the students. On December 18th, there was a special meeting of the Board of Directors of La Troupe des Anciens to discuss the celebrations planned for the Troupe's Golden Anniversary in 2019. This type of meeting would become more and more frequent as the date of the festivities got closer and closer and my involvement in it more and more pronounced.

By December, both of my fall courses had come to an end and it was time to take stock of what had happened. With regards to FSL 102, the online course that had intrigued me, I have to admit that I was disappointed with the way it unfolded. It was not the content of the course itself that was the source of the disappointment but rather the impersonal nature of the overall experience for myself and the students enrolled in it. I am not convinced that delivering a language course online is the best way for students to gain accuracy and fluency in the language under study. For one thing, the person-to-person interactions are severely limited. There is something to be said about the dynamics of in-person teaching and learning, a critical aspect of education that came to the forefront during COVID-19. As for the second, the FRE180 course at UTM, it was a pleasure to teach it and to deal with real students, in a classroom setting, who had just transitioned from high school to university, and to collaborate, once again, with Caroline. Alas, for the last time! From that point on I would not be involved anymore in the teaching of any course. I had started my teaching career in 1978 and now it was 2017. Thirty-nine years had flown by. I was more than ready to face other challenges and engage in pastimes for personal gratification alone. I was sixty-five years old and time was marching on faster and faster, so it seemed. And time, as everybody knows, is a luxury that nobody has the right to waste.

THREE

The Late Years

20

Retirement Living, 2018-

Looking forward to the immediate future, I was planning to devote most of my time to CEEF exchanges, the rehearsals and staging of the annual French Play at the University of Toronto and, almost immediately, the 2019 Golden Anniversary of La Troupe des Anciens. The remaining free time would be taken up by reading for pleasure and, perhaps, engaging in a bit of writing, too. My wife and I were also planning to do some travelling before it would be too late. Besides devoting myself to these activities, my daughter, from time to time, still needed my help in the realm of translating technical information from English to French for her work. Naturally, I would be glad to give her a hand.

In early January, my wife and I spent a lovely week in Bonita Springs, Florida. We needed the time to relax at the beach. We joined Eduarda, Constantino, her husband, and Gabriela, at the condo that they were renting for a month there. One of their daughters, Wendy, surprised us by being in the area on vacation at the same time with one of her sons, Nate.

In late January of 2018, the usual Pre-Departure meeting took place at the TCDSB. This one meant something special to me because at the beginning of February I would be taking one of the groups to Paris. Normally, on account of my obligations at the University of Toronto, I was only able to pick up students at the end of their exchange in late April or at the beginning of May. This time, my wife and I thought that it would be a great idea if, after dropping off the students in Paris, we could fly to Lisbon for a week or so. We had never been to Lisbon in February. To that end, we proceeded to rent a condo at Rua Ramalho Ortigão, fairly close to the Museu Calouste Gulbenkian and the extraordinary department store El Corte Inglés. The former, is a must stop for anyone who is interested in the arts. We were also lucky to be in Lisbon on a Sunday where concerts are for free at the Gulbenkian. The latter, is a paradise for fashion, food and drink. So, after leaving the students in the able hands of our CEEF partners in France, we took another flight to Lisbon. Unlike the weather in Paris, to our surprise, we found it to be quite pleasant in Portugal's beautiful capital city in February. The skies were consistently blue and the weather dry. The temperature wavered between fifteen and twenty degrees most days, a great temperature for exploring the city on foot. And, because the soccer season was well underway, we got tickets to see a game between Sporting CP and CD Feirense at the Estádio José Alvalade, the home of Sporting CP. On another day, we took the commuter train to lovely Cascais and walked along the board walk from there to Estoril where we visited the famous Casino. On yet another occasion, we took the ferryboat from Lisbon to Almada to purposely visit the Santuário de Cristo Rei from the top of which one can enjoy an amazing view of the Tejo, the river that goes by Lisbon on its way to the Atlantic Ocean, and Lisbon itself. And still on another occasion we made it to Parque das Nações. The rest of the time was devoted to exploring the *baixa*, downtown, stopping at cafés for a delicious *queijada de nata*, a Portuguese delicacy, and a shot of *Vinho do Porto*, a drink that is guaranteed to put you in the right mood every single time, and by going to different restaurants for dinner. It was a trip to remember.

Back in Canada, it was the season to conduct CEEF Home Interviews, attending rehearsals for the upcoming production of *Les Fourberies de Scapin* and *Huit jours à la campagne*, and numerous meetings related to the 50th Anniversary of La Troupe des Anciens, and still manage to get in the odd CEEF presentation in a high school.

On March 7th, 2018, the Board of Directors of La Troupe des Anciens met for a special meeting where the events of 2019 were discussed formally for the first time. We all agreed that a social event was desirable and Madame suggested that the publication of a "coffee table" type of book would be a wonderful legacy. In order to see this to fruition a couple of subcommittees were struck: one dealing with the reception and the second one having to do with the book. I was part of both of them. It was agreed that the two subcommittees would convene frequently to discuss progress. To that end, there were meetings on May 26th, June 18th, July 24th and August 1st and 20th. So, the summer was punctuated, every once in a while, with a meeting having to do with the "coffee table" book, a book that turned out to be quite time consuming for all those involved in the project on account of the gathering of the information and the writing itself which was revised many times. The final version was well worth it though. It's a beautiful book that traces the history of this unique troupe in Canada from its origin to 2019. Robert Quickert, a long-standing member of the troupe, myself and Madame were the members of the subcommittee dealing with the details of staging the party for the 50th Celebration. It involved searching the St. George campus of the University of Toronto for a suitable venue to accommodate about 100 guests for the reception, finding out prices, contacting food services and choosing an appropriate menu and refreshments, including wine and beer, drawing up a list of possible guests, etc. Because of the Troupe's long association with St. Michael's College, we finally settled on Charbonnel Lounge, a beautiful venue. A reservation was made for Saturday, May 4th, 2019.

In April of 2018, the two plays were staged with great success, especially *Les Fourberies de Scapin*, a play that contains a dream of a role for any actor who dares to play Scapin, the main character, to the delight of both students and the public at large.

In May, Filomena and I travelled to São Miguel. It was a last-minute type of trip. My wife suspected that her father was quite ill and that his wife was deliberately hiding this fact from his daughters. Her plan of action for the last four years had become abundantly clear to all of us: isolate the bugger as much as possible from his family so that he would be easily manipulated by her. In other words, make him as vulnerable as possible so that she could steal from him. We arrived in Ponta Delgada on May 11th and paid him a surprise visit at home. Filomena's suspicions proved to be quite right. The poor man was lying in bed wide awake, attached to all sorts of dirty buckets filled with urine. He was, for all intents and purposes, just skin and bones. Upon seeing us, one of the first things that he mentioned was that someone was stealing his money. Filomena pursued this line of inquiry and found out that he only had about 4,000 euros in his bank account in Ponta Delgada. That said, we knew that 14,000 US dollars had been withdrawn from his account in the US recently and wired to Ponta Delgada. Of course, he was referring to his wife when he said that someone was stealing his money although he did not have the courage to say so directly. In that, he was being true to his nature because he had been a coward all his life and, in his last few days alive, would remain the same. So, Filomena proceeded to tell him that there was only one person that could have done that transaction – his wife. Although present, she did not deny it and, by not denying it vehemently, she was admitting that she was the "thief". Many subjects were discussed during that first visit and his wife never left the bedroom, not even for a brief second. I am sure that she was afraid that the two of us would make him sign some sort of a document that would be detrimental to her financial well-being. One of the subjects discussed was that, given his weak condition, arrangements had been made for him to be hospitalized in the palliative care unit of the local hospital. The conniving bitch had covered up the extent of his illness to the rest of his family because she did not want anybody to show up unexpectedly in Ponta Delgada. The following day we paid him another visit at home and, after that, visited him every day at the hospital. We returned to Canada on May 25th and, on May 31st, he was dead. In the space of a mere four years of married life his wife had managed to pack him to the hospital on three different occasions. Miraculously, he had survived the first two stints there but he was just too weak to survive a third one. Family and friends suspected that she had been slowly poisoning him although, of course, no one could prove it. Also, the fact that she decided to cremate the old man right away, something that he had never discussed with his family all his life, raised the level of suspicions. He possessed in the US a plot in a cemetery for four people, one that he had purchased when his first wife had passed away with the intention of being buried in it one day and, eventually, his incapacitated daughter, Gabriela, too. So, the decision to cremate him was a surprise to all of us who were not consulted in the matter. He died on May 31st and, on June 1st, he was cremated. For the "happy" widow, it was an effective way of destroying the evidence if there was any. However, by acting so quickly, she added more credence to the belief that something untoward had occurred. In conclusion, he was a vain, foolish old man and paid the price for it.

On another front, June 21st marked the CEEF Pre-Arrival Meeting at the usual TCDSB. The European students had arrived in Canada. On June 28th, we went up to Bancroft to visit our daughter. We stayed at the Sword Inn, in the immediate vicinity of their apartment. Joel and her were living in a dump of a place, a tiny basement apartment which jokingly we referred to as the "fire trap". The good news was that they had started looking around with the intent of buying a house which in fact happened on September 24th. After moving from Finch, they had lived in no less than four different places, including a brief stay in Kirkland Lake. They purchased a chalet-type house just north of Bancroft in an established and safe residential area. They had decided to put down roots in that lovely area of our province. We were all ecstatic. Finally, they would have a place that they could call home.

As for us, we travelled by car to Massachusetts on September 27th to attend a family wedding on the 29th. Instead of driving straight through, a long and tedious drive, we decided to stay overnight in Schenectady, New York, and the following day proceed to Plymouth. In Plymouth, we had booked ourselves into Hotel 1620 where many other guests were staying. The festivities started that Friday evening at the East Bay Grille. The church ceremony itself took place in nearby Wareham, at St. Patrick's Church, and the reception at the Pinehills Golf Club. The celebration ended with a delicious brunch on Sunday at the Tavern on the Wharf. We had a great time. After a couple more days spent at Eduarda's home in Burlington, Massachusetts, we were on our way back to Mississauga by way of the Massachusetts Turnpike and the New York Thruway, a route very familiar to the two of us.

As I look at my agenda for 2018-2019, I count no less than thirty meetings having to do with the 50th Anniversary Celebration and the publication of the "coffee table" book. Those connected with the reception started with a meeting between myself, Robert Quickert and Ms. Jennifer DuRoss, Conference Services Supervisor, on September 5th. We had an appointment with her to check out two venues on campus: Father Madden Hall and Charbonnel Lounge. We preferred the second because it would be the perfect size for the number of guests that we were expecting and because of its closeness to Food Services. Next, on September 17th, there was a meeting with Ms. Jessica Barr, the archivist at the Kelly Library, about the possibility of making a donation of the upcoming "coffee table" book to the library as well as of all sorts of archival materials that several members of the troupe had accumulated over the many years (programs, posters, photos, DVDs, VHS tapes, congratulatory notes, etc.). She told us that the library would welcome such a donation. A few days later, on September 24th, the two of us met with Madame to bring her up to date on our findings. On November 14th, Madame and I met with the new Chairperson of the French Department, Professor Alexie Tcheuyap, to inquire to what extent La Troupe des Anciens could count on the Department for financial support in the publishing of the "coffee table" book and the use of Charbonnel Lounge. We were assured that the Department would definitely come up with some funds for the book. How much? We would find out soon, he promised. With regards to the use of Charbonnel, the Department would reserve it for the reception at no cost to us. Great news! On

November 25th, Robert and I met again with Madame to finalize the choice of a venue for the reception. Robert, in the meantime, had paid a visit to Hart House where many rooms exist that would be appropriate for our event. The Buttery, at Trinity College, next door to the George Ignatieff Theatre, and Burwash Hall, at Victoria College, the College closest to St. Mike's were also visited. Renting a venue in any one of these places would be too expensive for our budget. Therefore, the decision was made to go with Charbonnel Lounge, our first choice, anyways. The three of us picked a date: May 4th. On November 30th, Robert and I met again with Ms. DuRoss to make a formal reservation of the venue and to discuss who would be responsible to cater the event. She suggested we speak with Mr. Arsen Tauchelov, Food Service Director, Chartwells, responsible for the cafeterias at St. Mike's. A meeting with him was set up for March 27th.

In the meantime, while these meetings were going on, parallel ones were taking place too. On October 15th La Troupe des Anciens got together for the first rehearsal of *L'Avare*, the choice for our April shows. On December 9th, 16th and 30th, there were meetings with Madame, mostly having to do with the content of the book. The book was slowly but surely taking shape and, on the other front, the details of the social event were becoming clearer to all of us by the day.

January was a great month for Filomena and me. We returned to Naples, Florida, for a two-week stay at our *compadres'* condominium. Filomena's sister Eduarda, her husband and Gabriela were also in nearby Bonita Springs for their one-month in the sun. What made this particular trip different from the 2018 one was that Ana, our *comadre*, came to stay with us during the last few days of our trip. It was great to spend some quality time with her.

On January 25th, the rehearsals resumed and, two days later, on January 27th, the meetings of the two subcommittees as well. On February 7th, I left for Paris on CEEF business. After a few days in the City of Lights, my wife and I flew to Prague and, afterwards, took a train from there to Vienna. It would be our first time in both the Czech Republic and Austria. We took full advantage of the opportunity to see as much of the two cities as possible and a bit of the countryside during the train ride.

Now, every time that we found ourselves in Paris, we stayed at a comfortable little hotel called Hôtel Opéra Cadet, located on a peaceful pedestrian street full of *pâtisseries, boulangeries*, wine stores, mini markets, a couple of restaurants, and within a three-minute walk to a subway station, Cadet. On this particular trip, we had the pleasure of attending the performance of a comedy entitled *Un Week-end tranquille*, at the Grande-Comédie. As the title suggested, given that it was a comedy, there was nothing "peaceful" about the weekend. The play was hilarious. The theatre was packed, a good indication of the popularity of the show. It was a fun way to spend part of the evening. During our brief stay in Paris, we strolled down the Champs Élysées to the Louvre, went to the Trocadéro for a close-up view of Tour Eiffel, rested for a while at the peaceful Jardin du Luxembourg, made a mandatory stop at Notre Dame and even went as far as the Cathédrale Saint-Denis to check it out. Filomena also paid a couple of visits to Galleries Lafayette and Au Printemps, two of the most iconic department stores in France. They were a pleasant walk along Rue Lafayette from our hotel. It goes without saying that we walked alongside the Seine for a while just to enjoy the sights of the iconic Parisian monuments as they came into view.

I cannot continue this memoir without putting in a few words about two amazing cities: Prague and Vienna. With respect to the former, my friend André Tremblay, who had studied for a while at Charles University in the 1980s, gave me a few pointers with regards to the most important monuments and places of interest in *Matka Měst*, Mother of Cities. He also warned me about pickpockets and their preferred technique for taking a distracted tourist to the cleaners: they worked in twos in the subway system and also had a liking for trams and streetcars and, when the innocent tourist was about to disembark, they would block him or her, push the individual to the ground, and proceed to steal a purse or a knapsack. They liked to target older tourists like myself and my wife. Fortunately for us, his good-intentioned warning did not materialize. In fact, we found Praguers quite friendly and helpful. I guess the city's reputation had improved significantly ever since André's undergraduate experience there. In any case, we had our list of monuments to see and places to visit such as Prague Castle, St. Vitus Cathedral, Charles Bridge, Old Town Square, The Loreto, Wenceslas Square, Petřín Hill, the Spanish Synagogue, etc. Before leaving Canada, we had made a reservation to attend a performance of Mozart's opera *Don Giovanni* at the gorgeous Estates Theater, Stavovské divadlo, where it had been staged for the first time. After a short flight from Paris to Prague, we took the bus from the airport to the main train station and from there walked to the Hotel Grandium Praha, our hotel, just a short distance away on foot. The Grandium was not only very comfortable, but it also had a breakfast buffet that was something to die for, served with a complimentary glass of sparkling wine, first thing in the morning. It was also close enough to many of the places that we wanted to see. Upon checking in, thanks to Mr. Václav Roztočil, the concierge, a very helpful and friendly man, he suggested we take a guided tour of the city to get our bearings straight and to visit briefly a few key monuments. It was a great idea. We signed up for the Grand City tour which included the Prague Castle and Charles Bridge. He also informed us that he had received our tickets for the opera at the Estates Theater the following evening. The next morning, after breakfast, we found ourselves in the company of a young woman, Irena, a university graduate, who spoke very good English and who had just recently become a tour guide. My wife and I were the only ones with her. We spent an entire morning and part of the afternoon with our "private" guide. We were spoiled. At first, we did some sightseeing in a minivan and, afterwards, a lot of walking with her leading the way and explaining in detail all sorts of information about the Czech Republic and the monuments that we came across. It was obvious that she was a proud Praguer and that she enjoyed her job. At one moment, we stopped at a café shop, a Kavárna, of her choice to drink coffee and hot chocolate and to taste *ovocné knedlíki*, dumplings stuffed with strawberries. It was our treat. She eventually left us at the Old Town Square, in front of Astronomical Clock, where we watched in amazement the Prague *Orloj* in action, something that happens at the top of every hour to the delight of all in attendance.

Back at the hotel, before setting out to the opera, our friendly concierge alerted us that there would be a concert at the Spanish Synagogue on Thursday, April 14th, Valentine's Day. He did not have to waste his time to convince us that this would be a glorious opportunity. Of course, we signed up for it right away. He also pointed out a restaurant, almost in front of the Grandium, Restaurace Bredovský dvůr, that served typical Czech food, such as *guláš*, goulash, *utopence*, pickled sausages, *halušky*, plump little noodles, etc., and incredible beer, especially Pilsner Urquell and Staropramen, all to be had for a very modest price. That evening, we had a delicious meal there accompanied by Urquell that came directly from the vats that were in plain view of the patrons, by the bar area. They were a beautiful sight to behold. The restaurant was packed with locals, always a good sign that the food is great and that the prices are reasonable.

Don Giovanni turned out to be an unforgettable experience. It was sung in Italian with Czech and English surtitles. The theater itself is exquisite and it was packed with mostly natives dressed for a night at the opera, a sight to behold in itself. We felt privileged to be in attendance at this particular opera so many years after its premiere had taken place in that very theatre.

The next day, we returned to the Castle. We wanted to take another look at St. Vitus Cathedral and take a stroll down the Golden Lane, called thus because goldsmiths, in order to avoid paying guild dues, constructed tiny little houses built right into the thick castle walls. Franz Kafka (1883-1924), Prague's best-known writer, lived in one of them himself for a while and it is believed that he wrote a few of his novels while living there, perhaps even *The Trial*. After that, we went up to Petřín Hill to see the Loreto and, especially, a replica of the original Santa Casa in Loreto, in Italy, famous for two reasons: firstly, because it contains the miracle-working statue of Our Lady of Loreto and, secondly, because the Santa Casa is a replica of the Holy Family's house in Nazareth. Afterwards, we took a short walk to the Strahov Monastery, founded in 1140, which houses the magnificent Strahov Library where the nation's oldest books are kept, a must-see. Furthermore, the frescoes in the Theological Room are a sight to behold.

On our way back to Staré Mésto, Old Town, we stopped for a late lunch at U Medvídku, a very typical Czech restaurant, established in 1466. The waitress was courteous and the food hearty. The beer was, as usual, to die for.

Regarding the Spanish Synagogue, considered by many to be the "most beautiful synagogue in Europe", the least that can be said about its interior is that it is "opulent". The Jewish community holds regular services in it and it is also the home of Jewish Museum Exhibits, offices and a reference center. But that is not all; it also serves as a music venue. We heard pieces from Bernstein, Gershwin, Dvorak, Mozart, etc., performed by the Czech Collegium. The music was fantastic. The concert was a bonus that had, unexpectedly, come our way out of the blue.

And, because it was Valentine's Day, the Grandium was celebrating it with a special dinner menu at the Ingarden, its main restaurant. After the concert at the Spanish Synagogue, we returned to the hotel to take advantage of the offer. Dinner started with a glass of Prosecco Spumante DOC Seseníssimo, Extra Dry, followed by soup, cauliflower cream with homemade ravioli filled with mushrooms, truffle oil, succeeded by a main course, glazed supreme chicken breasts of corn chicken on saffron risotto with black olives and sugar peas, sauce with fresh oregano. The meal culminated with dessert, chocolate fondant with fresh strawberries and candied rose petals accompanied by either coffee or tea. After such a meal, both of us needed a good walk; we set out to the Old Town Square for the last time. It was our farewell walk as the next day we were taking the train to Vienna.

After a very pleasant train ride from Prague to Vienna, we made it to our hotel and right afterwards proceeded to explore the city. The weather in Vienna was much more pleasant than in Prague. It was sunny and mild and very conducive to walking everywhere. Although Vienna lacks the quaintness of Prague, it is a beautiful city with many charms of its own among them are: The Hofburg, Spanish Riding School, Stephansdom, The Belvedre, Karlskirche, Museum Quartier, Staatsoper, Schloss Schönbrunn, etc. Empress Maria Theresa and Emperor Franz Joseph so-called "creative splurges" during the time of the Austro-Hungarian Empire definitely put the city on the map of the world.

Before we had left Canada, we had already made reservations at the Volksoper to see *Eine Nacht in Venedig*, *A Night in Venice*, an operetta by Johann Strauss II, on February 17th. The best thing that we did upon arriving at the HBF Wien was the purchase of a 3-Day Vienna Ticket that entitled us to travel by subway, tram or bus everywhere within the city. We took full advantage of it to move about quickly from place to place. We found the Vienna subway system not only efficient, but also safe and clean. We also quickly realized that Vienna, just like Prague, was a very walkable city.

A word or two about a couple of landmarks and two shows. The first, St. Stephen's Cathedral, is Vienna's favorite landmark and Austria's best preserved Gothic religious building. Its interior is splendid, especially the high altar behind which are the five medieval stained-glass windows depicting biblical stories as well as the life and Passion of Jesus. In one of our visits, the choir was singing and the music was divine. The exterior, however, is just as impressive starting with its western towers, the Giant's Door and, of course, its unique Tiled Roof made up of nearly 230,000 colourful tiles displayed in symmetric patterns. The second, Schloss Schönbrunn, the summer residence of the Habsburgs, was built between 1695 and 1713 and Empress Maria Theresa had a major hand in its design. The interior is mostly in the Rococo style. It's decadent. The façade was redone between 1817-1819 and it was painted in "Schönbrunn yellow", the Habsburgs' favorite colour. The garden behind the palace is magnificent, too, reflective of an era where there was no shortage of money among the Austrian elite.

What hasn't been said about the world-renowned Spanish Riding School? It puts on a show to leave you speechless. The white, elegant, Lipizzaner stallions are simply beautiful to look at and the performance that the riders get out of them is incredible; it just proves how intelligent these animals are. On average, it takes about eight years of sustained training before the horses are ready to perform to the public at large. Given the fact that they are already four years old when they arrive at the Spanish Riding School, it means that they only start performing publicly when they are about twelve years old. It's interesting to note that the foals are born dark-skinned and only get their white coat between the ages of four and ten. As for the riders, they also have to put in quite a few years mastering classical dressage and other riding techniques before they are equally "ready". Although they have been mostly male over the centuries, there have been since 2008 a few female riders. The project is really a labour of love. Because we were in Vienna in the winter, the show took place in the Winter Riding School, an elegant 56 m long hall built in 1735. The horses originally came from Spain in 1562 thanks to Emperor Maximilian II, hence the name of the school.

Our evening at the Volksoper Wien, Vienna People's Opera, was enjoyable. Again, just like in Prague, we were amazed by how patrons tried their best to look spiffy for the occasion, in contrast with the relaxed manner in which many Canadians will dress for a similar show. The venue itself opened to the public in 1898 and is considered the "home" of the operetta in Vienna. An operetta is by its own definition a short opera that is amusing in character because the public knows in advance that "all is well that ends well". That said, at the Volksoper, operas, musicals and ballet are also performed. The venue stages close to three hundred performances per year. No small feat. It can accommodate 1,261 spectators and, for *A Night in Venice*, it was filled to capacity. The operetta itself was funny, the acting was excellent and the music engaging. It all made for a well-spent evening in Vienna.

We also enjoyed very much going for leisurely strolls from Stephansdom to Staatsoper, on Karntner Strasse and, from the cathedral to the

Hofburg Palace, along Graben and Kohl Markt. A lovely pedestrian zone with lots of shops, cafés and restaurants.

Back in Toronto via Paris, it was time to rejoin the rehearsals in progress for *L'Avare*, conduct In-home interviews for CEEF, complete revisions for the publication of the "coffee table" book, revisit Professor Tcheuyap to find out how much money the French Department was prepared to donate for the publication of the book, and finalize the menu for the reception with Mr. Tauchelov. On top of all these activities, when my former colleague at UTM Caroline Lebrec asked me to serve as a judge at the Soirée des Talents to be held on March 20th, I agreed to it.

On March 26th, Madame and I met again with Professor Tcheuyap. We brought with us a sample copy of the "coffee table" book for his perusal. He was most impressed with it and announced that La Troupe des Anciens could count on a significant gift from the Department toward its publication - $4,000.00. We were delighted. On the basis of his pronouncement, at the next meeting of the subcommittee in charge of the book, it was agreed that its sale price would be $50.00. There would be a limited edition of 100 copies, with the possibility of ordering additional copies if needed. The steps to make it available to the *fidèles* and the public at large were considered and agreed upon. Also, as a token of our appreciation to the teachers and their students who would be attending the matinées, and the general public who would come to the evening performances in April, Souvenir Pens with the following words engraved in them: *La Troupe des Anciens - 50 Ans de Théâtre français à Toronto* inscribed in them, would be given out for free, as a memento of the incredible milestone. Given our long association with St. Michael's College, the pens would be blue with white lettering. 700 hundred pens were ordered for the student audience and 400 pens for the adult patrons.

On another front, Robert and I met on March 27th with Mr. Tauchelov to discuss menu options, prices and the room's configuration for the reception. We left the meeting with two possible options and a cost estimate to share with the Board of Directors. On April 18th, we met and it was decided that La Troupe des Anciens would set aside a budget of $5,000.00 for the reception. All of us agreed that it had to be something special. On April 24th, we met with Mr. Ross D'Souza, Assistant to the Food Service Director, with our final choice regarding the menu and beverages. They were agreeable to Food Services. Once this important issue was dealt with, we requested to have Charbonnel Lounge available to La Troupe des Anciens from 3 to 6 o'clock with the reception itself starting at 4 o'clock. The request was promptly approved.

L'Avare, in the meantime, played on April 9th and 10th to the high school crowd and on the 12th and 13th to the public at large. The play, with François-Michel Pellequer interpreting the role of Harpagon, was a smashing success. It played to full houses. The shows arrived in the nick of time, so to speak, a perfect moment to publicize widely the sale of the "coffee table" book, hand out the Souvenir Pens, and remind the loyal fans that the reception for the 50th Anniversary was happening in three weeks. People were both appreciative and delighted with the unexpected souvenir and the upcoming celebration.

Now, during the final days before the reception, it was just a question of continuing to advertise the event widely so that the expected crowd would indeed materialize for it. The Board of Directors and the two subcommittees spared no effort in promoting the 50th Anniversary of La Troupe des Anciens. All of us had a vested interest in making it a tremendous success and, indeed, May 4th was so on all counts. Here is a description of how the event unfolded:

Set-up

15:00		Roberto Machado and Robert Quickert arrive
	15:00-15:45	Set up books, name tags, decorations
	15:30	Catering aim to be ready
15:45		Ready for early arrival check-in at book/name tag desk

Formal Start

16:00	Event begins
16:30-16:45	Marc di Ruggiero on the piano

17:00   Short speech by Professor Paulette Collet
17:15-17:20   Cake cutting
17:20-17:30   Roberto Machado announces Concours de citations
17:30-17:45   Marc di Ruggiero on the piano
17:50   Announcement of the three winners of the Concours de citations
18:00   Formal end of event

Tear Down

18:00   Removal of decorations, clean-up of name tags and book desk
18:15   Departure

The menu itself consisted of the following items:

Food
Cheese platters (Sauvagine, Aged Cheddar, Jarlsberg)
Pâté (Antoine's Black Pepper)
Bread and crackers
Fresh fruit platter (large)
Vegetable dip platter (large)
Bruschetta
Prosciutto Grissini
Smoked salmon & cream cheese crostini

Beverages
Alcoholic:
Niagara College Red and White wine
Cava sparkling wine
Beer (Stella Artois, Mill Street Organic)
Non-alcoholic:
Coffee (regular, decaf)
Tea
Canned pop
Sparkling water

As I mentioned before, it was a celebration worthy of a troupe that had existed for fifty years thanks to the dedication, persistence and vision of its artistic director, Professor emeritus Paulette Collet. It was a proud moment for the Board of Directors and all members of the Troupe des Anciens who had been part and parcel of the event in one way or another over the decades. Now that it was over, we could breathe a sigh of relief and move on to other challenges among which there would be one that was not in anybody's mind at the time – a pandemic which caused the cancellation of our 2020 to 2022 shows.

A few days after the reception, in May, the CEEF Matching of students took place in Barrie. Always an activity to look forward to on account of the friendly people who gathered there to engage in the process. Filomena, for her part, took advantage of the opportunity to visit our *comadre* at Grippen Lake. We reunited in Mississauga on May 10th and promptly took off to Bancroft to visit our daughter for a couple of days.

On May 15th, Robert and I met with Ms. Jessica Barr, the Kelly Library archivist, to discuss the details of the donation of La Troupe des Anciens' 50th Anniversary Book and the handing over of all the resources accumulated by individual members of the troupe to the Kelly Library archives. It was decided that Madame, accompanied by myself and Robert, would formally do that on September 10th, 2019, at 3:15, right at the beginning of the new academic year, at the library.

Another memorable moment in 2019 occurred when my wife and I attended Mitó's wedding in São Miguel. Mitó is, of course, a short form for Maria Antónia, one of Conceição's two daughters. The last wedding that I had attended in Ponta Delgada had been in the late 1960s, when I was still a teenager and living in the island. It had been a traditional one. We were curious as to what a modern-day wedding would look like. To that end, we flew to Ponta Delgada on June 7th and were greeted at the airport by Conceição and Noé, her husband. We had rented a car for the two and a half weeks that we would be in São Miguel. The idea was to stay in the summer family home in Furnas that belonged to Filomena's side of the family and to use the location as a springboard to revisit other towns and villages throughout the island that we were familiar with and that we enjoyed seeing every time that we returned to our birthplace. The wedding itself took place in Vila Franca do Campo, at five o'clock, in a lovely beachfront restaurant, and the reception was held under a huge tent adjoining it. It was a wonderful event that lasted until five o'clock in the morning. The company was delightful, the food delicious and the beverages abundant, which made for a memorable occasion. After it, we drove back to Furnas. We were, at that late hour, the only ones on the road. The moon was shining and the sky was full of stars. It was a gorgeous night.

We returned to Canada on June 26th because on June 29th my very good friend Sandra Hryhor, a colleague at the TDSB, was tying the knot with Roberto Freile, a wonderful guy from Ecuador. The exchanging of the vows took place in the Old Mill's Chapel and the reception at the Canadiana Reception Hall. Again, like Mito's wedding, it was a lovely event, one that marked the end of formal occurrences before the long days of summer.

On July the 25th, La Troupe des Anciens' Board of Directors met at Madame's residence, our usual meeting place, to take stock of the three 2019 accomplishments. It was agreed by all in attendance that the publication of the "coffee style" book, the play performances, and the 50th Anniversary Reception had not only met, but also exceeded all of our expectations. We congratulated one another on a job well done. I took the opportunity to inform the Board that Madame, Robert and I would be visiting the Kelly Library on September 10th and that Madame would formally hand over two copies of the Anniversary Book to the library and that, at the same time, I would be handing over a box containing memorabilia accumulated ever since 1969, the birth year of La Troupe des Anciens.

The rest of my summer was punctuated by several CEEF Airport duty days as Canadian students left for France or Spain on summer exchanges and as European ones began arriving in August for their three-month exchange. On August 26th, the CEEF General Meeting took place in Barrie. The next day, Robert and I met briefly with

Madame just to go over the details of the upcoming Kelly Library visit. For me, after an extremely busy winter and spring, the summer turned out to be a rather relaxing one which was much appreciated.

On September 10th, Madame formally presented two copies of La Troupe des Anciens' 50th Anniversary Book to the Kelly Library in the presence of the aforementioned Ms. Jessica Barr, Mr. Richard Carter, Reference Librarian, Mr. David Hagelaar, Associate Chief Librarian, and Mr. Korto Zambeli-Tardif, reporter for *The Mike*, the College's newspaper. Afterwards, I presented Ms. Barr with a good size box containing a treasure trove of materials having to do with the life and times of our beloved troupe.

A few days later, on September 24th, La Troupe des Anciens' Board of Directors Meeting took place. As usual, on the official agenda there were several items to be addressed such as: Artistic Director's Report, Report on ticket sales for student matinées, Financial Report, Election of Directors and Officers as needed, Announcement of play selection and performance dates for 2021, etc. Madame chose the ill-fated *Tartuffe* that, of course, never saw the light of day due to COVID-19.

September 27th marked the day that my friend André Tremblay, the now former Graduate Counsellor, retired. His retirement party took place in the little pub on Bay Street, across from the French Department, where we had had a pint every now and then over the years. Given André's friendliness and his competence at work, his party was well attended by the staff of the French Department, graduate students and fellow CUPE members.

October marked the beginning of CEEF school presentations and it also marked the month that my daughter and her husband went on vacation to the Azores. They would be visiting four of its islands: São Miguel, Faial, São Jorge and Pico from October 16th to the 31st. The highlight for them came when they climbed to the top of Pico, the mountain that gave the island its name and the highest point in Portugal, at a mere 2,351 m above sea level, on a glorious and clear day, so unusual at that time of the year. From its summit, they could see the islands of nearby São Jorge and Faial and, in the distance Graciosa and Terceira, an incredible sight.

On October 23rd, Filomena had to make a last minute one-week trip to São Miguel herself to sort out some legal matters having to do with her father's inheritance. At some point, she met up with Natasha and Joel and all three of them returned to Canada on the same flight on October 31st. It was an added bonus for my wife and her dear daughter as now they only saw each other from time to time.

Just a few days later, on November 17th, Filomena's aunt, her father's sister, who lived in Ponta Delgada, died at the ripe old age of 94. She was the last surviving member of her family. Filomena made another trip to Ponta Delgada on November 20th for the funeral and to dispose of the contents of the house where her aunt lived. She returned to Canada on December 4th. The last months of 2019 were proving to be quite busy and stressful after a relaxing summer, especially for my wife.

November marked an important month for me. After a regular visit to my friendly Optometrist, Dr. Brian Feldman, in 2018, it was discovered that I had cataracts on both eyes, a clear sign that I was ageing. He recommended I see Dr. Allan Slomovic, a Cornea, Anterior Segment and Refractive Surgeon, at Toronto's Western Hospital, to start the process leading to cataract surgery. After a long wait period, I finally got to see him on November 4th. Because I wear contact lenses, the first thing that I was told to do was that for the next month I could not wear them at all so that precise measurements could be taken. For someone with keratoconus like myself, believe me, it was a huge sacrifice not to be able to wear contacts. That said, you have to do what you have to do. My CEEF school presentations that were under way had to be interrupted, my eyesight was simply not good enough to drive from school to school without contacts. On December 1st, all measurements were taken and, a couple of days later, the CEEF presentations as well as the rehearsals for *Tartuffe* resumed for me.

On December 8th, Filomena left for Peterborough to give her cousin Ana Paula a hand. She is bipolar and every now and then goes through a bout of depression. Her cousin, however, has many other personality flaws: she is hypocritical, cowardly and, worse of all, a traitor towards her own family. Not surprisingly, after being looked after for a few days, reacting in typical fashion, Ana Paula did not have the courtesy to drive my wife to the local bus terminal and, instead, it was Filomena herself who had to call for a taxi in order to get there. Once again, her dear cousin had proved to be most ungrateful.

Shortly afterwards, it was Christmas with its many festivities. Natasha and Joel arrived on December 21st and left on Christmas Day to travel to Ottawa to spend some time with his mother and sister and, afterwards, to Cornwall, to be with his father. Because his parents are divorced, getting together with both of them, and with us, is always a challenge at festive times of the year. It is what it is.

Because Filomena and I would be in Europe on CEEF business once again in February and, therefore, not around to celebrate Natasha's birthday, we decided to drive up to Bancroft for a few days in early January. Now, driving to a snowbelt community in the winter is always a dicey affair. This time around was even worse as there was snow and frozen rain to contend with, always a deadly combination. I also made the huge mistake of driving there in our SAAB AERO 93 convertible, definitely the wrong type of car to drive in the winter time anywhere but, especially, in the countryside on account of the cabin being so close to the ground. It was a nightmare returning to Mississauga on Sunday, January 12th. Luckily, after a few detours on account of a road accident, we made it home. I swore never to repeat the experience.

On January 16th, the CEEF Pre-Departure Meeting took place. My wife and I would be taking a group of students to Frankfurt and Berlin on February 7th. After a few days in Germany's capital, we would be flying to Warsaw, followed by another flight to Budapest and, finally, a return trip to Toronto via Frankfurt. The two of us were especially looking forward to seeing Warsaw and Budapest. We were keen on discovering Warsaw's Old Town on foot. We also had made prior reservations to see *The Magic Flute* at the opera house, to attend a Chopin

Concerto and to visit the Warsaw Uprising Museum. In Budapest, it was the exquisite Hungarian Parliament Building, the Great Synagogue, St. Stephen's Basilica, the Gellért Hotel and Baths, where we were staying, and the Danube itself that interested us. More about these two amazing cities in the next paragraphs.

Regrettably, the weather in Berlin and Warsaw was not the best: grey skies, rain off and on and strong winds. In Budapest, however, it was perfect for walking about and very conducive to seeing the sights which were many. It was not our first time in Berlin. That said, it was a pleasure to be back; we went for a stroll on Unter den Linden from Brandenburger Tor to Alexanderplatz, joined a guided tour of the famous Philharmonie, home of the Berlin Philharmonic, one of the world's best if not the best orchestra, a venue praised worldwide for its acoustics. Because our hotel was so close to Tiergarten, we managed to get in a walk through the park in between showers. My wife also had in mind a visit to the amazing KaDeVe, the largest department store in Berlin, to look for a bargain or two. In one of our many walks, by pure chance, we discovered a brand-new family-run restaurant within a five-minute walk of our hotel on Budapester Strasse, La Sardegna. The food was delicious, the atmosphere great and the waiters most friendly, a fact that prompter the two of us to return there for a second meal. Before we knew it though, it was Tuesday morning and we were again on our way to the airport to catch a short flight to Warsaw.

Almost right after having made the reservation online for *The Magic Flute*, I realized, to my dismay, that I had made a mistake regarding our availability to attend it. The opera would play on February 15th but, lamentably, on the evening of February 15th we would be already in Budapest. In order to rectify my mistake, I wrote an email to Ms. Polokova, at Teatr Wielki Opera Narodowa, on February 2nd. I was hoping to be able to exchange my pair of tickets for *The Magic Flute* for any other show, hopefully *Halka*, probably Poland's most famous opera, which was scheduled to play on February 14th, Valentine's Day. My email to Ms. Polokova at the Opera House was left without an answer. Being one who does not give up easily, I asked my good friend, Renata Todros, on February 7th, who is Polish, speaks the language fluently and who, furthermore, was at one time a rehearsal pianist at the venue, to contact Ms. Polokova to explain the situation. It was all in vain, Ms. Polokova did not have the courtesy to reply. I tried to contact someone else, a Ms. Kacperczyk and, this time, I did get an answer which read like this:

Dear Sir,

We are really sorry but according to regulations tickets purchased online may only be returned if a performance is cancelled or rescheduled.

Your complaint cannot be taken, sorry.

Best regards,

Zespól Biuri...

It was clear to me that the people at the Opera House had not understood what I was asking for or if they had, they were not prepared to do anything about it. So, upon arriving in Warsaw, we made it a point of going personally to the Opera House's box office to see if we could resolve the issue. Looking at the floor plan for the Friday's performance of *Halka* on the computer monitor, we could see some available seats but, regrettably, the employee claimed that she did not have the authority to switch our Saturday tickets for ones for Friday's show. Nevertheless, she sent us around the corner to see a couple of managers who, perhaps, could do something about it. The two women we spoke with proved to be not only intransigent, but also unfriendly towards tourists such as ourselves. And that was the nature of the first contact that we had with real Varsovians. Intransigence personified. We decided that before leaving town we would offer the tickets to someone who might enjoy *The Magic Flute*. Fortunately, our contact with other natives was much more friendly and cordial than with the employees at the Opera House.

The evening of February 11th, while looking for a restaurant to have dinner in the immediate neighborhood of the Hampton, our hotel, we passed in front of the Marriott, right across from the Central Railway

Station, a hotel with a great view of the Palace of Culture. We looked up and saw that there was a restaurant on the second floor that was strategically located at the corner of Aleje Jerozolimskie and Emili Plater with an amazing, unobstructed view of the Palace of Culture. We decided to walk in and check it out. And that's how we met Bernard, one of the Maîtres d'hôtel at the restaurant in question who happened to be serving a platter of appetizers in the hotel's lobby. One conversation led to another and we could see why management had chosen him to be the point man for the restaurant – he had great interpersonal skills, was very knowledgeable about food and drink and, on top of all that, spoke excellent English. We quickly found ourselves on the restaurant enjoying a great view of Aleje Jerozolimskie below, Central Station right across from us, and the Palace of Culture lighted in purple just a short distance away. Thanks to Bernard, we enjoyed an excellent meal and talked with him about a variety of subjects. The man had travelled widely and was a fountain of knowledge. Before we left the restaurant, totally satisfied, he informed us that the Marriott was having a special Valentine's Day dinner, something that we might want to consider if we did not have any other plans for that evening. Since we were unable to get tickets for *Halka*, we were indeed free and so, on the spot, we made reservations for dinner for two, at eight o'clock, at the Floor No 2 Restaurant, to celebrate Valentine's Day in Warsaw. On the way back to our hotel, we considered whether Bernard would like to attend a performance of *The Magic Flute* with his wife to celebrate, albeit one day later, Valentine's Day. We would ask him if he would entertain the idea on the 14th, at the end of our dinner.

The next few days were busy ones. We had much to discover and much ground to cover. Warsaw, unlike Prague or Vienna, is a city spread over many kilometers. We found that the quickest and most efficient way to get around was by tram, bus or subway. All means of public transit were very efficient, clean and safe. We headed to Old Town first. We wanted to see Sigismund's Column, The Royal Castle, which was completely destroyed during World War II and lovingly rebuilt in the

1970s and 1980s, as was most of the Old Town, in an act of pure hate by the Nazis, St. John's Cathedral, the Old Town Market Square, and The Barbican. Aided by a travelers' book, we slowly made our way from place to place stopping frequently to drink something warm such as Rozgrzewający napar z hibiskusa z wódkąź, roughly translated as Warm elixir of hibiscus with vodka, a drink that indeed kept us walking and exploring. That afternoon, we strolled down Krakowskie Przedmiesci and Nowy Swiat from Sigismund's Column all the way to Charles de Gaulle's Roundabout. We made countless stops to admire the many outstanding buildings along the way: Church of St. Anne, the Presidential Palace, Hotel Bristol, University of Warsaw, the Church of the Holy Cross, etc. Needless to say, we had to enter this last one on account of the fact that in the nave, inside pillars, are urns containing the hearts of Chopin and the writer Reymont, the first Pole to win the Nobel Prize for literature in 1924.

After much walking, it was time to return to the hotel to refresh and go out for supper. We chose a restaurant nearby, Restauracja Sphinx, just up the street from the hotel. The atmosphere was good, the food acceptable and the beer great. Back at the hotel, we made reservations to attend a Chopin Concert the following evening at the Dean's Palace Warsaw Archdiocese Museum. The pianist would be Justyna Galant-Wojciechowska who graduated with distinction from the Łódź Academy of Music and proceeded to be the recipient of many awards in her chosen field. It turned out to be an intimate evening in the company of a very talented and accomplished performer. She played 4 Preludes Op. 28, Mazurka in F major, Waltzes Op. 64 and, after a brief intermission, Fantaisie-Impromptu C sharp minor Op. posth, Polonaise in C minor Op. 40 and, finally, Scherzo in B flat minor Op. 31. All in attendance left most satisfied with the performance and the unique experience of being in such an intimate setting.

Next on our list of places to visit was a mandatory visit to the Muzeum Powstania Warszawskiego, the Warsaw Uprising Museum, located at the corner of Przyokopowa and Grzybowska. I say "mandatory" because one needs to have a sense of the pain and suffering inflicted on Poland by the Nazis during the Second World War. They were bent on bringing the country to its knees and, for a while, succeeded. The exhibit itself is spread over several floors: Basement, Germans in Warsaw and Sewer Replica; Ground Floor, Before the Rising; Mezzanine, The Rising in August; First Floor, September and Surrender and the Liberator Hall with its huge replica of the B-24J Liberator bomber. The Warsaw Uprising Museum houses a most somber exhibit that demonstrates the courage and resilience of the Polish people who suffered tremendous horrors at the hands of the Nazis. In its brochure, one can read the following message:

The Warsaw Rising Museum focuses on events that took place in August and September of 1944. It pays homage to those who fought and died for a free Poland including its capital city. It also disseminates knowledge about the Warsaw Rising though [sic] diverse initiatives and helps today's visitors understand the history from over 70 years ago. The museum connects the past to the present by organizing cultural educational activity and innovative exhibits within a place of remembrance. Modern methods of communication help engage the visitor with the exhibition, facilitating their journey through time.

In my humble opinion, no visitor should ever leave Warsaw without paying a visit to this incredible museum.

Our next stop, to somehow counterbalance the seriousness nature of the first, was a stop at the Zlote Tarasy, The Golden Terrace, a central shopping mall located behind the Main Train Station and across from the Palace of Culture. After lunch in one of its restaurants, we went on a short walk to the Palace of Culture to view another exhibit, a fun one this time: Muzeum Domków Dla Lalek, The Dollhouse Museum. The museum was packed with young children, accompanied mostly by their mothers, who were fascinated and enchanted to be in front of dollhouses of all kinds that somehow resembled their own "toys". On account of the inclement weather, we passed on the opportunity to go up to the 30th floor of the Palac Kultury, Joseph Stalin's personal "gift" to Varsovians, to get a bird's eye view of Warsaw and, instead, opted to return to Old Town for another look around and to take another walk along Krakowskie.

After dinner at a popular hang-out for a younger crowd, Restauracja Vapiano, at the corner of Jerozolimskie and Emilii Plater, we decided to take the tram all the way to Stadion Narodowy, the National Stadium, built for the 2012 UEFA European Championships, on the east side of the Vistula, the river that crosses Warsaw, in an area called Saska Kepa. The lit stadium looked fabulous but the surrounding areas were deserted because there was a fine drizzle and light fog everywhere, not the most pleasant weather conditions to walk around. So, we decided to pack it for the night and returned to the hotel.

We took, the next day, the streetcar all the way to Arkadia, the biggest shopping mall in Warsaw. The ride took us through several neighborhoods and that, in and of itself, was entertaining. Once there, we noticed that the place was a beehive of activity. Varsovians, young, old and in-between, love shopping. After browsing for a while, we sat down for lunch in one of its many restaurants and, afterwards, took off to the nearest subway stop to return to Nowy Swiat. We wanted to explore on foot a couple of streets: Chimielna, a pedestrianized zone, and Foksal, a street whose buildings miraculously survived the bombings and now house plenty of restaurants and bars. After so much walking, we were tired and decided to return to the hotel to freshen up before going out to our Valentine's dinner at the Marriott at the end of which we would gladly give Bernard our tickets for *The Magic Flute*.

The restaurant was decorated for Valentine's Day. There was live music provided by a guitar player. Dinner itself was excellent and, over desert, when I asked Bernard if he had been to the opera recently, he told me that he had not. Furthermore, he had never seen *The Magic Flute*. At that point I presented him with a pair of tickets for the following evening at the Opera House. I explained to him that we could not attend the performance because we would be already in Budapest and that we would be very happy if he and his wife could take our place.

He was touched by the generosity of the gift. All in all, in spite of a frustrating start, we had enjoyed our brief stay in Warsaw.

The following morning, after breakfast, we boarded the airport bus and, shortly afterwards, arrived at Warsaw Chopin Airport where we began to see an inordinate number of Asian tourists wearing masks on their way to all sorts of destinations. We found it unusual, but did not give it a second thought.

Budapest was by far our favorite city during this European trip. The weather was mild, dry and sunny and, therefore, very conducive to long, pleasant walks. Also, some of the city's monuments along the Danube were simply gorgeous to look at and admire. We had chosen purposely to stay at the Danubius Hotel Gellért, a landmark in the city because it is a good example of what is referred to as Secessionist architecture and is reputed for its Thermal Spring Baths, considered the best in Budapest. It was also at the doorstep of a subway station, Szent Gellért tér, and trams stopped right next to it, major conveniences for any tourist without a car who wants to explore the city. We were not disappointed with our choice. What we did not know was that during the very weekend of our arrival the hotel was staging a three-day Indoor Beer Festival that culminated on Sunday, February 16th, with an All-You-Can-Eat and Drink Beer Brunch for 10.500 HUF per person. We were ecstatic and signed up for it right away. Mr. Gábor Müncz, the Gellért's executive chef, created a special menu for the occasion that was simply out of this world and the many craft beers on hand made it all even more appealing. We will never forget that Sunday in Budapest thanks to this unique and totally unexpected surprise.

We had checked-in at the Gellért in mid-afternoon the day before and, after resting for a while, we decided to explore the hotel's facilities and the immediate neighborhood. Eventually, we ended up at the Szeged Vendéglő, a typical Hungarian restaurant, with musicians and everything, located on Bartok Béla út, right next door to the Gellért. It was Saturday evening and, therefore, lots of locals were having dinner at the restaurant, always a great sign. We liked it so much that later on that week we returned there for another meal. After dinner, we crossed the Liberty Bridge, the closest one to our hotel, just to get a view of the Danube and the surrounding landmarks at night. It was a beautiful sight.

Our list of things to see and do, included the following: Hungarian Parliament, St. Stephen's Basilica, Váci utca, Mátyás Church, Fishermen's Bastion, Hungarian State Opera, Great Synagogue, Chain Bridge, Shoes on the Danube, Cave Church, Citadel, Liberation Monument, River Cruises (one at night and one during the day), etc. There was no time to waste.

The next morning, after a delicious buffet breakfast at the Gellért's Panorama Restaurant and Terrace, we were ready to go sightseeing. We started with the remarkable Cave Church, hewn into the Gellért hillside, next door to the hotel. From the church we proceeded to climb the Gellért Hill, named after Bishop Gellért, Budapest's patron saint, who met a violent death there in 1046, all the way to the Citadel and the Liberation Monument. There are several lookout points along the way that offer stunning views of Budapest and the winding Danube. At about 140 m above the majestic river, on a clear day, such as that Sunday, the views from the Hill were simply dazzling. After a most pleasant morning, we were ready to return to the hotel and enjoy the special brunch that would close the Indoor Beer Festival. We were not disappointed.

After such a big meal, accompanied by an array of delicious handcrafted beers, we were ready to explore the Pest side of Budapest. To that end, we crossed Liberty Bridge and headed for Váci utca, one of the city's best-known streets. It's definitely the city's commercial and social center. Luckily, most of it is pedestrianized and, therefore, one can walk peacefully along its length from north to south or vice-versa. On the south side, Váci utca ends at the doors of the Central Market Hall, a remarkable place worth a visit and, on the north side, at the Vörösmarty tér, named after the poet Mihály Vörösmarty whose statue adorns the plaza. The square's northern side houses the city's most famous coffee house, Gerbeaud Cukrászda, where we stopped for a cappuccino and a hot chocolate. The interior is spectacular and makes the price of the beverages well worth the experience. From there, we proceeded to the nearby subway station to take a ride in the Millennium Underground Railway, the first subway line to be constructed in Budapest in 1896 and the first electric railway in the world. The Vörösmarty station has to be one of the smallest and quaintest subway stations anywhere, and the smallness of the subway itself is something to behold. We got off at Opera with the intent of paying a quick visit to the Hungarian State Opera at Andrássy út 22 but, sadly, the building was undergoing renovations and, therefore, it was closed to the public. So, instead, we opted for a short walk along Andrássy to view the luxury boutiques, theatres and the many restaurants and cafés that line both of its sides. It was time to head back to the much more down to earth Váci utca and look for a restaurant for supper. Walking along it, we decided to enter Saint Michael's Church, located on the west side of Váci utca. We did not regret it. Although the outside of the church is unpretentious, the inside is really quite beautiful. Noteworthy are the High Altar, the Pulpit, the Fresco on the Dome in the Sanctuary and the Altar of Jesus' Heart where one can see the statues of Saint John of Nepomuk and Saint Anne, Jesus' grandmother. After this unexpected stop, we settled on Nagy Fa-Tál Konyhája, on Kígyó utca 4, a typical Hungarian restaurant with live music. After another great meal, we headed to the Liberty Bridge and our hotel. We had just had a great day in lovely Budapest. Before going to sleep, we planned our next day's activities. The Hungarian Parliament, Shoes on the Danube and St. Stephen's Basilica were on the list of things to do before returning to the hotel to enjoy the afternoon in the Gellért's swimming pool and thermal baths and, in the evening, after dinner, a cruise on the Danube.

 The following day, when we got to the magnificent Hungarian Parliament, we found out that it was closed for tours due to renovations. It was a major disappointment. We had to be happy with just admiring the extraordinary building from the outside. After admiring it from a variety of angles and witnessing the changing of the guard, we headed to

Shoes on the Danube, a most grave memorial to the hundreds of Jews who were murdered at the site by the fascist Arrow Cross militiamen in 1944-45. It displays sixty pairs of shoes, including those of children, lined up on the edge of the embankment. Another concrete example of the intolerance, racism and hatred, when left unchecked, displayed by human beings. It is, in its simplicity, an extremely moving tribute to those who perished needlessly on the spot at the hands of criminals. Afterwards, we went to St. Stephen's whose dome, 96 m high, is visible from all over the city. It is built in the shape of a Greek cross. It features a magnificent Main Altar with a life-size marble statue of St. Stephen; it also features the mummified forearm of the saint in the Holy Right-Hand Chapel, a relic that is venerated by believers.

After a light lunch at Séf Asztala Étterem Kft, across from the Hungarian Parliament, it was time to enjoy the Gellért's swimming pool and the thermal spring baths. We were not disappointed with the facilities. There is no doubt in my mind that the most dazzling part of the complex is the Neo-Classical main pool. It has a retractable roof and the high marble columns and galleries that surround it are something to behold while doing a few laps in its lukewarm waters. As for the medicinal baths, there are many to choose from and these, combined with the medical services and massages available on the premises, are sufficient enough reasons to want to stay at the Gellért. It's a unique experience not to be missed should you find yourself in Budapest.

And, after a most relaxing few hours of being pampered, it was time to get ready for dinner somewhere in the area as we were too tired to walk too far. We chose to return to the restaurant next door to the hotel, Szeged Vendéglő, where we enjoyed another very delicious Hungarian meal, *marhapörkölt tarhonyával*, traditional beef goulash in a hot paprika sauce which is served with soft noodles, accompanied by *sör*, beer, in this case, Dreher. Upon exiting the restaurant, we came upon a lovely evening conducive for a little stroll along the Buda embankment all the way to Elizabeth Bridge. The Danube was a beehive of activity with cruises going back and forth and we decided that the next afternoon we would partake in a river cruise ourselves. We also took notice that the departing and arrival point for these cruises was the Pest embankment, right by Elizabeth Bridge. It was time to return to the hotel and go to sleep after another marvelous day spent in Budapest.

The next morning, after breakfast, we headed to Mátyás Church, Fishermen's Bastion, followed by a visit to the Royal Palace grounds. What hasn't been said about Mátyás Church? It dates back to the XIII century and it has undergone many renovations ever since with the most recent ones being completed in 1896. On the outside, one notices right away the eye-catching colourful tile roof and the Béla Tower, named after King Béla IV. The inside is something to marvel at for a while in wonder on account of its beauty which explains why it was the site of so many royal weddings. We especially enjoyed admiring the Altar, the Stained-glass Windows on the south side, and the Tomb of King Béla III and Anne de Châtillon. From the terrace and turrets of Fishermen's Bastion, the view of the Hungarian Parliament, almost across the way, the Danube and the rest of the city is simply outstanding. It's unforgettable. The day that we visited Mátyás Church and the adjoining Fishermen's Bastion, the place was packed with high schoolers from Italy who happened to be in Budapest, accompanied by their teachers, on a school trip. They were boisterous and not very attentive to the explanations provided by their leaders, but still managed to be respectful. In retrospect, it's hard to believe that shortly after they returned home, especially to northern Italy, this part of the country would be declared a "red zone" due to COVID-19.

In the afternoon, we returned to Váci utca, had lunch at Anna Kávézó, at Váci utca 5, walked over to Deák Férenc Ter to check it out, returned to Váci utca before we boarded our boat cruise on the Danube by Elizabeth Bridge. It was a day full of highlights one after the other. Should you find yourself in Budapest one of these days, you must go on a boat cruise on the Danube. So many of the most iconic monuments in the city are in full display for your delight and pleasure with the most grandiose of them all being, of course, the majestic Hungarian

Parliament. The Silverline Cruise itself that we chose went as far north as Margaret Island and as far south as the Petófi Bridge covering, therefore, the most important city landmarks. The next evening, being our last one in Budapest, we promised to be back for an evening cruise as a sort of farewell to the city.

After the lovely cruise, we continued south on Váci utca on our way to the Central Market Hall and Corvinus University, situated next door to the market. The market itself is an enchanting place and, obviously, considering the number of Budapesters and tourists alike who were there, a favorite destination. We bought packages of hot Hungarian paprika for our family back in Canada since it seemed to be widely used in traditional Hungarian dishes. As far as Corvinus University of Budapest goes, the building was built between 1871-74 and it was destined to house the city's main customs' house; it became the University of Economics in 1951 in honour of Karl Marx where, to this day, a statue of him is still to be found. It is a Neo-Renaissance work of art, especially the part that faces the Danube with its colonnade, balcony and two rows of arched windows. And, because we were so close to the Bálna, the Whale, a super modern structure which we could see clearly from the Gellért, we decided to walk over to check it out. It so happens that it opened to the public in 2013 as a small shopping center but it also caters to cultural activities. The couple of restaurants that we looked into were half-empty and the entire place almost deserted. After all the sightseeing that we had done, we were ready to return to our hotel just a short distance away across the river. To that end, we crossed Liberty Bridge and found ourselves in the hotel's lobby. From there, we proceeded to the Gellért Söröző 7 Brasserie for a light dinner. We were tired from all the walking that we had done and needed to rest in view of being refreshed for our last full day in Budapest the following day. After dinner, over a beer, we planned our next day's activities. They included a visit to the Great Synagogue, Europe's largest; it was built in a Byzantine-Moorish style between 1854-59 and it can accommodate up to 3,000 worshippers. Afterwards, we also wanted to make a brief stop at the Inner-City Parish Church, a church that literally came within centimeters of being destroyed when Elizabeth Bridge was being rebuilt after the Second World War; and, like many tourists, we wanted to walk across the Chain Bridge, the most iconic of the Budapest bridges and, if time permitted it, to pay a visit to the Franz Liszt Museum, Hungary's greatest pianist. Finally, hopefully, we would still find a bit of time to go for a final swim in the Gellért's lovely indoor pool before going for dinner and taking our second cruise on the Danube when all the important monuments along both banks would be lit. Luckily, we had purchased at the Liszt Ferenc International Airport upon arrival the 3-Day Budapest Card, the Official City Pass, which allowed us to move quickly anywhere within the city by using public transit.

So, on Wednesday, February 19th, right after the tasty buffet breakfast at the hotel, we set out to the Great Synagogue, also called the Dohány Street Synagogue, where we had to line up in order to get tickets for a guided tour. Once inside, we were lucky to get as our guide an older Jewish gentleman who was a fountain of knowledge and, on top of that, possessed a great sense of humour. Although he had never been a teacher in his entire life, he was a born one who knew instinctively how to keep an audience engaged in his presentation by asking numerous questions and soliciting opinions of all kinds. The two hours that we spent in his company were most informative. The synagogue opened its doors in 1859 and, together with the adjacent Jewish History Museum, archives, the cemetery of the Holocaust victims, the Emmanuel Tree of Life, and the Raoul Wallenberg Park, is a magnificent tribute to the 600,000 Hungarian Jews killed during the Holocaust. Raoul Wallenberg alone, a Swedish diplomat, is believed to have saved about 100,000 Hungarian Jews during 1944-45. An architectural feature that strikes the visitor facing the synagogue is the twin Oriental-style Moorish towers topped with Byzantine onion domes. Once inside, one is awed by the size and beauty of the place, from the twin chandeliers, to the upper galleries, to the rose windows. The ark itself contains priceless scrolls that were saved by Catholic priests from the Nazis and that came from other synagogues.

As for the Inner-City Parish Church, also referred to as the Assumption Church, it is Budapest's oldest church, and it has had a turbulent past, as pointed out before, and most recently when Elizabeth Bridge was being reconstructed. Destroyed and rebuilt several times, now there is a section of its floor covered with glass through which one can see the foundation walls of the original building from the days of king Saint Stephen. Also noteworthy is a beautiful fresco of the Madonna that dates back to the XIV century. Finally, the great Ferenc Liszt himself was the conductor there for seven years and this last detail would be more than sufficient to attract the visitor to the building.

After visiting the church, we walked along the Duna Corso and the Belgrad Rakpart to the Széchenyi Chain Bridge, perhaps Budapest's most recognizable icon and the first permanent bridge to be built across the Danube in Budapest. We walked to the middle of it and stood there for a while watching the boat traffic on the Danube and admiring the beautiful buildings on the Buda side as well as on the Pest side. We both agreed that Budapest was not only located in a terrific spot but that the aesthetic beauty of the buildings on both sides of the Danube justified its popularity with all tourists, young and old. It was time for a late lunch followed by a visit to the Franz Liszt Memorial Museum.

The Museum itself was quite interesting. It contains the furniture, musical instruments and every day common objects used by the pianist. It's also a research center and its archives are considered the second most important in Europe. After the visit, we returned to Váci utca where my wife had seen a handbag that she wanted to purchase.

Before dinner, we found an hour or so for a final swim in the Gellért main indoor pool. Dinner itself was at the Gellért pub. It was a light affair. Before retiring for the night, we made it back to the Silverline Cruises dock, to take our evening cruise along the Danube. If the daytime cruise had been good, the evening one was magical. The night was clear, all the major buildings were lit, including the bridges, and for the next couple of hours we were in a sort of wonderland.

The next morning, after the buffet breakfast, we were off to the airport to catch a flight to Frankfurt and, three hours later, another one to Toronto. All in all, the entire European trip had been amazing.

Back in Toronto, on February 20th, CEEF In-Home Interviews resumed in earnest as well as rehearsals for *Tartuffe*. And then, the much-anticipated day for my right eye surgery finally arrived on March 9th. It took place at the Kensington Eye Institute and I am happy to report that everything went well. Luckily, all CEEF In-Home Interviews had been completed beforehand. It meant, however, that I had to interrupt my participation in the rehearsals because I could not see properly. That said, just a few weeks later the decision to cancel the shows on account of COVID-19 came about. It was the responsible thing to do. The schools who had made reservations for the matinées were contacted and told the "bad" news, news which they were expecting anyway, and the ones who had already paid for a specific performance were reimbursed for it. It was the first time that La Troupe des Anciens had ever cancelled a show in its long history. It took a pandemic to do it. We all felt terrible about it but there wasn't much that we could do about it anyways.

Meanwhile, CEEF made the decision to repatriate all Canadian students who were on exchange in Europe. Parents were concerned for the health of their children and, as things got progressively worse in Italy, Spain, France and Germany, some of them began to panic and the demands for their children's repatriation grew louder and louder. Gord, aided by Dorothy, and our friends at the Barrie office, Ingrid, Karen and Pat, worked hard to get all students back to Canada as quickly as possible. It goes without saying that it was a stressful time for all concerned. Regrettably, CEEF ceased operations on April 1st, 2020. It fell victim, like so many other not-for-profits, companies, and all sorts of businesses across Canada, to COVID-19. We, CEEF volunteers, felt awful about its demise but, given the uncertain times ahead, there was no other choice, drastic action needed to be taken and it was taken.

Regarding my left eye surgery which was scheduled to take place on March 23rd, it got cancelled, of course, too. It was considered elective surgery and, therefore, not a priority. Eventually, it would occur on July 16th, to my great relief. Afterwards, it was just a question of seeing my friendly optometrist, Dr. Brian Feldman, and get him to prescribe new contact lenses so that I could see once again where I was going. It took quite a few visits to his office, with all sorts of restrictions in place, to get things straightened out. Luckily for me, as things stand, my vision hasn't been this good in years.

The rest of the summer was mostly uneventful. Natasha came to visit for a week in July and, then, we drove her home staying in Bancroft for a couple of days. This particular trip was different from previous ones in that Joel and Natasha had acquired two beehives and were now amateur beekeepers. So, on the way to Bancroft we stopped in Scarborough to buy a honey extractor and proceeded to extract quite a bit of honey during the weekend. It was amazing how much delicious honey the busy bees had produced in such a short period of time. On Saturday, August 8th, my cousin Paula and John, her husband, came over for a barbecue and the following day we visited Sandra and Roberto at their RV (Recreation Vehicle) parked at Lake Belwood, near Erin. Both occasions were lots of fun and they made us realize how much we had missed socializing with family and friends alike on account of the nasty pandemic.

In August, our daughter, once again, visited us for another week and, before we knew it, it was September again. Filomena and I were thinking of doing renovations to the main bathroom in our home and, since there wasn't much else to do, it seemed to be the right time for it. In retrospect, it was the wrong time for it because of the pandemic and its many restrictions that eventually delayed considerably the completion of the project. Live and learn. John, my cousin's husband, was our contractor and our point man when dealing with carpenters, electricians, tilers, etc., and Filomena and I pitched in whenever needed as a way to while the time away and, in the process, save some money.

Living with COVID-19 brought about many and varied challenges to everybody. We are social beings who thrive in personal contact with our fellow human beings on a daily basis. Not being able to see and interact with one another has caused much suffering, especially to older Canadians who are isolated in nursing homes many of which lack the essential upgrades and the experienced personnel to keep them safe from the virus. The sheer number of seniors in nursing homes who succumbed to COVID-19 highlights convincingly their vulnerability and the government's negligence in not doing its utmost to keep them safe. Seniors, in this country and everywhere, became sitting ducks waiting for the invisible virus to hit them. It's another tragedy of our times and it took a pandemic to bring it to the fore. It is shameful that people who contributed so much to this country are put in such an untenable situation. It remains to be seen what all levels of government will do to rectify this wrong going forward.

Politically speaking, I have voted in every single municipal, provincial and federal election in my adopted country. I consider it my duty and obligation as a citizen to participate in the political system by having my voice heard and my vote counted when it's most important – during elections. I have voted for candidates who belonged to either the Liberal Party or the New Democratic Party, that is to say to candidates who positioned themselves slightly to the left in the political spectrum. The first Prime Minister that I voted for was Pierre Elliott Trudeau, just after becoming a Canadian citizen in 1977. I had been following his political career ever since arriving in Canada in December of 1969 and had the pleasure of attending, together with a few friends of mine, back in the summer of 1974, an election rally at Varsity Stadium where he was the main speaker. Intellectually and politically-speaking, I admired the man. Another federal politician that drew my attention in the 1970s was David Lewis, the leader of the New Democratic Party, whose good intentions, integrity and unwavering support of the working class were never in doubt. It's interesting to note that both men begot children who followed in their fathers' footsteps. The latter, by giving life to

Stephen Lewis who was very much active in Ontario politics at the provincial level and, the former, by producing the current Prime Minister of Canada, Justin Trudeau. I have witnessed personally, to my disappointment and frustration, over the decades, what happens when right-wing conservative governments get elected with the inevitable cuts that occur to education, healthcare and social programs in the name of so-called fiscal responsibility and reducing the deficit. I have also witnessed how these same conservative governments align themselves with the rich minority to the detriment of the many who are just trying their best to keep afloat. At the federal and provincial levels respectively, former Prime Minister Brian Mulroney, and a former Premier of Ontario, Mike Harris, come to mind, just to mention two of the most notorious ones. Mulroney introduced a most unpopular tax, the Goods and Services Tax (GST), produced the Charlottetown fiasco and, if that were not enough, promoted Western alienation causing directly the birth of an ultra-conservative party, the Reform Party, led by Preston Manning. Harris, on the Ontario scene, was responsible for causing much damage in the areas of education, healthcare and welfare. Clearly, the 1980s and 1990s were not the best of times for the advancement of social justice causes in Canada. I pride myself in the fact that I have never voted for a single conservative candidate in my lifetime.

In spite of the inevitable *contretemps* along the way, I have had a wonderful life in Canada!

EPILOGUE

Looking back at my life and times in Canada, I am the first one to realize and admit how lucky I have been to live in this incredible country. I have enjoyed a privileged lifestyle thanks to the many opportunities that came my way among which I consider education the most valuable one, one that opened all sorts of rewarding professional doors for me which, in turn, permitted me to enjoy a standard of living unimaginable to so many other people around the world, especially in the Azores. In my particular case, I give credit to my father for firmly believing that higher education was one of the keys for success and a rewarding life. I am a prime example of that. Back in August of 1961, just days before his ill-fated second trip to the US, he left a handwritten note to his wife, my mother, in which he expresses the wish that if he were not to return from his trip for whatever reason, she do everything in her power for me, his son, to get a university education, something that he had been unable to obtain himself on account of his own father's demise, in 1930, when he was just thirteen years old. When my father's death occurred, I had just turned nine years old myself and the long road ahead looked insurmountable to my mother, I am sure, given that she was left with limited financial resources to turn her husband's dream into a reality. But, in spite of it all, she persevered and her perseverance enabled me to realize his dream. It was rendered possible, however, thanks to a lot of personal sacrifices on her part. So, she is equally responsible for my own professional and personal successes.

Lately, I have been taking stock of my travels and I have realized that after travelling in the 1970s in this land to such faraway places as Vancouver and Victoria, in 1971, and to Montréal and Québec City,

EPILOGUE

in 1972, followed by a trip in December of that same year to windy Winnipeg and a stint of four months of work at Camping La Loutre, halfway between Québec City and Chicoutimi, in 1975, and another trip in 1979 to Québec City, Montréal and Ottawa, followed by several school trips in the 1980s, 1990s and early 2000s to Montréal and Québec City, my other travels in this country have been limited mostly to cities, towns and villages in Ontario. Fortunately, interspersed with these trips in Canada, I have had the chance to travel widely in Europe, to such countries as Portugal, Spain, France, England, Germany, Switzerland, Poland, Czech Republic, Austria, Hungary, Italy, Greece, and far away as Egypt, in Africa. I have been to Mexico, Venezuela, Cuba, Dominican Republic, other Caribbean islands, and numerous times to the United States. That said, there is so much more about my beloved and adopted country that I have not discovered except for reading and seeing images of it on TV. In part, of course, it's the vastness of the country itself that creates a challenge to realizing the goal of getting to know all of its regions personally. That, however, is a poor excuse. It's high time to rectify this state of affairs and start travelling widely in Canada once again.

So, nowadays, I find myself making plans about possible trips within Canada. Filomena and I would like to visit the Maritimes, Newfoundland and Labrador, on the east coast, and take a train trip all the way from Union Station, in Toronto, to Vancouver, in British Columbia, a dream of a trip that has been in the back of my mind for many years. I believe that before dying every Canadian should have the opportunity to embark on such a trip in order to gain an understanding of the sheer size and natural beauty of this country. And, in particular, there is Alberta and the unparalleled Rocky Mountains to admire and Banff and Jasper National Parks to discover. And, what about the appeal of Northern Canada? Yukon, Northwest Territories, Nunavut? Those are possibilities too. Still so much to discover before one's time is up.

Canada is not a perfect country, far from it, as one of the most recent national scandals, this one involving Residential Schools, which

EPILOGUE

were run mostly by the Catholic and Anglican Churches, has shown; no country is. Ever since the French and the English set foot in North America, they proceeded systematically to annihilate First Nations (FN), the people who already inhabited the land. Alas, to this day, many Canadians know very little about the history of their country and much less about the atrocities that were committed by the Whites through the ages simply because they have not been taught anything about them in either elementary or high school. Back in the early 1970s, for instance, when I was a student at Bloor Collegiate and was taking grade 13 Canadian History, these terrible deeds never came up for analysis and discussion, which was unfortunate because this glaring omission has contributed to the widespread biased views that non-Natives harbor towards the Native people of Canada. In this regard, if non-Native attitudes and behaviours are to improve and change for the better, Canadian History courses must address past wrongs head-on. I was constantly reminded, to my continued chagrin later on as an educator, of the sheer ignorance of my students regarding the history of this country and, in particular, everything pertaining to the relationships between the political elite and the Aboriginal people. In my humble opinion, a good starting point would be to make it available for every high schooler Thomas King's *The Inconvenient Indian, A Curious Account of Native People in North America*, a comprehensive analysis of the various policies put in place by different levels of government to "eliminate" the perceived "Indian problem" including the most recent one, "assimilation through education". Worse, these cruelties have been either consistently denied or conveniently covered up by past generations of politicians of all political stripes.

Thus, in this latest fiasco, callousness, negligence, incompetence, outright racism on the part of school administrators and the staff responsible for running Residential Schools and, in the absence of any oversight measures put in place by the federal government of Canada, which established the schools in the first place, made it possible for the uprooted and vulnerable FN children to be abused physically, sexually, and psychologically. Canada's policy of "Take the Indian out of the child", attributed to John A. MacDonald, the country's first Prime Minister, prepared the groundwork for the enormous tragedy that unfolded afterwards. It remains to be seen if the Final Report 2008-2015 of the Truth and Reconciliation Commission of Canada (TRC), will finally force all levels of government to rectify the past wrongs done to Native people. Justice delayed is, indeed, justice not served and, when it comes to Canada's Indigenous people, any reasonable Canadian has to agree that they have been victimized in every conceivable way: they were abused, discriminated against, murdered, robbed of their land (the greatest land robbery ever!) and dignity and, if that were not enough, put in reservations/reserves where they live in substandard conditions away from the rest of the populace. Sadly, the last chapter of their story has yet to be written. In the meantime, their struggle for survival goes on and on and on.

Since we are speaking of past wrongs, let's not forget what was done to Japanese and Italian-Canadians during the Second World War and, nowadays, what is being done to Muslims across the land, too. In the name of nationalism, atrocities were committed and continue to be committed worldwide, including in Canada. That said, I think we are witnessing the beginning of a general willingness on the part of our citizenry to face its past and present mistakes honestly and directly to avoid similar blunders from occurring in the future. If that is indeed the case, hopefully, history won't repeat itself. All of us Canadians are responsible for the lack of honesty, transparency and moral integrity on the part of politicians who made it a point of ignoring the atrocities as they were unfolding nationwide before their very eyes. It's unbelievable and, yes, tragic, that we have let them get away with such blatant injustices without paying a political price at the polls.

As I am about to wrap up relating my adventures and misadventures as an Azorean in Canada, I cannot let this opportunity pass without uttering a few words about the so-called "Freedom Convoy" that blockaded border crossings between Canada and the US and laid siege

EPILOGUE

to downtown Ottawa for a few weeks in 2023. I have come to the conclusion, like the vast majority of Canadians, that the people who participated in it were fanatics. Here was a minority group, made up mostly of white men with a sense of entitlement and privilege, who wanted to impose their version of "freedom" on the rest of the population. Their overall ignorance regarding COVID-19 itself, and the recommended mass vaccination of Canadians to prevent unnecessary deaths, as put forth by the medical profession and leading scientists alike, and supported by all levels of government, combined with heavy doses of disinformation and misinformation that they held, all coming from dubious sources such as Internet conspiracy sites, and their attitudinal arrogance, are beyond rational comprehension. The hooligans were not only against pandemic restrictions and vaccine mandates, but they were also bent on the ousting of a democratically elected federal government which they perceived as being Nazi-like and "antifreedom". These protesters seemed to have taken the cue from their American brothers and sisters who brought chaos to Washington on January 6th, 2020, encouraged by former President Trump, in a blatant attempt to stop the peaceful transition of power from Republicans to Democrats at the Capitol and with the sole purpose of retaining power at all costs. He apparently was willing, if need be, to tear his own country apart in the process. Therefore, it was not at all surprising that reactionary Americans, the vast majority aligned with the alt-right movement, were using the opportunity to contribute millions of dollars in donations to the cause of the "Freedom Convoy" in an attempt to disrupt daily life in Canada just like they continue to do in their own politically troubled country.

One cannot expect yahoos with personal grievances of all sorts to understand, and much less appreciate, the quality of life that science has afforded all of us including, directly or indirectly, themselves and their loved ones. What remains certain is that if a similar protest had been organized by Black Lives Matter or, for that matter, by First Nations folks, it would have been quenched rapidly by the police with the full backing of the authorities, local and national. Racism and discrimination are alive and well in Canada too, I am afraid, just like in America. In any case, it would be a sure bet that the response to such a hypothetical event would have been met with prompt and decisive action within days, not weeks, as was the case with the trucker blockade in Ottawa and elsewhere. This state of affairs points to the fact that there is definitely a double standard when it comes to who is participating in the protesting. The colour of one's skin does matter!

Eventually, to clear the truckers and their sympathizers from downtown Ottawa, the federal government, led by Prime Minister Justin Trudeau, felt compelled to invoke the Emergencies Act, a first since its inception in 1988, hereby giving the police the necessary tools to arrest the leaders of the "Freedom Convoy", and the anti-government demonstrators associated with the movement, for mischief, a federal offence. The Emergencies Act, among many measures, enabled authorities to freeze their bank accounts, thereby stopping the flow of money and goods that were keeping them fed and fueled, allowed tow trucks to remove illegally parked vehicles from the streets of Ottawa, cancelled drivers' licenses and insurance policies, prohibited minors to be in the no go zone, etc. All these measures brought finally the illegal occupation of Ottawa to a speedy grand finale.

Nevertheless, all these troubles put aside, one must admit that Canada is a beautiful country in its geographical diversity, rich in its many and varied natural resources and, socially speaking, an experiment in progress in the area of multiculturalism and democracy. It's a country that seems to be much more open than our neighbors to the immediate south when it comes to dealing with ethnic, religious, political and social differences that can and often do pull us apart as humans, especially in hard economic times. We, Canadians, pride ourselves in the fact that we are a "multicultural society", a characteristic that we think enriches all of us, instead of the so-called "melting pot" that characterizes the United States, an unfortunate trait that diminishes all of its citizens. I would like to think that most Canadians are generous, reasonable, kind, decent folks who decry injustices whenever and wherever they spot them, and who are willing to stand up for fairness and justice for the betterment of society and humanity.

When everything is said and done, COVID-19 forced me to sit down and tackle something that had been in the back of my mind for some time – writing what I have entitled *An Azorean Trilogy*. Three volumes connected by a common thread – me. Book One, *An Azorean in Canada: A Memoir* has as the main protagonist myself and deals with my life as an immigrant in Canada; Book Two, *A Proud Azorean: A Biography* is about my father and his unexpected death at the age of forty-three years old; finally, Book Three, *The Making of an Azorean Coward, Hypocrite and Traitor: A Biography* concerns a cowardly man, my father-in-law, and the impact that his cowardice had on his entire family. The three books were a project that gave me much to think about as I recalled, to the best of my ability, and aided in the process by a treasure trove of archival material, life in the Azores from the 1920s to the end of the 1960s and, afterwards, in Canada and in the United States for myself and my wife, respectively, until 1978, the year we got married. From 1978 onwards, it deals we our common life experience in Canada. Every immigrant has a unique story to tell. There are many challenges that face recent immigrants in their adopted countries. My wife and I were not immune to some of them. That said, we were fortunate to have fared better than most. The three books also give voice to people in my family who did not, or could not, put into words their own particular life story and all three books are, when everything is said and done, a labour of love.

ACKNOWLEDGMENTS

I would like to thank the following people who helped me bring, either directly or indirectly, this project, *An Azorean in Canada: A Memoir*, to fruition: my father who spoiled me rotten until my 9th birthday; my mother who, after his premature death, protected a psychologically vulnerable child, me, until I could stand on my own two feet; my maternal grandparents who were kind enough to welcome the two of us into their home when my mother became a widow and had nowhere else to go; my elementary and high school friends, both in Ponta Delgada and in Toronto, whose friendship towards me never wavered, especially Marco António Tavares de Moura and Emanuel da Costa Melo Vasconcelos, in elementary school, and Luís França Machado, José Cabral, Mario Amato, Joseph Curatola and Orlando Buonestella, among so many more, in high school; Gerri, James Hastings and Paul Adams, three indispensable friends during the summer of 1972 at École française d'été, in Montréal; John Gelder for sharing my incredible experience at Parc des Laurentides in the summer of 1975; João Medeiros, at the West End YMCA, who employed me from 1976 to 1978 in Summer Camps and as a teacher of ESL and whose commitment to the Portuguese community in Toronto was nothing short of exemplary; my teachers at Bloor Collegiate who welcomed a "lost" immigrant with open arms and took an interest in me and in my struggles with English, namely Mrs. Angela Goyeau, my ESL teacher, Mr. Juergen Hoffmann, my grade 11 History teacher and my home form teacher, who rewarded my hard work in his class by choosing me, under the umbrella of the Young Voyageurs Program, to represent the school in a wonderful trip to British Columbia in 1971, and Mrs.

ACKNOWLEDGMENTS

Margaret Carter, my teacher of grade 13 French, who encouraged me to apply for the Summer Language Bursary Program in 1972; my professors at Saint Michael's College, among them Jean-Claude Susini and Paulette Collet, for recognizing promise in an undergraduate student; my newly found friends at St. Mike's, especially Antoinette Liscio who, as I did, participated in the French Plays and who invited me to participate in the summer program at Université Canadienne en France in the summer of 1988 and whom, in turn, I invited to be my daughter's godmother when Natasha was baptised in 1989, Joyce Krnc who, although she was not studying Spanish at all, volunteered to type my essays in that language to save a friend who could not even type with one finger, and Charles Campisi with whom I shared many lunches and laughs along the way; my professors at the Faculty of Education, notably Carl Theodore and Ross Jones who recommended me for my first real teaching interview at Grand River Collegiate; Mr. Ross Shaver, my first principal, for seeing potential in an unknown quantity and my fellow teachers in the Languages Department at that school, especially Zelda Thomas, who took the time to show the ropes to a novice teacher; Principal Ralph Peters who hired me to teach Portuguese and Spanish at Harbord Collegiate in 1980 thereby gifting me with a dream of a job and who was succeeded, in turn, by the following principals at the school: Douglas Lougheed, who supported unconditionally all the Noite de Teatro productions during his tenure at the school, Donald Creighton who saw leadership skills in me and appointed me Assistant Head of Moderns thereby opening the door for possible future positions of responsibility in the teaching profession, James McCarron who put in a good word when I applied for the headship at Malvern Collegiate, Frances Parkin, the first female principal of Harbord Collegiate for, three years later, making me Curriculum Leader of Languages back at my former school, Mary Jane McNamara for showing leadership, vision, determination and commitment to see to it that the teaching of Modern Languages such as Cantonese, Mandarin, Portuguese and Spanish had to begin in grade 9 and, finally, Rodrigo Fuentes, my last

ACKNOWLEDGMENTS

principal, for his unwavering support and his kind remarks during my retirement party in June of 2010. And, last but not least, David Wells, principal at Malvern Collegiate, who hired me as the Head of Modern Languages at his school in 1997 and, by doing so, showed confidence in my leadership skills. Together with them, there were countless vice-principals with whom I had the distinct pleasure of working during my long career in education. Thanks to you all. Not to mention, of course, the wonderful teachers who taught alongside me at Grand River Collegiate, Harbord Collegiate and Malvern Collegiate; they became part of my extended family. At Harbord Collegiate there was Jack Harryman, the Head of Moderns and Classics, who was followed by Jim Rayner in that position, and my esteemed colleagues, incredible teachers such as Penny Vincent, Paulette Kuehn, Margherita Manuele, Peter Liu, Lena Winesanker, Claire Soper, John Hilbish, Françoise Cockburn, Lydia Lubinski, Sophie Berezosky, Linda Anthony, Daniel LeBlanc, Richard LeBlanc, Teresa Kwok, RuiYing Zhang, Justina Gadouchis, Alice Freitas and Millee Zhao, people who stayed for the long haul giving the Department a sense of stability and continuity; at Malvern Collegiate, I met Richard Mehringer, Janine Geddes, Joanne Cortes, Paul Leclerc, Danny Lamontagne, Bill Mighton, Richard Beaudry and others, all committed to providing students with the best possible public education. At Grand River Collegiate, the aforementioned Zelda Thomas for mentoring me and Principal Ross Shaver for his professional advice and availability; the numerous Teacher Candidates, over sixty of them, that I welcomed into my classes starting, in 1981, with Barbara Santamaría and finishing, in 2010, with Monica Paraghamian whose energy, enthusiasm, dedication and love of teaching was a source of inspiration to me and my students. Honestly, I owe all my successes in the classroom to these fine educators. They were amazing role models to emulate in one way or another.

That said, schools are just empty shells without the students that fill their classes and halls. I was truly blessed, throughout my entire career, to have taught in three amazing high schools: Grand River Collegiate,

ACKNOWLEDGMENTS

Harbord Collegiate and Malvern Collegiate. Thanks to the young people that I came across daily, I was able to accomplish all the goals that I had set for myself in the realm of education. None of those ideals would have been met without their active collaboration and participation in the learning process. I owe to them all my gratitude and, as we say in French, *je tire ma révérence*.

Regarding the School of Graduate Studies at the University of Toronto, I owe a huge debt of gratitude to Professors Michel Lord, my thesis director, and Professors Pascal Riendeau and Salvatore Bancheri who were part and parcel of my thesis committee. Their academic expertise, sound advice and moral support were much appreciated during the six years that it took me to finish the degree. All three of them displayed the patience of saints for which I am eternally grateful.

Along my life, I have been also privileged to be friends with some extraordinary people such as Professor Laura Bulger whom I replaced at Harbord Collegiate when she moved on to teach at the university level and our unforgettable fight for the establishment of a Minor Program in Portuguese Studies at Glendon College; Professor Paulette Collet who recruited me into what became, years later, La Troupe des Anciens, an opportunity that taught me much about staging plays, acting, and the French language and literature; thanks to her, I met countless new friends who all shared one common trait, that is to say a deep love for theatre. People such as Julie MacLaughlin, Frank Milani, Antoinette Liscio, Caro Simard, Edward Miczek, Basile Hacetoglu, Elizabeth Bucci, Elisabeth Widner, Moore Miller, Grant Weaver, Éli Morad, Robert Quickert, Peter Carayiannis, and countless others. Truly, it has been quite a privilege and honour to have been part of this amateur troupe ever since 1975; Lucien Benacem, a former instructor of mine at Saint Mike's and, later, a colleague at the TDSB but also, for a decade, the President of UFE. Thanks to his friendship, I met Marie-Thérèse Saladin, Timothee Li, Jean-Paul Martyniuk, Colette Owen and so many more people who continue to be committed to the well-being of the francophone community in and around Toronto; Gord Berg, a former Head of Languages, also at the TDSB, who invited me to be part of a most valuable not-for-profit organization called CEEF; he opened new horizons for me after my retirement from teaching in 2010 by enabling me to stay engaged with adolescents and, in the process, to embark in fresh travel adventures in Europe.

Finally, I would like to thank my wife, Filomena, and my daughter, Natasha, for being an indispensable part of my life journey and for, implicitly or explicitly, supporting my personal and professional goals; without a loving family and its support, none of my dreams would have become a reality. So, to the two of them I say *muito obrigado*.

PHOTOGRAPH CREDITS

Photograph Insert

All photographs courtesy of the Machado Family Archives.

ABOUT THE AUTHOR

Roberto A. Machado was born in Ponta Delgada, São Miguel, Azores, in 1952. He emigrated to Canada in 1969 to avoid being drafted into the Portuguese army which was involved in an unjust war of attrition against the natives of its former colonies of Angola, Mozambique and Guiné-Bissau. He settled down in Toronto where he attended Bloor Collegiate Institute and, afterwards, the University of Toronto. He is the proud recipient of four university degrees including a Ph.D. in Québec literature. He began his teaching career in 1978 at Grand River Collegiate Institute, in Kitchener, Ontario, where he taught French and Spanish. Beginning in 1980, he taught French, Portuguese and Spanish at Harbord Collegiate Institute, in Toronto, for twenty-seven years and was the Head of the Modern Languages Department at that school for the last ten. He also served as Head of Modern Languages at Malvern Collegiate Institute for three years. Now retired, he devotes his spare time to being an active member of La Troupe des Anciens de l'Université de Toronto, traveling, gardening and writing for pleasure. *An Azorean in Canada: A Memoir* is the first volume of *An Azorean Trilogy*. Roberto is married and the boastful father of a wonderful daughter. He lives in Mississauga, Ontario, Canada.

www.ingramcontent.com/pod-product-compliance
Lightning Source LLC
Chambersburg PA
CBHW042322090526
44585CB00025BA/2794